Fast Learning and
Invariant Object Recognition

Sixth-Generation Computer Technology Series

Branko Souček, Editor
University of Zagreb

Neural and Massively Parallel Computers: The Sixth Generation
Branko Souček and Marina Souček

Neural and Concurrent Real-Time Systems: The Sixth Generation
Branko Souček

*Neural and Intelligent Systems Integration: Fifth and Sixth Generation
Integrated Reasoning Information Systems*
Branko Souček and the IRIS Group

*Fast Learning and Invariant Object Recognition: The Sixth-Generation
Breakthrough*
Branko Souček and the IRIS Group

Dynamic, Genetic, and Chaotic Programming: The Sixth Generation
Branko Souček and the IRIS Group

*Fuzzy, Holographic, and Parallel Intelligence: The Sixth-Generation
Breakthrough*
Branko Souček and the IRIS Group

Fast Learning and Invariant Object Recognition

The Sixth-Generation Breakthrough

BRANKO SOUČEK
and
The IRIS GROUP

A Wiley-Interscience Publication

JOHN WILEY & SONS, INC.

New York-Chichester-Brisbane-Toronto-Singapore

Copyright © 1992 by John Wiley & Sons, Inc.

Library of Congress Cataloging in Publication Data:
Souček, Branko.
    Fast learning and invariant object recognition : the sixth-
generation breakthrough / Branko Souček and IRIS Group.
        p.   cm—(Sixth-generation computer technology series)
    "A Wiley-Interscience publication."
    Includes index.
    1. Image processing.   2. Machine learning.   3. Electronic digital
computers.   I. IRIS Group.   II. Title.   III. Series.
TA1632.S65 1992
006.3'7—dc20   91-47113
    ISBN 0-471-57430-9 (cloth : alk. paper)   CIP

Printed and bound in the United States of America by Braun-Brumfield, Inc.

10 9 8 7 6 5 4 3 2 1

CONTRIBUTORS

The IRIS Group presents a forum for international cooperation in research development and applications of intelligent systems. The IRIS International Center is involved in projects, design, measurements, and experiments, as well as in teaching courses and workshops, and consulting. The IRIS invites inquiries and operates under the auspices of the Star Service S.p.A., director V. L. Plantamura. The IRIS research coordinator is Professor B. Souček, IRIS, Star Service—Via Amendola 162/1, 70126—Bari, Italy.

ANDREAS ALBRECHT
TH Leipzig
Leipzig, Germany

NIRWAN ANSARI
Department of Electrical and
  Computer Engineering
New Jersey Institute of Technology
Newark, New Jersey

JAI-HOON CHUNG
KAIST
Seoul, Korea

A. DOBNIKAR
Department of Electrical and
  Computer Engineering
University of Ljubljana
Ljubljana, Slovenia

ANGELA FRANICH
Department of Informatics
University of Bari
Bari, Italy

B. JURČIČ-ZLOBEC
Department of Electrical and
  Computer Engineering
University of Ljubljana
Ljubljana, Slovenia

F. KOZATO
Department of Computer Science
Queen Mary and Westfield College
London, United Kingdom

KWOWEI LI
Department of Electrical and
   Computer Engineering
New Jersey Institute of Technology
Newark, New Jersey

A. LIKAR
Department of Electrical and
   Computer Engineering
University of Ljubljana
Ljubljana, Slovenia

SEUNG RYOUL MAENG
KAIST
Seoul, Korea

ALI A. MINAI
Department of Electrical
   Engineering
University of Virginia
Charlottesville, Virginia

MANAVENDRA MISRA
Department of Electrical
   Engineering Systems
University of Southern California
Los Angeles, California

SELWYN PIRAMUTHU
Dept. of Decision and
   Information Sciences
University of Florida
Gainesville, Florida

D. PODBREGAR
Department of Electrical and
   Computer Engineering
University of Ljubljana
Ljubljana, Slovenia

VIKTOR K. PRASANNA KUMAR
Department of Southern California
Los Angeles, California

MAX B. REID
NASA Ames Research Center
Moffett Field, California

G. A. RINGWOOD
Department of Computer Science
Queen Mary and Westfield College
London, United Kingdom

BRANKO SOUČEK
IRIS International Center
Bari, Italy

LILLY SPIRKOVSKA
NASA Ames Research Center
Moffett Field, California

RONALD H. SILVERMAN
Department of Ophthamology
Cornell University Medical College
New York, New York

RONALD D. WILLIAMS
Department of Electrical
   Engineering
University of Virginia
Charlottesville, Virginia

STEPHEN S. WILSON
Applied Intelligent Systems
Ann Arbor, Michigan

DAVID H. WOLPERT
LANL
Los Alamos, New Mexico

HYUNSOO YOON
KAIST
Seoul, Korea

CONTENTS

PART II INVARIANT OBJECT RECOGNITION

PREFACE

Learning, generalization, seeing, and recognition are the major features of natural intelligence. Each of these features has been also investigated by a technology. The ultimate solution are man-made systems that integrate all these features into

LEARNING–GENERALIZATION–SEEING–RECOGNITION HYBRIDS.

Nature shows that learning, object and pattern recognition are inseparable features in living organisms.

Although man recognizes physical objects and conceptual patterns with ease, it is very difficult to explain the mechanism of recognition. For this reason it is not easy to make computer systems for pattern and object recognition.

This book presents the latest advances in learning and in generalization, and their integration into object recognition systems. It describes high-speed architectures and system organizations, suitable for industrial applications. This book is divided into two parts.

Part I deals with learning systems. Different learning rules have been developed so far.

Backpropagation, a local iterative technique, is the most popular method for training multilayered networks. However, the backpropagation is slow, unstable, and it could produce inferior solutions when the problem to be solved is moderately complex or the network is large. Significant improvements and numerous new algorithms and speed-up modifications to backpropagation are described. They are based on holographic networks, adaptive decoupled momentum, feature construction, the second-order gradient method, and the combination of learning in neural networks and symbolic processing.

Generalization is a major issue in intelligent systems. This book describes multiple possible generalizers and confronts and compares different infinitesimal and discrete methods in learning and in neural network synthesis.

Long computational time had been a critical obstacle for progress in neural networks. Hence extensive efforts are being devoted to the parallel implementation of neural networks. This book presents parallel, systolic implementations of neural networks.

Part II deals with object recognition systems. An important aspect of the human visual system is the ability to recognize an object despite changes in the object's position in the input field, its size, or its angular orientation. This book investigates position, scale and rotation invariant object recognition systems.

Invariant Object Recognition includes industrial applications of machine vision. Detailed description of concrete systems and applications is given, covering the testing of IC chips, flying object recognition including the space shuttle and aircrafts, the detection of moving objects, shape recognition in manufacturing, biomedical image classification and three-dimensional ultrasonic imaging in clinical ophthalmology.

Newly developed computer systems designed to handle the speeds for real-time vision applications are presented. These include massively parallel-vision processors with raw power of up to 2 billion operations per second which perform logical operations on an entire image in 0.1 milliseconds, special high speed parallel SIMD systems with close to a billion connection per second, and new systolic array implementations with over 300 billion connections per second. The system must be noise and distortion immune.

Several high-speed object recognition systems, suitable for real-time applications are described. They include:

Translation invariant object recognition systems. An orthogonal set of feature layers is defined and provides a complete description of image features to serve as inputs to the final layer. Simulated annealing and Hebbian learning are found to be successful methods for training and for industrial applications.

Higher-order neural networks in position, scale, and rotation invariant object recognition. This system requires only a single layer of neural interconnections to provide the required nonlinear separation of a pattern space into subsets representing the object to be identified. This allows a simple learning rule to be used to modify the interconnection weights, leading to rapid convergence.

Visual tracking with object classification using specialized neural networks. These results are compared to Kalman filtering and to Fourier transformations procedures.

Partial shape recognition by means of a modified Hopfield neural network. Each object is represented by a set of landmarks. The hypothesis of a model object in a scene is completed by matching the model landmark with the scene landmarks. A heuristic measure is then computed to decide if the model is in the scene. This method is scale invariant and it can be implemented on parallel systems.

Neural networks for segmentation of three-dimensional ultrasonic images. This includes use of competitive learning as an undirected learning procedure and backpropagation for directed learning.

Neural network models on the reduced mesh of trees (RMOT) architecture. Dynamic link architecture for invariant object recognition is implemented on a linear array of processors.

This book presents unified treatment of material that is otherwise scattered over many publications and research reports. Previously unpublished methods and results based on research of the Integrated Reasoning Information Systems, IRIS Group, are presented. The IRIS Group reports the results of over 300 men-years of frontier research in leading American, European, and Asian laboratories and projects.

This book has been written as a textbook for students, as well as a reference for practicing system designers and users. An undergraduate-level background is assumed. The treatment is rounded out with a large number of examples, experimental results, details of working systems, illustrations, flowcharts, and a bibliography of over 300 items. The examples are designed as practical exercises for students, programmers, engineers and users.

Readers interested in other related topics, and in the background on neural, concurrent and intelligent systems, should combine this book with the other Sixth-Generation Computer Technology Series books listed opposite the title page. In particular, the complementary solutions using different paradigms are described in B. Souček and the IRIS Group: *Fuzzy, Holographic, and Parallel Intelligence; The Sixth-Generation Breakthrough*, Wiley 1992.

BRANKO SOUČEK

Bari, Italy
February 1992

ACKNOWLEDGMENTS

We acknowledge the encouragement, discussions, and support received from our teachers, collaborators, friends, and colleagues. We are grateful for the grants supporting our research. We thank the institutions where we performed the experiments and research with intelligent systems. The institutions are listed next to the contributors' names. Special thanks to Mrs. Vladimira Zlatič, Mrs. Lisa Van Horn, and John Wiley's editors and reviewers for an outstanding job in preparation, supervising, and copyediting the manuscript.

PART I

Fast Learning

CHAPTER 1 ———————————————

Learning to See

ANGELA FRANICH
BRANKO SOUČEK

1.1 INTRODUCTION

Learning, generalization, seeing, and recognition are the major features of natural intelligence. Each of these features has been also investigated by technology. The ultimate solution is a man-made system that integrates all these features into learning–generalization–seeing–recognition hybrids.

An important aspect of the human visual system is the ability to recognize an object despite changes in the object's position in the input field, its size, or its angular orientation. Many laboratories investigate position, scale, and rotation invariant object recognition systems.

Invariant object recognition includes industrial applications of machine vision involving translation, rotation, and scale invariant processing. The influence of rotation and scale is minimized through the proper transformation. Translation invariance means that the relative neighborhood connection topology and weights of cells are identical for every pixel. The problem leads to an orthogonal set of feature layers mapped into fine grained, massively parallel systems. Partially visible objects are represented by a set of shape relevant points, called "landmarks." The hypothesis of a model object in a scene is completed by matching the model landmark with the scene landmarks.

Newly developed computer systems designed to handle the speeds for real-time vision applications include massively parallel vision processors with raw power of up to two billion operations per second, performing logical operations on an entire image in 0.1 msec, special high speed parallel SIMD systems with close to a

Fast Learning and Invariant Object Recognition, By Branko Souček and the IRIS Group.
ISBN 0-471-57430-9 © 1992 John Wiley & Sons, Inc.

billion connection per second, and new systolic array implementations with over 300 billion connections per second, among others.

1.2 FAST LEARNING

Learning is one of the basic features of intelligence. The concept of learning machines comes from biological models. Learning is effective self-modification of the organism that lives in a complex and changing environment. Learning is any directed change in the knowledge structure that improves the performance.

Even lower animals exhibit features of learning and adaptation. Souček and Carlson [1] performed computer aided experiments with insects and birds and with frog synapses. These experiments show that learning and language present the base for adaptive communication.

Different learning rules have been developed so far [1–5].

Back propagation, a local iterative technique, is the most popular method for training multilayered neural networks. However, the back propagation is slow and unstable, and it could produce inferior solutions when the problem to be solved is moderately complex or the network is large. Numerous speedup modifications to the back-propagation algorithm exist, with significant improvements.

Holographic networks are a new brand of neural networks, which have been developed by Sutherland [6, 7]. This type of networks significantly differs from the conventional back-propagation layered type. The main difference is that a holographic neuron is much more powerful than a conventional one, so that it is functionally equivalent to a whole conventional network. Therefore there is no need to build massive networks of holographic neurons for most applications one or few neurons are sufficient. In a holographic neuron there exist only one input channel and one output channel, but they carry whole vectors of complex numbers. An input vector S is called a stimulus and it has the form:

$$S = [\lambda_1 e^{i\theta_1}, \lambda_2 e^{i\theta_2}, \cdots, \lambda_n e^{i\theta_n}].$$

An output vector R is called a response and its form is:

$$R = [\gamma_1 e^{i\phi_1}, \gamma_2 e^{i\phi_2}, \cdots, \gamma_m e^{i\phi_m}].$$

All complex numbers above are written in polar notation, so that modules are interpreted as confidence levels of data, and phase angles serve as actual values of data. The neuron internally holds a complex $n \times m$ matrix X, which enables memorizing stimulus-response associations. Learning one association between a stimulus S and a desired response R reduces to the (noniterative) matrix operation

$$X + S^T R.$$

Note that all associations are enfolded onto the same matrix X. The response $R*$ to a stimulus

$$S* = [\lambda_1^* e^{i\theta_1^*}, \lambda_2^* e^{i\theta_2^*}, \cdots, \lambda_n^* e^{i\theta_n^*}].$$

is computed through the following matrix operation:

$$R* = \frac{1}{c^*} S*X.$$

Here c^* denotes a normalization coefficient which is given by $c^* = \Sigma_{k=1}^{n} \lambda_k^*$.

The response $R*$ to a stimulus $S*$ can be interpreted as a vector (i.e., a complex number) composed of many components. Each component corresponds to one of the learned responses. If $S*$ is equal to one of the learned stimuli S, then the corresponding response R occurs in $R*$ as a component with a great confidence level (≈ 1). The remaining components have small confidence levels ($\ll 1$) and they produce a "noise" (error).

1.3 THE LEARNING TO SEE SYSTEM

Object and pattern recognition are natural features of living organisms. A child learns to recognize visual, acoustic, and tactile sensations. At the first level are the elementary sensations: the face of a mother or father, basic words, warm and cold objects, and so on. The second level includes complex features: the recognition of a smiling face or angry face, noise versus music, a beautiful painting or a plain one. The third level includes abstractions and conceptual recognition: a good answer or a wrong one; ideas, reasons, models.

Although humans recognize physical objects and conceptual patterns with ease, it is very difficult to explain the mechanism of recognition. For this reason it is not easy to make computer systems for pattern and object recognition.

The physical world communicates with the pattern recognition system through sensors, transducers, and input/output channels. The pattern enters the system as a multidimensional vector, with a large number S of sensory components.

The first task of the system is to reduce the complexity of the problem, and to extract F features that describe the pattern in the best possible way. The number of features F should be much smaller than the number S of sensory components ($F \ll S$).

The second task of the system is to categorize patterns into C classes.

Example. Recognition of a hand written character. The sensory field is composed of a matrix 12×12. Hence $S = 124$. The recognition is based on $F = 7$ features, following Grunlund [8]. The characters are grouped into $C = 36$ classes.

A human subject is able to recognize most of the objects in the scene independent of where they may be in the visual field. The object can be translated, rotated or distorted to a certain degree or scaled up or down without degrading the accuracy of recognition. A variety of models inspired by the biological systems have been designed with the goal of reproducing these characteristics in machine vision systems. They include trees, such as Quinlan's ID3 [9]; backpropagation based methods; higher-order neural networks; and Sutherland's holographic networks.

One of the more standard approaches in pattern recognition (i.e., linear search) implements a convention whereby several pattern templates, whether in original or compressed form (i.e., frequency domain), must be stored and individually compared against the input reference pattern. These standard methods generally tend to require large amounts of memory and are computationally intensive and rather limited in their generalization capabilities. The linear search, for instance, indicates only a level of closeness for all stored pattern prototypes as compared against the input reference. Scaling problems are often encountered whereby a slight distortion of the input pattern often incurs a large increase in the computed pattern variance (poor generalization properties).

Figure 1.1 presents a visual to auditory associator based on the holographic network.

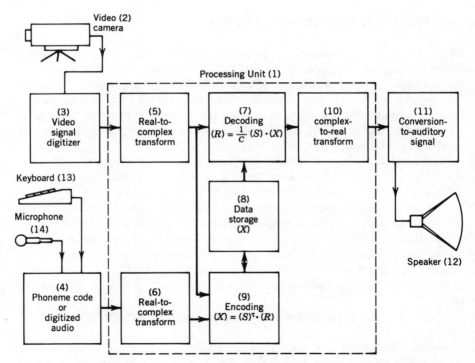

Figure 1.1 *A visual to auditory holographic associator and an intelligent multimedia integrator that merges learning, object recognition, and Sutherland's [6] Holographic Neural Technology.*

External visual and auditory fields are converted from real to complex domain. The processing Unit (1) stores multiple stimulus-response associations, using complex number or vector matrices. The system behaves as an image (or voice) addressable memory.

Input field represents the stimulus, and it is transformed in an inherently parallel manner through all the patterns enfolded within the holographic cell, finding the desired content in one single pass. Hence the system learns to see.

The holographic neural process performs a function analogous to pattern recognition, although pattern templates are effectively enfolded onto the same storage space, thus reducing memory requirements to only the amount of storage needed for a single pattern prototype. The complex-valued response generated within the holographic neural process indicates both a degree of confidence (magnitude component of the response vector) and an associated component of analog information (phase angle). Analog stimulus-response associations or mappings as learned and expressed within the holographic neural process are presented to neuron cells as arrays of such complex-valued numbers. The holographic neuron cell displays both the capability to learn associations on a single encoding transformation and within the individual neuron cell.

1.4 TOWARDS 10^{10} BIT COMPUTERS

It is now generally accepted that the central nervous system consists of about 10^{11} individual neurons. Each neuron supports several thousands synapses and is capable of storing about 10^4 bits of information. This makes the intelligence capacity of the human brain about 10^{15} bits. The snail, which has about 10^3 neurons in its central nervous system, would have the intelligence capacity of 10^7 bits, equivalent to that of the typical 1990s computer.

The amount of high-speed, random-access memory increases by an order of magnitude every six years. By the year 2040, we could expect computers with 10^{15} bits, which is the estimated cognitive power of the human brain. How do we design and program such machines? How do we fill them with data?

Bock [10] points out the following facts. Today, the average rate of software production is about four lines of code per person-hour, and by the year 2000, it could improve to 10 lines of code per person-hour. If we assume that an average line of high-level code will generate about 100 bits of machine code, 1 hour of programming will fill up 1000 bits of memory. Hence to program a 10^{10} bit computer in the year 2000 would take 10^7 person-hours. This is approximately 5000 person-years. Using similar arithmetic, Bock [10] speculates that in the year 2040, it would take 10 million person-years to program a 10^{15} bit computer, and concludes that classical programming is out of the question.

The solutions are in the areas of automated application integration, dynamic, genetic, and chaotic programming (See Refs. 1 to 5). Another solution is a mixture of learning, recognition, and association techniques, like in living organisms: accepting a vast amount of data through video, audio, and other fast I/O channels;

learning based on evaluations received by sensors from the environment and on associations coming from the memory; reasoning and generalization.

The visual to auditory associator, presented in Figure 1.1, shows the way into this new computing paradigm. It involves a marriage of learning and recognition, with fuzzy, holographic and parallel intelligence. In other words, the system Integrates Reasoning, Informing and Serving (IRIS). The IRIS paradigms are defined and described in [1 to 5].

REFERENCES

[1] B. Souček and M. Souček, *Neural and Massively Parallel Computers: The Sixth Generation*, Wiley, New York, 1988.

[2] B. Souček, *Neural and Concurrent Real—Time Systems: The Sixth Generation*, Wiley, New York, 1989.

[3] B. Souček and IRIS Group, *Neural and Intelligent Systems Integration*, Wiley, New York, 1991.

[4] B. Souček and IRIS Group, *Dynamic, Genetic and Chaotic Programming: The Sixth Generation*, Wiley, New York, 1992.

[5] B. Souček and IRIS Group, *Fuzzy, Holographic, and Parallel Intelligence*, Wiley, New York, 1992.

[6] J. Sutherland, "The holographic neural method," in B. Souček and IRIS Group, *Fuzzy, Holographic, and Parallel Intelligence*, Wiley, New York, 1992.

[7] J. Sutherland, A holographic model of memory, learning and expression, *Internat. J. Neural Syst.*, 1 (3), 259–267 1990.

[8] G. H. Grunlund, Fourier preprocessing for hand print character recognition, *IEEE Trans. Computers*, 192–201, (Feb. 1972).

[9] J. R. Quinland, Introduction of decision trees, *Machine Learning*, 1, 81–106 (1986).

[10] P. Bock, "Building the ultimate machine: The emergence of artificial cognition," in H. P. Schwefel and R. Manner (eds.), *Parallel Problem Solving from Nature*, Springer-Verlag, Berlin, pp. 474–481, 1991.

CHAPTER 2 ───────────────

Fast Back Propagation with Adaptive Decoupled Momentum

ALI A. MINAI
RONALD D. WILLIAMS

2.1 INTRODUCTION

The back-propagation algorithm is a very popular gradient descent method for training feedforward neural networks. In its simplest form, it performs fixed step size, steepest descent on an error surface in parameter space. Frequently, these error surfaces are highly nonlinear and quite complicated, forcing the use of very small step size to ensure stable convergence of the search procedure. This, in turn, makes the algorithm painfully slow, and causes it to get trapped in suboptimal local minima. Recently, numerous methods have been proposed to overcome these problems, and most have shown some degree of success. However, given the difficulty of completely describing neural net error surfaces in closed form, there is always room for better heuristics. Two very successful improvements to back propagation are the addition of an inertial *momentum* term, and the *delta-bar-delta* method for the adaptive variation of step size during learning. In the research reported here, a hybrid of these two techniques was used to produce improvements beyond those given by either technique alone, and without compromising the stability of the search procedure. This was done by using careful heuristics to adapt both step size and momentum in a decoupled fashion, thus allowing the search more flexibility than was available in the original algorithms.

In recent years, the back-propagation algorithm [1, 2, 3] has emerged as the leading method for training feedforward neural networks. These networks are being widely used in artificial intelligence applications, pattern recognition, signal processing, adaptive control, and speech-understanding systems. In its standard form,

Fast Learning and Invariant Object Recognition, By Branko Souček and the IRIS Group.
ISBN 0-471-57430-9   © 1992 John Wiley & Sons, Inc.

back propagation is a simple steepest descent algorithm, searching for minima on an appropriately specified error surface, using small steps of fixed size (specified by the *learning rate* or *gain parameter*). Like all such algorithms, back propagation suffers from certain drawbacks. Since the learning rate cannot be adaptively changed, it must be kept small to avoid divergence, which makes the algorithm very slow. Furthermore, the steepest descent policy is best suited to searching quadratic surfaces with a single minimum. On the very complex surfaces that occur in neural network optimization, more sophisticated techniques are necessary to achieve satisfactory performance. One such technique is presented in this chapter.

The decoupled momentum (DM) Algorithm is based on two previous methods developed by other researchers. These are momentum [2, 4], and the delta-bar-delta (DBD) Algorithm [5]. Momentum adds an intertial term to the basic learning equation, which enables the search to avoid small local minima, thus reducing the time to convergence. The DBD algorithm uses decoupled learning rates for the network parameters, and changes these rates adaptively, based on experiential error surface information. Both methods have shown remarkable success. The decoupled momentum algorithm is a hybrid of these two techniques. It uses the basic decoupling philosophy of the DBD algorithm but also adds a decoupled momentum term to each parameter's learning equation. Momentum is adapted just like the learning rate, thus producing a very flexible algorithm with a sophisticated response to the complex situations it encounters. In particular, the algorithm overcomes problems posed by error surfaces dominated by large flat areas with sudden, sharp minima. It has been demonstrated that the decoupled momentum algorithm (and other related versions) provides significant speedup over and above that given by momentum or DBD alone [6, 7]. More importantly, this speedup is obtained without compromising the stability of the search process in any way. This is a direct consequence of a carefully contrived hybridization scheme.

This chapter describes the DM algorithm in detail, discusses the philosophy behind it, presents comparative results on a number of problems, and suggests directions of further research in this and related areas.

2.2 THE BACK-PROPAGATION ALGORITHM

Originally, the back-propagation algorithm was designed for training feedforward systems only [2, 3], although it has since been generalized to handle recurrent systems as well [8–14]. In the research reported here, only feedforward networks are considered, since they are conceptually simpler to handle and account for the vast majority of the algorithm's applications.

A feedforward network N can be seen as a collection $\mathbf{P} = \{i\}$; $i = 1, 2, 3, \ldots, n$ of n processing elements (neurons) connected together in an *acyclic graph* with edges $\mathbf{W} = \{w_{ij}\}$; $i, j \in \mathbf{P}$. Typically, each neuron's output y_i is determined as:

$$y_i = \sigma(z_i) = \frac{1}{1 + e^{-z_i}} \qquad (2.1)$$

$$z_i = \sum_{j \in I_i} w_{ij} y_j + \theta_i \tag{2.2}$$

where I_i is the set of neurons that feed i and θ_i is a bias; $\sigma()$ is a simple sigmoid function between 0 and 1, and is called the *activation function* (or *transfer characteristic*) of neuron i. Activation functions other than the sigmoid have also been used with some success [15–18]. The acyclic connectivity ensures that no neuron can influence its own state directly or indirectly. A well defined set of m neurons, $X \subset P$, is designated the *input set*, and the neurons in this set receive input only from some external source. They can, thus, be seen as belonging to the lowest hierarchical level. Typically, these input neurons simply distribute signals to the next layer without transforming them in any way. At the other end of the hierarchy, a set $O \subset P$ of p units is designated the *output set*. The outputs of these neurons are taken to encode the network's state. Usually, the neurons in the net are arranged in *layers* L_k, such that $L_k \cap L_l = \varnothing$ when $k \neq l$, and $\cup_k L_k = P$. Such a network is shown in Figure 2.1. When an input vector $x = [x_1 x_2 \cdots x_m]$ is applied to the input neurons, a response $o = [o_1 o_2 \cdots o_p]$ is produced at the output neurons through direct forward propagation of signals. Thus, the network can be considered a nonlinear mapping from m to p dimensions, with parameter set W:

$$o = N(x; W) \tag{2.3}$$

The purpose of training is to modify the parameters until N represents a desired mapping.

Let $T = \{\tau_k\} = \{(x_k, o_k^*)\}$ be a *training set* of desired input/output pairs for the mapping to be learned. Then, the error of the network on training input τ_k can be

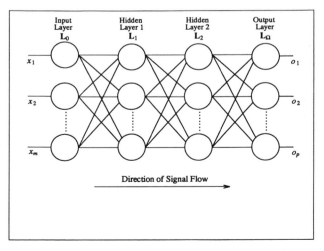

Figure 2.1   *A layered feedforward neural network.*

defined as

$$E_k(N) = \tfrac{1}{2} \sum_{i \in \mathbf{O}} (N(\mathbf{x}_k) - \mathbf{o}_k^*)^2 \qquad (2.4)$$

(though other definitions can also be used). The overall error over training set T of input/output pairs is

$$E = \sum_{k \in T} E_k \qquad (2.5)$$

Since the error metric used is smooth, E defines a smooth surface in the space of all network weights (*weight space*), and in order to do steepest descent, back propagation modifies the weights as

$$\Delta w_{ij} = -\eta \, \frac{\partial E}{\partial w_{ij}} \qquad (2.6)$$

where η is the *learning rate* parameter. The calculation of the partial derivative of the error with respect to weights deep in the network requires the backward propagation of error values from output to input—hence the name "back-propagation." The procedure used for this purpose was first developed by Werbos in 1974 [3], and is called *dynamic feedback*.

2.3 BACK-PROPAGATION PROBLEMS

In its simple gradient descent form, back-propagation suffers from serious drawbacks. Some of the more important among these are

1. **Slow Speed:** Since the error surface is nonlinear and only local gradient information is available at any time, η must be kept very small to ensure stable convergence. This, of course, slows down the learning process considerably.
2. **Local Minima:** The error surface on which gradient descent occurs may have local minima [19], which will always trap a strict descent algorithm.
3. **Misdirection of Descent:** It is well known from adaptive filter theory [20] that the performance of a steepest descent algorithm on quadratic error surfaces depends on the contours of the surface. On surfaces with noncircular contours, the gradient points in the direction of the minimum *only* when the current parameter setting happens to be on one of the principal axes of the surface, which is extremely unlikely. In all other cases, the direction of steepest gradient is not the best one, and descent occurs in a descending spiral rather than a straight (shortest) path, thus increasing the time to convergence. Given the complexity of back-propagation error surfaces, a

steepest descent policy will lead to a misdirection of the search in all but the rarest of cases. Typically, following this rule will reduce error, but at a rate far below optimal efficiency. (Jacobs [5] provides a more detailed discussion of this problem in the back-propagation context.)

4. **Oscillations:**   When the local noncircularity of the error surface becomes extreme, it approximates a narrow "ravine," sloping very gently toward the real minimum and very strongly in an almost orthogonal direction. Under such circumstances, a steepest descent algorithm with a finite step size can get into an oscillatory situation, jumping to and fro over the ravine rather than progressing toward the minimum. To complicate matters even further, these ravines may themselves be curved due to the nonlinear nature of the network being trained.

5. **Reversed Priorities:**   In the standard version of back propagation given by Eq. (2.6), the *physical* size of the horizontal step (Δw_{ij}) taken is directly proportional to the magnitude of the gradient ($\partial E / \partial w_{ij}$). Thus, for a fixed η, the horizontal step is large on *steep* slopes and small on flat areas. Strictly, this policy is appropriate only if there is a single minimum and if the gradient levels out as the minimum is approached (e.g., on quadratic surfaces). On surfaces where high error plateaus abound, and where slope can change rapidly, arbitrarily and nonlinearly, this "fixed step size" policy can easily lead to serious problems.

2.4   IMPROVING BACK PROPAGATION THROUGH STEP SIZE ADAPTATION

The fundamental problem in performing gradient descent on complicated surfaces is that the optimal learning rate (η_{opt}) is different at different points. Since it is usually impossible—or at least intractable—to work with a closed form of the error surface, the only information available to the algorithm is *local*. However, any calculation for η_{opt} made on the basis of this local information applies only *at* that particular point on the error surface. Typically, simplifying assumptions are made in order to extrapolate this information over a larger area. For example, the algorithm may assume that the gradient remains constant over a neighborhood of the point for which the calculation was made. A more sophisticated approach is to assume that the *curvature* of the surface remains constant in a neighborhood around that point. The latter may be done implicitly by assuming that the error surface is locally quadratic [21]. A somewhat different approach is to make intuitive heuristic assumptions about the error surface, and to vary the learning rate η on this basis throughout the learning process. All these methods, taken together, may be termed *adaptive step size methods* for improving back propagation. Numerous such techniques have been suggested in the literature [5, 21–29]. Of these, two are fundamental to the method presented in this chapter and are briefly discussed below.

2.4.1 Momentum

The most important step size method for back propagation is *momentum* [2, 4]. Essentially, the momentum method adds an *inertial parameter* μ to the gradient descent process of Eq. (2.6), thus damping out oscillations across error surface ravines and providing some speedup. The learning equation in this case is

$$\Delta w_{ij}(t) = -\eta \frac{\partial E}{\partial w_{ij}} + \mu \Delta w_{ij}(t - 1) \qquad (2.7)$$

where t indexes the iteration number. This can be considered a step size method because it implicitly adapts the size of the learning step on the basis of recent experience. The acceleration provided by momentum has been analyzed by Watrous [30], and is shown to approach $1/(1 - \mu)$ in the limit in situations where the gradient does not change too rapidly.

2.4.2 The Delta-Bar-Delta Algorithm

Another very successful method for back-propagation speedup is the *delta-bar-delta (DBD) algorithm* of Jacobs [5]. This algorithm is based on the principle that global assumptions cannot be made about error surfaces found in back-propagation training of nonlinear networks. The shape of the surface at any specific point might differ considerably along different weight directions. This means that the optimal step size may be quite different in each direction. In general, the exact determination of these optimal step sizes is not possible because of the nonlinear and complex nature of the error surface. However, intelligent heuristic assumptions can be made to improve performance considerably over the default case.

The fundamental insight of the DBD method is the *decoupling* of learning along the different weight directions. Using the same learning rate for all weights (as back propagation normally does) creates a strongly coupled process of high dimensionality. Giving each weight its own independent learning rate decomposes this process into multiple autonomous, one-dimensional processes, and descent on the error surface occurs as a *superposition* of these independent processes. The heuristic basis of the DBD method can be summarized [5] as follows:

1. Each weight (i.e., each dimension of the search space) is given its own, independent learning rate, effectively *decoupling* the system.
2. Each learning rate is varied independently based on error surface information.
3. When the error surface gradient $\partial E/\partial w_{ij}$ has the same sign for many iterations, the corresponding learning rate is increased, since this indicates that a minimum lies ahead.
4. When the error surface gradient changes signs for several consecutive time

steps, the learning rate is decreased, since this indicates that a minimum is being jumped over.

Based on these heuristics, the scheme for modifying learning rates is

$$\eta_{ij}(t + 1) = \eta_{ij}(t) + \Delta\eta_{ij}(t) \tag{2.8}$$

$$\Delta\eta_{ij}(t) = \begin{cases} \kappa & \text{if } \bar{\delta}_{ij}(t - 1)\delta_{ij}(t) > 0 \\ -\phi\eta_{ij}(t) & \text{if } \bar{\delta}_{ij}(t - 1)\delta_{ij}(t) < 0 \\ 0 & \text{otherwise} \end{cases} \tag{2.9}$$

$$\delta_{ij}(t) = \frac{\partial E(t)}{\partial w_{ij}} \tag{2.10}$$

$$\bar{\delta}_{ij}(t) = (1 - \theta)\delta_{ij}(t) + \theta\bar{\delta}_{ij}(t - 1) \tag{2.11}$$

where κ, ϕ and θ are parameters specified by the user. The quantity $\bar{\delta}(t)$ is basically an exponentially decaying trace of gradient values. Learning rates are increased additively to prevent them from becoming too large, while decrementing is exponential to ensure positive rates at all times and to allow rapid decrease [5].

2.5 DRAWBACKS OF THE DELTA-BAR-DELTA ALGORITHM

Experience has shown that the DBD algorithm is an excellent method for speeding up the learning process. However, because of its heuristic basis, there is always the possibility of further improvement, though this must be done without abandoning the essential features of the method.

Results cited by Jacobs [5] indicate that using momentum along with the delta-bar-delta algorithm can enhance performance considerably. However, it can also make the search diverge wildly—especially if κ is even moderately large. The reason is that momentum "magnifies" learning rate increments and quickly leads to inordinately large learning steps. One possible solution is to keep the κ factor very small, but this can easily lead to slow increase in η and little speedup.

Another related problem is that, even with a small κ, the learning rate can sometimes increase so much that the small exponential decrease is not sufficient to prevent wild jumps. Increasing ϕ exacerbates the problem instead of solving it because it causes drastic reduction of learning rate at inopportune moments, leaving the search stranded at points of high error. Simulations bear out the suspicion that DBD is very sensitive to small variations in the value of its parameters—especially κ.

In order to overcome these problems, several modifications to the basic DBD algorithm have been investigated. These, in turn, have led to the development of the *decoupled momentum (DM) algorithm*. The next section provides some background for the modified approach.

2.6   ARGUMENTS FOR A MODIFIED APPROACH

Most feedforward neural networks in current use have neurons with saturating activation functions, for example, sigmoids or hypergaussians. Thus, stimuli from large parts of the input space of these units produce virtually identical response, and even significant modifications to the input line weights have little effect on the neurons' output. This naturally translates into a very small (perhaps negligible) gradient in weight space. For example, suppose a sigmoidal output neuron i is fed by two hidden neurons j and k. Let the weights from these neurons to i be $w_{ij} = 5.0$ and $w_{ik} = 5.0$, and let the outputs from them be $y_j = 0.8$, $y_k = 0.6$. If the threshold of i is $w_{i0} = 2.0$, the net input to i is $z_i = 5 \times 0.8 + 5 \times 0.6 + 2 = 9$. By the definition of the sigmoid, the output of i is $y_i = \sigma(9) = 0.9998766$. Now, if w_{ij} is changed by ± 0.5 (which is a large change), the impact on y_i is as follows: For $w_{ij} = 4.5$, $y_i = \sigma(8.6) = 0.9998159$; and for $w_{ij} = 5.5$, $y_i = \sigma(9.4) = 0.9999172$. Thus, a change of 0.5 in w_{ij} changes the response of i only by the order of 10^{-5}. Clearly, then, the error surface gradient along the direction of w_{ij} will be very small, and standard back propagation will proceed *very* slowly. This problem is less serious when weight magnitudes are relatively small (because this produces activation functions with wide regions of well differentiated response). Nevertheless, it has been suggested [1] that the error surface of a typical feedforward network with many neurons is dominated by flat areas. Interspersed among these flat areas are minima, whose approach is signalled by *increasing* steepness of the gradient. Of course, the exact error surface characteristics close to a minimum can be quite unpredictable.

The problems of DBD can be traced to its uniform increment rule. As the search climbs down into a minimum, learning rate increases in fixed increments. If the gradient magnitude is decreasing at the same time, this keeps the actual horizontal step (Δw) fairly constant where normal back propagation would have made it smaller. However, if the gradient magnitude is increasing (i.e., if the shape of the minimum departs significantly from convexity), the effect of the increment is magnified, and the actual step size Δw increases very rapidly. This increase might be enough to throw the search entirely clear of the minimum. The problem becomes even more serious if momentum is used.

Based on these factors, the following two questions arise:

1. How can the step size explosion on steep slopes be avoided without sacrificing acceleration on flat areas?
2. If momentum improves the speed of the DBD algorithm, how can it be used without compromising the stability of the search?

These issues have been investigated using small training problems, and the following key points [6, 7] have emerged:

1. The idea of using adaptive, decoupled learning rates for individual weights can be fruitfully extended to momentum, giving the learning equation:

$$\Delta w_i(t) = -\eta_i(t)\delta_i(t) + \mu_i(t)\Delta w_i(t-1) \tag{2.12}$$

which is basically a decoupled system with independent memory in each direction. Momentum, in this case, can be adapted by rules similar to those used for the learning rate.

2. If the error surface in some direction w_i has been flat for some time, learning rate and momentum can be increased significantly because the very small values of $\delta_i(t)$ and $\Delta w_i(t-1)$ will keep the absolute step size Δw_i in check. When the gradient is appreciable, however, the increments should be made significantly smaller to avoid an explosion in Δw_i.

3. When a minimum along direction w_i is jumped over, both η_i and μ_i should be immediately decreased using the delta-bar-delta rule. To avoid losing minima, the decrease in momentum must be very drastic, so as to effectively erase the memory of recent weight changes. Conversely, a lower decrement factor can be used to introduce noise into the search and allow escape from shallow local minima.

4. Momentum μ_i must always be such that $0 \le \mu_i < 1$. Negative momentum defeats descent, while momentum of 1 or greater creates a positive feedback situation and leads to divergence. Some implementations of back-propagation scale η by $1 - \mu$, but that is not typical and has little significance [27].

These heuristic conclusions are the basis for the decoupled momentum algorithm.

2.7 THE DECOUPLED MOMENTUM ALGORITHM

The decoupled momentum algorithm has the following basic features:

1. Each weight w_{ij} has its own adaptive learning rate $\eta_{ij}(t)$ and momentum $\mu_{ij}(t)$.

2. Learning rate increase is made an exponentially decreasing function of $|\bar{\delta}(t)|$ instead of being a constant κ. This means that learning rate increases rapidly on very flat areas but quite slowly on areas of significant slope. The algorithm can thus adapt to largely flat error surfaces which must be covered quickly, and rough error surfaces which must be explored more carefully and without rapid growth of step size. Also, using an exponential ensures that deviations from the steepest descent direction would be significant only when different slopes are markedly disproportionate and compensating distortion is needed [5].

3. Momentum is varied just like the learning rate. Thus it is increased on plateaus and decreased exponentially near minima. The DBD criterion is used for this purpose too, but the increment factor is again a decreasing exponential function of $|\bar{\delta}(t)|$.

4. To prevent momentum from becoming too high, a *ceiling* is defined at which it is hard limited.

The equations for the DM algorithm can be written as follows:

$$\eta_{ij}(t+1) = \eta_{ij}(t) + \Delta\eta_{ij}(t) \tag{2.13}$$

$$\mu_{ij}(t+1) = \text{MIN}\,[\mu_{\max}, \mu_{ij}(t) + \Delta\mu_{ij}(t)] \tag{2.14}$$

$$\Delta\eta_{ij}(t) = \begin{cases} \kappa_l \exp\,(-\gamma_l|\bar{\delta}_{ij}(t)|) \\ -\phi_l\eta_{ij}(t) \\ 0 \end{cases}$$

$$\Delta\mu_{ij}(t) = \begin{cases} \kappa_m \exp\,(-\gamma_m|\bar{\delta}_{ij}(t)|) & \text{if } \bar{\delta}_{ij}(t-1)\delta_{ij}(t) > 0 \\ -\phi_m\mu_{ij}(t) & \text{if } \bar{\delta}_{ij}(t-1)\delta_{ij}(t) < 0 \\ 0 & \text{otherwise} \end{cases} \tag{2.15}$$

where $\delta_{ij}(t)$ and $\bar{\delta}_{ij}(t)$ and $\bar{\delta}_{ij}(t)$ are as in Eqs. (2.10) and (2.11), and $\kappa_l, \phi_l, \gamma_l, \kappa_m, \phi_m, \gamma_m$ and $\mu_{\max}$ are specified by the user. Note that DM reduces effectively to delta-bar-delta, back propagation with momentum (BPM), or standard back propagation with appropriate parameter settings.

2.8 SIMULATIONS

To investigate the performance of the DM algorithm, four learning problems of varying difficulty have been used. The first two require the learning of one-dimensional continuous mappings from a small data set, while the other two involve the learning of difficult Boolean functions given the complete truth tables. The problems are

Quadratic Map.   To learn the one-dimensional quadratic mapping,

$$y = f(x) = 3.95x(1-x), \quad 0 \le x \le 1 \tag{2.12}$$

given 20 randomly generated training points. The network used has one input neuron, one linear output neuron, and a layer of two sigmoidal hidden neurons. Performance is averaged over 30 runs.

Quartic Map.   To learn the severely bimodal one-dimensional quartic mapping,

$$y = f(f(x)); \quad f(x) = 3.95x(1-x), \quad 0 \le x \le 1 \tag{2.13}$$

given a randomly generated training set of 30 points. The network used has one input neuron, one linear output neuron, and a layer of four sigmoidal hidden neurons. Performance is averaged over 10 runs.

4-Bit Parity.   To learn the 4-bit parity function given all 16 patterns as the training set. The network has four input neurons, a layer of eight sigmoidal hidden neurons, and one linear output neuron thresholded for one above 0.75 and zero below 0.25. Performance is averaged over 30 runs.

3-Bit Binary-to-Local Mapping.   To learn to uniquely map 3-bit binary vectors to specified one of eight outputs. All eight patterns are used for training, and performance is averaged over 10 runs. The network used has three input neurons, two hidden layers of one and eight sigmoidal neurons respectively, and eight linear output neurons thresholded at 0.75 and 0.25 (as above). This problem with this particular network architecture was selected because Jacobs [5] cites it as being especially difficult due to the single unit hidden layer.

Results are reported for simulations with four learning algorithms: (1) back propagation with momentum (BPM), (2) delta-bar-delta (DBD), (3) decoupled momentum (DM), (4) delta-bar-delta with adaptive decoupled momentum (DBD-M). The DBD-M algorithm used the momentum modification rule of Eqs. (2.14) and (2.15) but the learning rate modification rule of Eq. (2.9). Some trial and error was used to find the settings that gave good results. If settings for DBD were available from Jacobs [5], these were also tried. Each run was started at a random point in weight space, with weights uniformly distributed between −1.0 and 1.0. All training was done in the "batched mode": Weight changes were accumulated over a pass through the entire data set and the average of this accumulated value applied at the end of the pass. One such pass is termed an *epoch*.

The results for all four problems are shown in Figures 2.2 through 2.7.

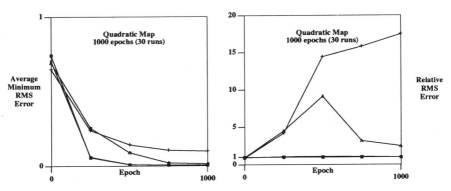

Figure 2.2 *Performance of different algorithms on the quadratic map problem.*

  + BPM: $\eta = 1.0$, $\mu = 0.9$

  $\triangle$ DBD: $\eta_i = 1.0$, $\kappa = 0.1$, $\phi = 0.3$, $\theta = 0.7$

  × DBD-M: $\eta_i = 1.0$, $\mu_{max} = 0.9$, $\kappa_l = 0.1$, $\phi_l = 0.3$, $\gamma_m = 5.0$, $\kappa_m = 0.1$, $\phi_m = 0.5$, $\theta = 0.7$

  ■ DM: $\eta_l = 1.0$, $\mu_{max} = 0.9$, $\gamma_l = 20.0$, $\kappa_l = 0.1$, $\phi_l = 0.3$, $\gamma_m = 5.0$, $\kappa_m = 0.1$, $\phi_m = 0.5$, $\theta = 0.7$

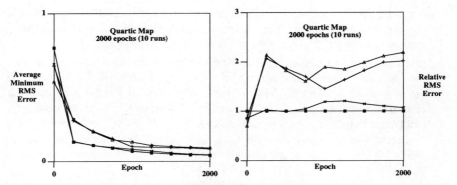

Figure 2.3 *Performance of different algorithms on the quartic map problem.*

$+$ BPM: $\eta = 1.0$, $\mu = 0.9$

$\triangle$ DBD: $\eta_i = 1.0$, $\kappa = 0.05$, $\phi = 0.3$, $\theta = 0.7$

$\times$ DBD-M: $\eta_i = 1.0$, $\mu_{max} = 0.9$, $\kappa_i = 0.1$, $\phi_i = 0.3$, $\gamma_m = 5.0$, $\kappa_m = 0.1$, $\phi_m = 0.5$, $\theta = 0.7$

$\blacksquare$ DM: $\eta_i = 1.0$, $\mu_{max} = 0.9$, $\gamma_l = 20.0$, $\kappa_l = 0.05$, $\phi_l = 0.3$, $\gamma_m = 5.0$, $\kappa_m = 0.1$, $\phi_m = 0.5$, $\theta = 0.7$

2.9 RESULTS AND DISCUSSION

Figure 2.2(a) is a plot of RMS error against the number of training epochs for the quadratic map problem, while figure 2.2(b) presents the same information with each algorithm's error divided by the error of the DM algorithm at the corresponding step. It is obvious that DM gives the best performance over the training period,

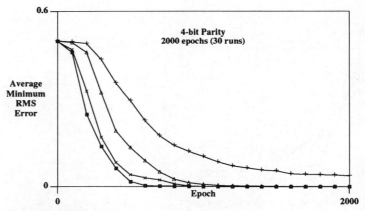

Figure 2.4 *Performance of different algorithms on the 4-bit parity problem.*

$+$ BPM: $\eta = 0.5$, $\mu = 0.9$

$\triangle$ DBD: $\eta_i = 1.0$, $\kappa = 0.1$, $\phi = 0.1$, $\theta = 0.7$

$\times$ DBD-M: $\eta_i = 1.0$, $\mu_{max} = 0.9$, $\kappa_i = 0.1$, $\phi_i = 0.1$, $\gamma_m = 1.0$, $\kappa_m = 0.1$, $\phi_m = 0.3$, $\theta = 0.7$

$\blacksquare$ DM: $\eta_i = 1.0$, $\mu_{max} = 0.9$, $\gamma_l = 10.0$, $\kappa_l = 0.1$, $\phi_l = 0.1$, $\gamma_m = 1.0$, $\kappa_m = 0.1$, $\phi_m = 0.3$, $\theta = 0.7$

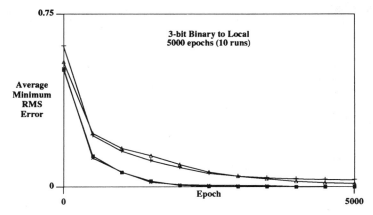

Figure 2.5 *Performance of different algorithms on the binary-to-local problem.*

+ BPM: $\eta = 0.5$, $\mu = 0.9$

△ DBD: $\eta_i = 0.05$, $\kappa = 0.05$, $\phi = 0.1$, $\theta = 0.7$

× DBD-M: $\eta_i = 0.05$, $\mu_{max} = 0.9$, $\kappa_I = 0.05$, $\phi_I = 0.1$, $\gamma_m = 1.0$, $\kappa_m = 0.1$, $\phi_m = 0.3$, $\theta = 0.7$

■ DM: $\eta_i = 0.05$, $\mu_{max} = 0.9$, $\gamma_I = 10.0$, $\kappa_I = 0.05$, $\phi_I = 0.1$, $\gamma_m = 1.0$, $\kappa_m = 0.1$, $\phi_m = 0.3$, $\theta = 0.7$

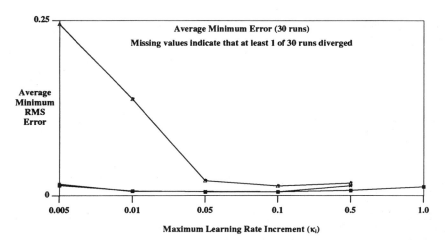

Figure 2.6 *Stability of algorithms with different learning rate increments. Quadratic map problem:* $y = 3.95x(1 - x)$, *1000 Epochs, 20 data points.*

△ DBD: $\eta_i = 1.0$, $\mu = 0.9$, $\kappa = x$, $\phi = 0.3$, $\theta = 0.7$

× DBD-M: $\eta_i = 1.0$, $\mu_{max} = 0.9$, $\kappa_I = x$, $\phi_I = 0.3$, $\gamma_m = 5.0$, $\kappa_m = 0.1$, $\phi_m = 0.5$, $\theta = 0.7$

■ DM: $\eta_i = 1.0$, $\mu_{max} = 0.9$, $\gamma_I = 20.0$, $\kappa_I = x$, $\phi_I = 0.3$, $\gamma_m = 5.0$, $\kappa_m = 0.1$, $\phi_m = 0.5$, $\theta = 0.7$

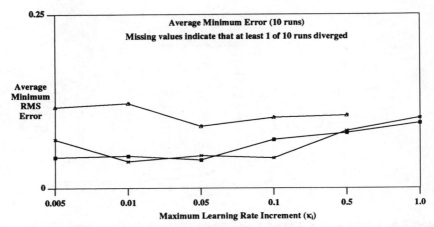

Figure 2.7 *Stability of algorithms with different learning rate increments. Quartic map problem: $y = f(f(x)); f(x) = 3.95x(1 - x)$, 2000 Epochs, 30 data points.*

△ DBD: $\eta_i = 1.0$, $\mu = 0.9$, $\kappa = x$, $\phi = 0.3$, $\theta = 0.7$

× DBD-M: $\eta_i = 1.0$, $\mu_{max} = 0.9$, $\kappa_l = x$, $\phi_l = 0.3$, $\gamma_m = 5.0$, $\kappa_m = 0.1$, $\phi_m = 0.5$, $\theta = 0.7$

■ DM: $\eta_i = 1.0$, $\mu_{max} = 0.9$, $\gamma_l = 20.0$, $\kappa_l = x$, $\phi_l = 0.3$, $\gamma_m = 5.0$, $\kappa_m = 0.1$, $\phi_m = 0.5$, $\theta = 0.7$

though DBD-M has almost the same performance. DBD is initially no better than steepest descent with momentum, and is outperformed over the whole training period by a factor of at least three.

Figures 2.3(a) and (b) present the same data for the quartic map problem. Here again, it is obvious that the modified algorithms outperform DBD and BPM by a factor of two throughout the learning period. Indeed, DBD does a little worse than BPM on this problem.

Figures 2.4 and 2.5 show the learning curves for the 4-bit parity problem and the binary-to-local problem, respectively. On the parity problem, the modified algorithms converge several times faster than DBD. Indeed, of the 30 runs made, DBD found the solution 29 times, while DM and DBD-M found it every time. Steepest descent with momentum fared much worse on both speed and number of converged solutions. On the binary-to-local problem, DBD once again did little better than steepest descent with momentum, while the DM and DBD-M algorithms had far better and virtually identical performance. Remarkably, all 10 runs of DM and DBD-M found perfect solutions, while both DBD and BPM had poorer performance.

Finally, Figures 2.6 and 2.7 illustrate the sensitivity of the three adaptive algorithms to the learning rate increment factor κ_l. It is obvious that, for the quadratic map, DBD is very sensitive to κ_l. Small values slow the algorithm down, while an increment of greater than 0.5 causes some runs to diverge. The same is true for the quartic map problem, though here a small increment (in the range tested) seems to be a lesser handicap—presumably because the error surface is more complex and requires careful descent. Among the other algorithms, DBD-M also diverges (in some cases) for increments greater than 0.5—though only on the quadratic map—while DM does not. The remarkable point is the stable performance of DM over the entire range of κ_l for both problems. It also consistently produces excellent performance in terms of error. This clearly indicates the advantage of using an adjustable increment rather than a flat one.

2.10 CONCLUSION

The main purpose of the experiments reported here is to demonstrate that adaptive momentum can be safely and usefully combined with the delta-bar-delta algorithm (and presumably other step size algorithms), provided that learning rate and momentum increments are made sensitive to the gradient magnitude. The main price of the improved performance shown by the decoupled momentum algorithm is the proliferation of user-specified parameters—five more than delta-bar-delta. Though most of these parameters can be set within fairly wide ranges, some recommendations can be made:

- The initial learning rate should be set very small in most cases, especially for "complicated" problems (e.g., the binary-to-local problem).
- The more "complicated" a problem, the smaller should learning rate and momentum increments be. This makes learning slower but provides better assurance of finding minima on very sharply convoluted surfaces. In general, the momentum increment (κ_m) should be kept fairly small (≤ 0.1).
- The smaller the maximum increment (κ) used, the less important the corresponding γ parameter. In general, large γ should be used with a large κ, so that the effect of the large increment is confined to very flat areas.
- Learning rate and momentum decrement factors (ϕ_l and ϕ_m) should be quite large (in the 0.1 to 1.0 range). In particular, making ϕ_m close to 1.0 ensures that momentum is completely damped whenever a minimum is jumped over. This will prevent the search from "skipping" out of a minimum just because of momentum. On the other hand, making ϕ_m smaller will allow the search to jump out of some minima and perhaps find a better minimum. If there is reason to believe that wide minima are likely to be deeper than narrow ones, it might be good policy to set ϕ_m around 0.5.
- The maximum value for momentum can safely be set fairly high, as long as the increment value is not too large.
- Since θ acts as the memory parameter for adaptation, it should be made small in situations where rapid adaptation is needed (e.g., if there is reason to believe that the error surface is very convoluted) and vice versa.

From the perspective of computational complexity, the DM algorithm requires the calculation of momentum as well as learning rate for each weight at each step. However, both these computations use the same information (the DBD criterion) and, therefore, entail no extra passes through the network. The time complexity of DM is, therefore, the same as that of DBD, provided that the exponential function is efficiently implemented. Extra storage is required for momentum values but is a small overhead over DBD's storage of gradient traces and learning rate values.

On the basis of the experiments reported here, it may be safely claimed that the decoupled momentum algorithm considerably improves on the performance of the delta-bar-delta algorithm for many problems of reasonable complexity. However, generalizing these claims over all possible situations would be irresponsible. Like all other heuristic methods applied in complex nonlinear situations, the DM method will probably fail to improve performance under certain circumstances. The results presented here indicate that such circumstances are likely to be rare—especially if the above guidelines are followed.

2.11   ISSUES FOR FURTHER RESEARCH

Several insights have emerged from the research reported here and can be the topic of further research. Some of these are listed below.

- As pointed out above, the parameters of the DM algorithm could be used in a *simulated annealing* setting, providing a better probability of escaping local minima. However, there is some danger of parameter proliferation with such schemes, and it might be necessary to simplify the current adaptive scheme to allow the inclusion of annealing.

- It is noticeable from experiments that momentum's decisive advantage is mostly in the *early* part of the search—presumably because gradients are larger and the minima are wider. As the search descends to a "floor," perhaps with narrow minima, it might be worthwhile to cut momentum out and do a detailed, slow search in a small neighborhood in order to achieve further improvement. For example, the maximum momentum parameter could be made proportional to current error.

- A very large number of back-propagation heuristics have been suggested by researchers over the years. It would be worthwhile to assess the compatibility of some of these, and perhaps combine them with DM type algorithms to achieve even greater improvement. Again, this might require simplification of the DM algorithm or even a return to DBD.

- Given the complicated nature of the optimization problem solved by back propagation, it might be appropriate to consider *multistage methods*. For example, the search could be divided into three serial parts: (1) a high energy, coarse-grained search to locate a wide minimum; (2) a quick descent to the wide floor of this minimum (if it exists); and (3) a careful exploration of the floor and slow descent to the lowest point in the basin. Totally different strategies may be suited to each stage, and it may be that a multistage procedure consisting of three different algorithms will prove better than a global, adaptive procedure such as DBD or DM. Such a "modular" procedure could be much simpler than the adaptive ones simply because the internal homogeneity of each stage will require less complicated adaptation.

ACKNOWLEDGMENT

This research was supported by the Virginia Center for Innovative Technology and was conducted at the Center for Semicustom Integrated Systems, University of Virginia, Charlottesville.

REFERENCES

[1] R. Hecht-Nielsen, Theory of the back-propagation neural network, *Proc. Internat. Joint Conf. on Neural Networks*, Vol. I, 593–606 (June 1989).

[2] D. E. Rumelhart, G. E. Hinton, and R. J. Williams, "Learning Internal Representations by Error Propagation," in D. E. Rumelhart and J. L. McClelland, Eds., *Parallel Distributed Processing: Explorations in the Microstructure of Cognition*, Vol. 1: *Foundations*, MIT Press, Cambridge, Mass., 1986, pp. 318–362.

[3] P. Werbos, "Beyond Regression: New Tools for Prediction and Analysis in the Behavioral Sciences," Ph.D. thesis, Harvard University (August 1974).

[4] D. Plaut, S. Nowlan, and G. Hinton, "Experiments on Learning by Back-Propagation," Tech. Rep. CMU-CS-86-126, Dept. Computer Science, Carnegie Mellon University, Pittsburgh, Pa. (1986).

[5] R. A. Jacobs, Increased rates of convergence through learning rate adaptation, *Neural Networks*, 1, 295–307 (1988).

[6] A. A. Minai and R. D. Williams, Acceleration of back-propagation through learning rate and momentum adaptation, *Proc. Internat. Joint Conf. on Neural Networks 90*, Vol. I, 676–679 (January 1990).

[7] A. A. Minai and R. D. Williams, Back-propagation heuristics: A study of the extended delta-bar-delta algorithm, *Proc. Internat. Joint Conf. on Neural Networks 90*, Vol. I, 676–679 (June 1990).

[8] L. B. Almeida, A learning rule for asynchronous perceptrons with feedback in a combinatorial environment, *Proc. 1st Internat. Conf. on Neural Networks*, Vol. II, 609–618 (1987).

[9] B. A. Pearlmutter, Learning state space trajectories in recurrent neural networks, *Neural Computation*, 1, 263–269 (1989).

[10] F. J. Pineda, Generalization of back-propagation to recurrent neural networks, *Physical Review Lett.*, 59, 2229–2232 (1987).

[11] R. Rowher and B. Forrest, Training time-dependence in neural networks, *Proc. 1st Internat. Conf. on Neural Networks*, Vol. II, 701–708 (1987).

[12] P. J. Werbos, Generalization of backpropagation with application to a recurrent gas market model, *Neural Networks*, 1(4), 339–356 (1988).

[13] R. J. Williams and D. Zipser, A learning algorithm for continually running fully recurrent neural networks, *Neural Computation*, 1, 270–280 (1989).

[14] R. J. Williams and J. Peng, An efficient gradient-based algorithm for on-line training of recurrent network trajectories, *Neural Computation*, 2, 490–501 (1990).

[15] E. Hartman, J. D. Keeler, and J. M. Kowalski, Layered neural networks with gaussian hidden units as universal approximators, *Neural Computation*, 2(2), 210–215 (Summer 1990).

[16] J. Moody and C. Darken, "Fast Learning in Networks of Locally-Tuned Processing Units," Research Rep. YALEU/DCS/RR-654, Dept. Computer Science, Yale University (March 1989).

[17] M. Niranjan and F. Fallside, Neural networks and radial basis functions in classifying static speech patterns, *Neural Networks*, 2, 359 (1988).

[18] M. Stinchcombe and H. White, Universal approximation using feedforward networks with non-sigmoid hidden layer activation functions, *Proc. 1st Internat. Joint Conf. on Neural Networks*, Vol. I, 613–617 (1988).

[19] J. M. McInerney, K. G. Haines, S. Biafore, and R. Hecht-Nielsen, Back propagation error surfaces can have local minima, *Proc. 1st Internat. Joint Conf. on Neural Networks*, Vol. II, 627 (1988).

[20] B. Widrow and S. D. Stearns, *Adaptive Signal Processing*, Prentice-Hall, New York, 1985.

[21] S. E. Fahlman, "An Empirical Study of Learning in Backpropagation Networks," Depart. Computer Science Tech. Rep. CMU-CS-88-162, Carnegie-Mellon Univ., (1988).

[22] L. G. Allred and G. E. Kelly, Supervised learning techniques for backpropagation networks, *Proc. Internat. Joint Conf. on Neural Networks 90*, Vol. I, 721–728 (June 1990).

[23] J. P. Cater, Successfully using peak learning rates of 10 (and greater) in back-propagation networks with the heuristic learning algorithm, *Proc. 1st Internat. Conf. on Neural Networks*, Vol. II, 645–651 (1987).

[24] E. D. Dahl, Accelerated learning using the generalized delta rule, *Proc. 1st Internat. Conf. on Neural Networks*, Vol. II, 523–530 (1987).

[25] M. R. Devos and G. A. Orban, Self adaptive backpropagation, *Proc. NeuroNimes 1988*, Vol. EZ (1988).

[26] D. E. Rumelhart and J. L. McClelland, Eds., *Parallel Distributed Processing: Explorations in the Microstructure of Cognition*, (2 volumes), MIT Press, Cambridge, Mass., 1986.

[27] T. Tollenaere, SuperSAB: Fast adaptive back propagation with good scaling properties, *Neural Networks*, 3(5), 561–573 (1990).

[28] T. P. Vogl, J. K. Mangis, A. K. Rigler, W. T. Zink, and D. L. Alkon, Accelerating the convergence of the back-propagation method, *Biological Cybernetics*, 59, 257–263 (1988).

[29] R. H. White, "The learning rate in back-propagation systems: An application of Newton's method," *Proc. Internat. Joint Conf. on Neural Networks 90*, Vol. I, 679–684 (June 1990).

[30] R. L. Watrous, Learning algorithms for connectionist networks: Applied gradient methods of nonlinear optimization, *Proc. 1st Internat. Conf. on Neural Networks*, Vol. II, 619–627 (1987).

CHAPTER 3 ⸺⸺⸺⸺⸺⸺⸺⸺⸺⸺⸺

Second Order Gradient Methods in Back Propagation

SELWYN PIRAMUTHU

3.1 INTRODUCTION

The back-propagation algorithm, as it pertains to a multilayered perceptron, has been shown to be able to learn any function to a very close approximation [1, 2, 3]. The classic back-propagation algorithm [4, 5] uses the simplistic steepest descent method for searching in feature space. This chapter presents a modified Newton–Raphson type algorithm, along with various attempts at improving the back-propagation algorithm, specifically using second order gradient search methods.

The major problem with the steepest descent method is that the step lengths are always the same regardless of the current point in the search space. This prevents the algorithm from taking advantage of the fluctuations in the search space and also the proximity of current point of search to the optimal point. The second order methods that have been explored to date for back-propagation fall under the general category of Newton-type methods. Although these are all based on the same principle of modifying the step length during gradient search, each of these take advantage of various characteristics of the gradient search algorithm.

The second order methods incorporate gradient information at current search points into the search strategy, thus avoiding the pitfalls associated with a constant step length. One of the disadvantages of using second order methods is the inversion of the Hessian matrix, which increases in dimension proportional to the number of units in the layers in the connectionist network. To circumvent the problem due to the inversion of Hessian matrix, various approximation assumptions have been made by researchers. These assumptions improve the overall performance of

Fast Learning and Invariant Object Recognition, By Branko Souček and the IRIS Group.
ISBN 0-471-57430-9 © 1992 John Wiley & Sons, Inc.

the back-propagation algorithm in situations where the assumptions are valid. This chapter discusses these assumptions, along with their validity and shortcomings, in order to explore various alternatives and their consequences in improving the convergence speed of the back-propagation algorithm.

In this section, we briefly discuss previous research aimed at utilizing the second order derivatives in gaining more information about the search surface, to aid in the speed of convergence. Second order methods converges faster than gradient methods by taking into account additional information about the objective function. Most of the previous attempts have been in the realm of quasi-Newton methods as applied to back propagation due to the difficulty in deriving the Hessian matrix in a second order algorithm.

Waltrous [6] implemented the Broyden–Fletcher–Goldfarb–Shanno (BFGS) algorithm in a connectionist learning framework, and compared it with back propagation. BFGS converged in significantly fewer iterations as compared to back propagation. BFGS is a quasi-Newton method and hence only an approximation to the inverse Hessian need be computed.

Becker and le Cun [7] use a diagonal approximation to the Hessian to compute approximate curvature information, ignoring the off-diagonal terms in the Hessian matrix. Instead of the weight update rule in back propagation, $\Delta w_{ij} = -\eta \frac{\partial E}{\partial \text{net}_j}$, a "pseudo-Newton step"

$$\Delta w_{ij} = -\frac{\dfrac{\partial E}{\partial \text{net}_j}}{\dfrac{\partial^2 E}{\partial \text{net}_j^2}}$$

was used.

The pseudo-Newton method has the effect of scaling the descent step in each direction unlike Newton method which performs both scaling and rotation of the steepest descent step. In their study, the diagonal Hessians were approximated using a finite difference method. The validity of this method depends on how well the diagonal Hessian approximation models the true Hessian.

Parker [8] derived a second order LMS algorithm for linear functions. Several assumptions and approximations are made in the process. For example, the derivation of $\frac{\partial^2 w}{\partial t^2}$, the second order derivative, is valid only for linear functions. Approximations are also made on estimating a matrix in the process wherein average values are taken for the estimates. Since these average values may prove not as effective as instantaneous values, the resulting expression is only approximate.

Fahlman [9] proposed a second-order method (*quickdrop*) using heuristics based loosely on Newton's method. The quickprop algorithm is valid only if the assumptions (discussed later in this section) hold. The quickprop algorithm is similar to the back-propagation algorithm, in addition to which, copies of $\frac{\partial E}{\partial w(t-1)}$ and $(w(t) - w(t-1))$ are kept for each weight. The $\Delta w(t)$ values

$$\Delta w(t) = \frac{S(t)}{S(t-1) - S(t)} \Delta w(t-1)$$

where $S(t) = \frac{\partial E}{\partial w(t)}$ are used to jump directly to the bottom of the parabola, individually for each of the weights that are being computed.

These methods have shown promising results by utilizing second order gradient search procedures to improve the performance of back-propagation algorithm. However, the assumptions and simplifications that were made in the process could be avoided to a certain extent by proper assumptions on the error function and also by approaching the problem a little differently. For example, Fahlman's quickprop algorithm is based on ". . . two risky assumptions: (1) the error vs. weight curve for each weight can be approximated by a parabola whose arms open upward, and (2) the change in the shape of the error curve, as seen by each weight, is not affected by all the other weights that are changing at the same time." (Fahlman [9], p. 46) Assumption (1) is unwarranted since this is a much stronger assumption than assuming convexity of the error space, which is encompassed by this assumption. But if the error space is convex it defeats the purpose of using a second order method at all, when a simplistic steepest gradient search would suffice. Since the weights are dependent on activations (step 3 of the back-propagation algorithm in Section 3.2), which in turn are dependent on the weights in other links (step 4 of the back-propagation algorithm in Section 3.2) assumption (2) may not always hold unless in special circumstances. Similarly, the method proposed by Becker and Le Cun [7] depends on how well the diagonal Hessian approximation models the true Hessian, and in Parker the derivation of $\frac{\partial^2 w}{\partial t^2}$ and the effects that average values (as opposed to instantaneous values) might have on the solution procedure are unknown. In the next section, we develop a modified algorithm that avoids some of the problems encountered while dealing with second-order methods for back propagation.

3.2 MODIFIED BP ALGORITHM

In the steepest gradient method [4], the objective (error) function that is minimized is

$$E = \sum_p E_p = \tfrac{1}{2} \sum_p \sum_j (o_{pj} - a_{pj})^2 \tag{3.1}$$

where, p corresponds to the pattern that is currently under consideration, o_{pj} is the target output value of the j th unit in the output layer when pattern p is input, a_{pj} is the actual output value of the j th unit in the output layer when pattern p is input, and E is the sum of errors over all the patterns that are input. Once the threshold (θ) values are set, the θ terms can be ignored for further analysis. For unit j receiving input from unit i's in the lower layer,

$$\text{net}_j = \sum_i w_{ij} a_i, \tag{3.2}$$

where

$$a_i = f(\text{net}_i) = \frac{1}{1 + e^{-\text{net}_i}} \tag{3.3}$$

and f is a sigmoid (squashing) function. Since the change in weight in a link is directly (negatively) proportional to the rate of change of the error function with respect to a change in weight in the link of interest, that is,

$$\Delta_p w_{ij} \propto -\frac{\partial E_p}{\partial w_{ij}}.$$

By chain rule, the derivative can be written as the product of two parts: the derivative of the error with respect to the output of the unit times the derivative of the output with respect to the weight

$$\frac{\partial E_p}{\partial w_{ij}} = \frac{\partial E_p}{\partial \text{net}_{pj}} \frac{\partial \text{net}_{pj}}{\partial w_{ij}}. \tag{3.4}$$

From Eq. (3.2), we get

$$\frac{\partial \text{net}_{pj}}{\partial w_{ij}} = \frac{\partial}{\partial w_{ij}} \sum_k w_{kj} a_{pk} = a_{pi}. \tag{3.5}$$

Define

$$\delta_{pj} = -\frac{\partial E_p}{\partial \text{net}_{pj}} = -\frac{\partial E_p}{\partial a_{pj}} \frac{\partial a_{pj}}{\partial \text{net}_{pj}}. \tag{3.6}$$

From Eq. (3.3),

$$\frac{\partial a_{pj}}{\partial \text{net}_{pj}} = f'(\text{net}_{pj}) \tag{3.7}$$

which is the derivative of the squashing function f for the j th unit, evaluated at the net input net_{pj} to that unit. If j is an unit in the output layer of the network, from Eq. (3.1),

$$\frac{\partial E_p}{\partial a_{pj}} = -(o_{pj} - a_{pj}). \tag{3.8}$$

It follows from Eqs. (3.6, 3.7, 3.8) that

$$\delta_{pj} = (o_{pj} - a_{pj})\, f'\,(\text{net}_{pj}). \tag{3.9}$$

In the proposed method, the idea of optimizing a quadratic function is utilized. The original objective function, in the classical steepest gradient method, of minimizing the squares of the differences between the actual and the desired output values summed over the output units and all pairs of input/output vectors is replaced by an equivalent exponential function. This is done in order to allow for the second derivative to be derived from the objective function. The direction of descent which minimizes $(o_j - a_j)^2$ is equivalent to the direction of descent which minimizes $e^{(o_j - a_j)^2}$, and the transformation is justified since the exponential of a nonnegative function reaches its minimum when the function reaches its minimum.

Recall that the first three terms of a Taylor series expansion gives

$$h(x_p + p) \approx h(x_k) + g_k^T p + \tfrac{1}{2} p^T G_k p$$

so that the gradient is approximated by $G_k + g_k p_k$. In our modification the function to be minimized (ignoring the subscript p) is

$$h(a) = e^{(o_j - a_j)^2} \tag{3.10}$$

where o_j and a_j are the target and actual outputs (active values) of the j th unit in the output layer. Hence,

$$g_i = -2(o_j - a_j)e^{(o_j - a_j)^2}$$
$$G_j = 2e^{(o_j - a_j)^2} + 4(o_j - a_j)^2 e^{(o_j - a_j)^2}$$

The gradient is thus:

$$G_i(o_j - a_j) + g_j = 4(o_j - a_j)^3 e^{(o_j - a_j)^2} \tag{3.11}$$

Substituting Eqs. (3.11) and (3.7) into Eq. (3.6), we get

$$\delta_j = 4(o_j - a_j)^3 e^{(o_j - a_j)^2} f'\,(\text{net}_j) \tag{3.12}$$

where $f'\,(\text{net}_j)$ is the derivative of the activation function with respect to a change in the net input to unit j.

This is the modification in step 5 of the modified back-propagation algorithm as given below. In the regular back propagation (using steepest gradient), step 5 if unit j is an output unit is

$$\delta_j = (o_j - a_j)f'\,(\text{net}_j)$$

which is replaced by Eq. (3.12) in the modified back-propagation algorithm.

3.2.1   Modified Back-Propagation Algorithm

1. **Initialize**   Set number of units in input (N_o), output (M), and hidden

$$(N_k; \; k = 1, \ldots, h) \text{ layers,}$$

   where h is the number of hidden layers. Specify links between units with no links between two units in the same layer. Set random values for weights in all the bias levels for all the units (except those in the input layer).

2. **Input**   Present input/output vectors $i_1, \ldots, i_{N-1}, o_1, \ldots, o_{M-1}$.

3. **Update weights**

$$w_{ij}(n + 1) = w_{ij}(n) + \eta \delta_j a_i + \alpha(w_{ij}(n) - w_{ij}(n - 1))$$

   where $w_{ij}(n + 1)$ is the weight in the link from unit i to unit j in the nth iteration (epoch), η is the learning rate, and α is the momentum term.

4. **Calculate actual outputs**   for hidden layers ($x_i = i_i$ if unit i is an input unit),

$$a_j = f\left(\sum_{i=0}^{N_k - 1} w_{ij}x_i - \theta_j \right), \quad 0 \le j \le N_k$$

   for output layer,

$$a_j = f\left(\sum_{i=0}^{M - 1} w_{ij}x_i - \theta_j \right), \quad 0 \le j \le N_h$$

   where θ_j is the threshold in the jth unit in the layer under consideration.

5. **Update δ-values**   If unit (j) is an output unit:

$$\delta_j = 4(o_j - a_j)^3 e^{(o_j - a_j)^2} f'(\text{net}_j)$$

   if unit (j) is a hidden unit:

$$\delta_j = f'(\text{net}_j) \sum_k \delta_k w_{jk}$$

6. **Repeat**   Go to step 2.

It is readily seen that in the modified algorithm the connection weights change according to the product of the standard BP adjustment terms and a random scaling factor $4(o_j - a_j)^2 e^{(o_j - a_j)^2}$.

3.3 EXAMPLES

In this section, we discuss the implementation details of two encoding problems (4-2-4 and 8-3-8) that were used to compare the performances of the back-propagation algorithms. The two encoding problems are used to illustrate the relative performances of the two algorithms (SG, NR) on standard problems with no external noise. The purpose here is to study the convergence rates (in terms of both the (run) time as well as the number of epochs taken to converge) of the two algorithms for comparable final tss values across all the patterns.

In the 4-2-4 and 8-3-8 encoding problems [9] (Ackley, Hinton, and Sejnowski, 1985; Ballard, 1987; Bremermann and Anderson, 1990), a set of orthogonal input patterns are mapped to a set of orthogonal output patterns through a lesser (relative to input and output) number of hidden units. For an equal number (N) of input and output units, the number of hidden units is taken to be $\log_2 N$. The $\log_2 N$ hidden units form a binary code with a distinct binary pattern for each of the N input patterns. The network is allowed to learn an encoding of an N-bit input pattern into a $\log_2 N$-bit pattern, which is then decoded into an N-bit output pattern. Hidden units act as efficient encoders of the input signal, which is the natural mode of operation in multilayered perceptrons. Hence encoding problems were selected in this study to compare the different back-propagation algorithms on multilayered perceptrons.

In the 4-2-4 encoding problem, there are four input and four output nodes and two nodes in a hidden layer (Fig. 3.1). The inputs and outputs for the 4-2-4 encoding problem are as follows:

pattern #	input	output
one	1 0 0 0	1 0 0 0
two	0 1 0 0	0 1 0 0
three	0 0 1 0	0 0 1 0
four	0 0 0 1	0 0 0 1

As can be seen, both the input and the output patterns are the same. To account for scalability of the results, a slightly larger problem, the 8-3-8 encoding problem, was also used (Fig. 3.2). The principle underlying the 8-3-8 encoding problem is the same as that in the 4-2-4 encoding problem. The input and output patterns for the 8-3-8 encoding problem are as follows:

pattern #	input	output
one	1 0 0 0 0 0 0 0	1 0 0 0 0 0 0 0
two	0 1 0 0 0 0 0 0	0 1 0 0 0 0 0 0
three	0 0 1 0 0 0 0 0	0 0 1 0 0 0 0 0
four	0 0 0 1 0 0 0 0	0 0 0 1 0 0 0 0
five	0 0 0 0 1 0 0 0	0 0 0 0 1 0 0 0
six	0 0 0 0 0 1 0 0	0 0 0 0 0 1 0 0
seven	0 0 0 0 0 0 1 0	0 0 0 0 0 0 1 0
eight	0 0 0 0 0 0 0 1	0 0 0 0 0 0 0 1

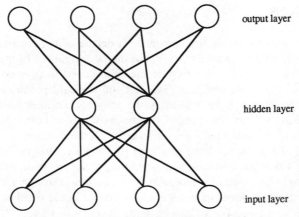

output layer

hidden layer

input layer

Figure 3.1   *The 4-2-4 encoding network.*

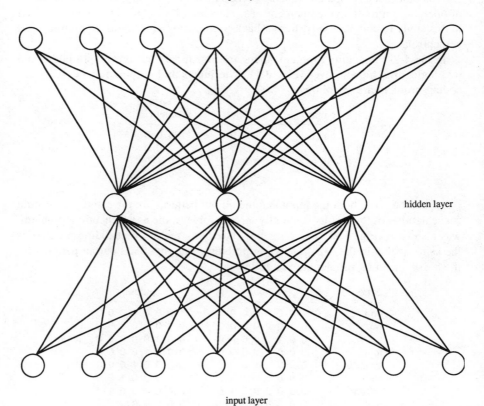

output layer

hidden layer

input layer

Figure 3.2   *The 8-3-8 encoding network.*

The modified algorithm, the steepest-gradient-type algorithm, and the hybrid method in a multilayered perceptron are used to solve the two standard encoding problems.

Simulations were performed using steepest gradient (classic) back-propagation (SG) algorithm and back propagation with the modified algorithm (NR). Since the weights in the nodes and the threshold values in the individual units were set at random initially, the initial tss values varied across different simulation runs. To average out the effects due to randomization of the weights in the links and the threshold values in the units, repetitions of the simulation runs were performed.

The programs were run on a Convex-C240 machine in a UNIX environment. Twenty repeated simulation runs were made for the two cases (SG, M) for the 4-2-4 as well as the 8-3-8 encoding problems. As can be seen from Table 3.1, the number of epochs taken by M to converge is less than that for the steepest descent algorithm. The times taken by the different algorithms (in run time seconds) are also correspondingly different. NR converged much faster than the SG algorithm, with almost similar tss values across all the different patterns. The tss values are given in the tables just for comparison purposes.

Since there is no external noise in the 4-2-4 and 8-3-8 encoding problems (as can be seen from Tables 3.1 and 3.2), as the problem size is increased (from 4-2-4 to 8-3-8) the differences in performances of the different algorithms are significant. The number of epochs required for SG to converge is about five times

TABLE 3.1   4-2-4 Encoding Problem

	SG	NR
epochs	342	115
time(sec.)	138	69
tss(one)	0.0101	0.0085
tss(two)	0.0202	0.0197
tss(three)	0.0295	0.0312
tss(four)	0.0397	0.0383

TABLE 3.2   8-3-8 Encoding Problem

	SG	NR
epochs	1008	189
time(sec.)	274	75
tss(one)	0.0049	0.0041
tss(two)	0.0103	0.0091
tss(three)	0.0151	0.0143
tss(four)	0.0201	0.0203
tss(five)	0.0250	0.0249
tss(six)	0.0303	0.0304
tss(seven)	0.0352	0.0346
tss(eight)	0.0398	0.0387

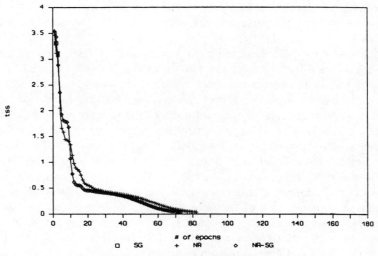

Figure 3.3 *4-2-4 encoding problem.*

that for NR for the 8-3-8 encoding problem, whereas the factor is only about three for the 4-2-4 encoding problem. Similarly, the time taken for SG to converge is about thrice that of NR for the 8-3-8 encoding problem, whereas it is about twice for the 4-2-4 encoding problem.

Figures 3.3 and 3.4 illustrate the convergence for a sample run of the two algorithms (SG, NR), as implemented in back propagation, using both 4-2-4 and 8-3-8 encoding problems, respectively.

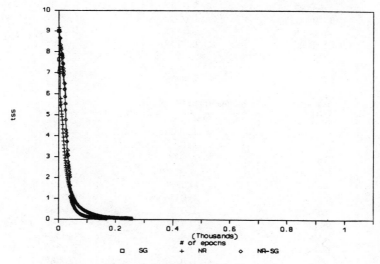

Figure 3.4 *8-3-8 encoding problem.*

3.4 DISCUSSION

The difference between the classical back-propagation algorithm and the modified algorithm is the product term $4(o - a)^2 e^{(o - a)^2}$. This term behaves beneficially when the current position in the search space is both far as well as near the optima. When the current search position is far from the optima, the exponential term dominates, and longer steps are taken. When the current position is near the optima, the $(o - a)^2$ term dominates, effectively rendering smaller steps to be taken during the search. Thus, the step size is modified as per current point of search relative to the optimum point of interest. The benefits are further enhanced by the hybrid algorithm, which avoids very large step sizes during the initial stages of search, thus narrowing on the optimum point.

The algorithm NR performs better than SG in terms of accuracy and speed of convergence. This is due to an increase in the granularity of the search process, by means of the exponential transformation of the objective function, and also due to the second order gradient search procedure. The increase in granularity increases the step size taken during search through the solution space, hence increasing the speed of convergence of NR algorithm. The second order gradient search process in NR utilizes information about curvatures in the search space, thus modifying the search process appropriately, leading to faster convergence to the final value.

Becker and LeCun [7], Fahlman [9], Parker [8], and Waltrous [6], among others, have suggested the use of second order gradient methods for accelerating the back-propagation procedure. However, these methods rely on matrix inversion and thus are more computationally expensive. The NR method uses an exponential objective function, along with modifications to the SG algorithm, avoiding matrix inversion at the same time taking advantage of second order process, thus making the computation tasks in the learning process easier.

REFERENCES

[1] G. Cybenko, "Continuous Valued Neural Networks with Two Hidden Layers are Sufficient," Tech. Rep., Dept. of Computer Science, Tufts University, Medford, Mass., 1988.

[2] E. J. Hartman, J. D. Keeler, and J. M. Kowalski, Layered neural networks with Gaussian hidden units as universal approximations, *Neural Computation*, 2, 210–215 (1990).

[3] K. Hornik, M. Stinchcombe, and H. White, Multilayer feedforward networks are universal approximators, *Neural Networks*, 2, 359–366 (1989).

[4] David E. Rumelhart, James L. McClelland, and the PDP Research Group, *Parallel Distributed Processing—Explorations in the Microstructure of Cognition*, Vol. I: *Foundations*, MIT Press, Cambridge, Mass., 1987, pp. 319–364.

[5] P. Werbos, "Beyond Regression: New Tools for Prediction and Analysis in the Behavioral Sciences," Ph.D. thesis, Harvard University (1974).

[6] Raymond L. Waltrous, Learning algorithms for connectionist networks: Applied gra-

38

dient methods of nonlinear optimization, *Proc. IEEE Internat. Conf. on Neural Networks*, 619–627 (1987).

[7] S. Becker and Y. Le Cun, Improving the convergence of back-propagation learning with second order methods, *Proc. 1988 Connectionist Models Summer School*, Pittsburgh (1988).

[8] D. B. Parker, Optimal algorithms for adaptive networks: Second order back-propagation, second order direct propagation, and second order Hebbian learning, *Proc. IEEE Internat. Conf. Neural Networks*, (1987).

[9] S. E. Fahlman, Faster-learning variations on back-propagation: An empirical study, *Proc. 1988 Connectionist Models Summer School*, Morgan–Kaufman, D. S. Touretzky et al., Eds., Pittsburgh (1988).

CHAPTER 4 ⸻

Constructing Efficient Features for Back Propagation

SELWYN PIRAMUTHU

4.1 INTRODUCTION

Back propagation (BP) is one of the most widely used of artificial neural network algorithms because of its powerful problem solving capabilities. The parallel problem solving process in a (single-or multilayered) perceptron is derived in an attempt to mimic similar structures found in nature. Recent progress in developing *artificial neural networks* (ANNs) and their use in varied domains have spurred the interests of researchers in studying various means of improving them. Although it has excellent characteristics for learning concepts [1], one of the inherent drawbacks with the BP algorithm is that it is very slow to converge. Researchers have approached this problem through disparate means ranging from modifications to the BP algorithm per se to appropriate implementations of the algorithm in VLSI components.

Unlike previous attempts through modifications to the BP algorithm itself, this chapter deals with an attempt to increase the convergence speed of the BP algorithm through *feature construction*, which is used to *preprocess* the data before being used by BP. *Feature construction* is the process of detecting potentially useful relationships as new features [2]. By using feature construction, the subset of the initial set of features and newly constructed features, which are deemed to have more cumulative information, are used as input to the BP algorithm. The newly constructed features possibly have fewer peaks per class [3], thus making the search space less complex, which in turn increases the convergence speed of BP. The importance of using efficient features for learning is discussed in the next

Fast Learning and Invariant Object Recognition, By Branko Souček and the IRIS Group.
ISBN 0-471-57430-9 © 1992 John Wiley & Sons, Inc.

section. Feature construction is briefly discussed in Section 4.2. Learning using back-propagation algorithm, as pertaining to this chapter, is briefly discussed in Section 4.3. Using an example, the effects of preprocessing input data for BP using feature construction is shown in Section 4.4. Section 4.5 concludes with comments on the proposed methodology.

Features, along with their respective values, are the source of information with which a feature space can be searched for required results. This also signifies the importance of the characteristics of a given feature space to be amenable to yield the expected solution. Given a problem, the best we can do is to search for the solution in the space covered by the range of values of the known features that are deemed to be important. The performance of any learning algorithm could only be as good as the quality of the feature set that is used for learning the concepts of interest. Hence, selection of the initial set of features plays a major role in the learning process.

One of the means of measuring the importance of a feature for a given problem domain is to measure the information content [3] of all the available features to be able to distinguish the good features from the rest. The good features for classification purposes would entail a lesser number of peaks in a search space with good overall information content, along with a lesser number of features. Thus, ideally, a feature set with the least possible number of features and the appropriate information content to be able to solve the problem at hand is desirable.

Feature construction is a methodology by which newer features can be constructed from the original set of features, resulting in a less complex representation. The number of features that are required for learning concepts is effectively reduced [5], while also reducing the number of peaks that are present in the feature space. Ragavan and Piramuthu [6] use a dispersion measure to measure the complexity of the feature space. They show that the complexity of a feature space could be reduced by using feature construction, resulting an increased ease of learning the concepts represented by the feature set. The reduction in the complexity of the feature space is very beneficial for learning algorithms such as BP. As the number of peaks are reduced in the feature space, the number of hyperplanes that are required to separate examples belonging to different classes are drastically reduced, thus improving the learning process.

4.2 FEATURE CONSTRUCTION

Feature construction [1, 2, 7, 8, 9] is used to develop higher order features that represent the concepts under consideration more concisely as well as reduce the number of peaks that are required to describe a concept. Some of the learning systems that perform feature construction are BACON [10], CITRE [8], DUCE [11], and FRINGE [12]. Matheus [8] considers feature construction using the AND ($\wedge$) operator. By restricting the operators, the space of potential constructors is reduced. In this chapter, we consider only Boolean features to avoid the potentially infinite number of features that could be constructed using numerical features.

During feature construction, the new features that are constructed are defined using only existing features, including features that have already been constructed in a similar manner.

For explanation purposes, CITRE [8] is used to discuss the use of feature construction as a preprocessor for BP. The FRINGE [12] module of CITRE constructs features iteratively from decision trees. It forms new features by conjoining two nodes at the fringe of the tree. The parent and grandparent nodes of positive leaves are conjoined to give a new feature. The new features thus constructed are added to the original set of features, and a new decision tree is constructed. In CITRE, a decision tree is constructed from examples using information-theoretic [3] measures. This is similar to ID3 [13], an algorithm for generating decision trees. Let the number of decision alternatives (e.g., a concept is either true or false) in the instance space of interest be $C(C_1, C_2)$. At any given node in the decision tree, the expected information that is required to classify the instances at that node as belonging to class C_i, or otherwise, is given by

$$I(p, n) = - \frac{p}{(p + n)} * \log_2 \left[\frac{p}{(p + n)} \right] - \frac{n}{(p + n)} * \log_2 \left[\frac{n}{(p + n)} \right]$$

where, p is the proportion of the instances that belong to class C_i and n ($= 1 - p$) is the proportion of instances that do not belong to class C_i.

Let the features in the instance space be a_i ($i = 1 \cdot \cdot \cdot n$). At a given node, let the number of instances that take on different values for a_i for class C_i be p_i and let n_i be the number of instances that do not belong to class C_i. The expected information required for that branch of the tree with a_i as the root node is

$$E(a_i) = \sum_i \frac{(p_i + n_i)}{(p + n)} * I(p_i, n_i)$$

a weighted average of the proportion of instances that are present at the node of interest. The information that is gained by branching on a_i is

$$\text{gain } (a_i) = I(p, n) - E(a_i)$$

The feature that gains the most information at a node is chosen as the one based on which the branching is performed. The process is used recursively at each node of the tree until all the terminal nodes (leaves) are reached.

Feature construction in CITRE is performed whenever disjunctive regions are detected in a decision tree, as evidenced by the presence of more than one positively labeled terminal node. As new features are constructed, they are added to the *active* feature set and decision trees are constructed iteratively. Since the number of features can grow disproportionately large, CITRE has a maximum limit on the number of features it can keep at a time. The information-theoretic measure is again used in evaluating the features that are to be retained.

4.3 LEARNING BY BACK PROPAGATION

A number of previous studies have compared BP with other classification methods including statistical tree induction, with results favoring BP in terms of classification accuracy. One of the major drawbacks of BP is that it is very slow. Several researchers [14, 15] have worked on this problem trying to increase the convergence speed of the BP algorithm by disparate means. There are four primary means of increasing the convergence speed of BP: (1) by appropriately preprocessing the data used as input to the algorithm, (2) by improving the BP algorithm itself, (3) by hard-wiring the algorithm using VLSI circuits, and (4) by utilizing the inherent parallelism in the BP algorithm through implementations in parallel machines.

Several researchers [14, 15] have successfully modified the BP algorithm using second order gradient search methods, resulting in improved performance. Kung, Vlontos, and Hwang [16] describe a VLSI architecture for implementing BP using a programmable systolic array. Hinton [17] and Deprit [18] describe the use of parallel processing computers to implement the BP algorithm with each unit in the network assigned to a processor.

In this chapter, no attempt is made to improve the BP algorithm itself as in previous studies. Instead, the data used as input to the BP algorithm is preprocessed [5]. More specifically, the complexity of the concept is reduced in the features used as input to BP, to enable it to learn more effectively. As discussed in Section 4.2, feature construction can be used to reduce the complexity of concepts. Using feature construction, a subset of the initial and newly constructed features that are deemed to be better for representation are used as input to the BP algorithm. The new representation has fewer concept regions per class. This makes the search space less complex, which in turn increases the convergence speed of BP.

4.4 AN EXAMPLE OF BP USING FEATURE CONSTRUCTION

In this chapter, no attempt is made to improve the BP algorithm as such as in previous studies. Instead, the data used as input to the BP algorithm are preprocessed to enable the BP algorithm to perform more effectively. Feature construction decreases the resulting number of peaks in the search space, thus simplifying the learning process for the BP algorithm. The convergence speed of the BP algorithm is directly proportional to the input units, as determined by the number of input features. Reduction in both the number of peaks in the search space and the number of input units required speeds up the convergence of BP algorithm as a result of a decrease in complexity of the overall search space.

The following are results obtained using a sample data set [1] consisting of 200 examples with 9 (Boolean) features and 2 classes (true/false). The features used in the trees that were generated for the data set using the FRINGE module of CITRE are given as follows:

Tree Generation 1:

features used: a3, a4, a5, a6, a7, a8, a9.
new features:
f1: and(equal (a4,true), equal(a8,false))
f2: and(equal (a7,true), equal(a5,true))
f3: and(equal (a8,true), equal(a6,false))
f4: and(equal (a9,false), equal(a8,false))

Tree Generation 2:

features used: a3, a5, a7, f1, f3.
new features:
f5: and(equal(a3,false), equal(a5,true))
f6: and(equal(a7,false), equal(f1,true))
f7: and(equal(a7,false), equal(f3,true))
f8: and(equal(a7,true), equal(a3,false))

Tree Generation 3:

features used: a7, f1, f5, f6, f7.
new features:
f9: and(equal(a7,true), equal(f5,true))
f10: and(equal(f6,true), equal(f5,false))

Tree Generation 4:

features used: f6, f7, f9.
new features:
f11: and(equal(f6,true), equal(f9,false))
f12: and(equal(f9,true), equal(f7,false))

Tree Generation 5:

features used: f6, f7, f9 (*same as in tree generation 4*).

The decision trees constructed by CITRE are represented by their generation numbers (n) for the tree constructed after the $(n - 1)^{th}$ iteration. The identical entries for the last two trees (4 and 5) are due to the identical final trees that CITRE produces on convergence. The decision features in the final trees are fewer than those in the initial set (9). This reduces the number of input units, in turn reducing the hidden units that are necessary. The number of hidden units is taken to be roughly half the total number of input and output units for all the networks. Thus the total number of units used in the network is reduced.

TABLE 4.1   BP Results Using the Example Data Set

	# of epochs				
trial #	t1	t2	t3	t4	t5
1	219	54	40	17	11
2	45	42	34	16	14
3	45	57	34	27	13
4	44	50	33	16	13
5	47	95	41	25	10
6	46	96	40	29	10
7	50	66	40	19	12
8	144	55	33	23	12
9	56	46	35	29	13
10	56	55	40	17	15
average	75.2	61.6	37	21.8	12.3

Notes:
t1: result using all 9 features (BP network: 9 + 5 + 1)
t2: result using 7 features that were used for tree generation 1 (7 + 4 + 1)
t3: result using 5 features that were used for tree generation 2 (5 + 3 + 1)
t4: result using 5 features that were used for tree generation 3 (5 + 3 + 1)
t5: result using 3 features that were used for tree generation 4 (3 + 2 + 1)
where, $a + b + c$: a, b, and c are the number of input, hidden, and output units, respectively.

As the initial weights in the network were set randomly, the BP algorithm was run 10 times for each set of features corresponding to the various trees constructed by CITRE. Both the individual and the average values from the 10 runs are given in Table 4.1.

As can be seen from Table 4.1, the number of epochs required for the BP network to converge is lesser for t5 (12.3), which is the tree of interest, than for t1 (75.2). The number of *active* features also decreased to 3 (t5) from 9 (t1) in the initial data set. Although not shown in Table 4.1, the classification accuracy was a 100 percent in all five cases (t1, t2, t3, t4, t5), and the corresponding speed of convergence of BP also improved with feature construction. Thus by preprocessing data using constructive induction, the convergence speed of BP was increased.

Neural networks require fewer epochs to learn a concept if the complexity of the representation of the input data is decreased by using good features. By constructing new features, we not only reduce the number of effective features that are needed to define the concepts, but also increase the average information content at each of the constructed input units. This is achieved by considering the interaction effects of the features in addition to the main effects, through feature construction.

4.5   DISCUSSION

The BP algorithm is being successfully used in commercial applications such as credit risk rating of companies, among others. There have also been developments in the area of creating expert systems using neural networks. In a commercial credit risk rating situation, for example, the learning speed of the BP algorithm is critical for the firm to be able to make quicker decisions for it to remain competitive. This chapter presented a means of getting closer to the goal of achieving faster learning using a feedforward neural network by automating the input feature selection process. This methodology also eliminates the least important features from the training data, thus facilitating efficient use of computing resources by directing attention only to those features that are deemed important for a given classification problem.

Advantages of neural networks such as good performance in high feature interaction domains are combined with advantages of decision-tree based induction by this method. Incorporating a front-end-like CITRE to the BP algorithm also provides a facile technique for introducing domain knowledge in neural networks. Knowledge gets compiled into the constructed features.

Given a data set, using feature construction, the ratio of the number of features to the number of examples in the input to the BP algorithm is reduced, which makes learning using BP more statistically valid. In this chapter, feature construction was done only for Boolean features, since the search space gets to be complex for continuous features. In this chapter, an attempt was made to improve the speed of convergence of BP algorithm without any improvement of the BP algorithm per se. Feature construction, when used along with other methods of improving the BP algorithm itself, such as second order gradient search methods, can significantly increase the speed of convergence of the BP algorithm.

REFERENCES

[1] C. J. Matheus, "Feature Construction: An Analytic Framework and An Application to Decision Trees," Ph.D. thesis, Dept. Computer Science, University of Illinois at Urbana-Champaign (December 1989).

[2] P. Mehra, L. A. Rendell, B. W. Wah, Principled constructive induction, *Proc. 11th Internat. Joint Conf. on Artificial Intelligence*, Detroit, Morgan-Kaufman, 651–656 (1989).

[3] C. E. Shannon, A mathematical theory of communication, *Bell Systems Tech. J.*, 27, 379–423 (1948).

[5] S. Piramuthu, Feature construction for back-propagation, *Proc. Internat. Workshop on Parallel Problem Solving from Nature*, Springer-Verlag, Heidelberg, 264–268 (1990).

[6] H. Ragavan and S. Piramuthu, The utility of feature construction for back-propagation, *Proc. 12th Internat. Joint Conf. on Artificial Intelligence*, Sydney, Australia, Morgan-Kaufman, 844–848 (1991).

[7] G. Drastal, Informed pruning in constructive induction, *AAAI* (1990).

[8] C. J. Matheus, Feature construction in CITRE, *Machine Learning Conference* (1990).

[9] C. J. Matheus and L. A. Rendell, Constructive induction on decision trees, *Proc. 11th Internat. Joint Conf. on Artificial Intelligence*, Detroit, Morgan-Kaufman, 645–650 (1989).

[10] P. Langley, H. A. Simon, G. L. Bradshaw, and J. M. Zytkow, *Scientific Discovery: Computational Explorations of the Creative Process*, MIT Press, Cambridge, Mass., 1987.

[11] S. Muggleton, Duce: An oracle based approach to constructive induction, *Proc. 10th Internat. Joint Conf. on Artificial Intelligence*, Morgan-Kaufman, 287–292 (1987).

[12] G. Pagallo, and D. Haussler, Two algorithms that learn DNF by discovering relevant features, *Proc. 6th Internat. Workshop on Machine Learning*, Morgan-Kauffman, 119–123 (1989).

[13] J. R. Quinlan, Induction of decision trees, *Machine Learning*, 1(1), 81–106 (1986).

[14] S. Becker and Y. Le Cun, Improving the convergence of back-propagation learning with second-order methods, *Proc. 1988 Connectionist Models Summer School*, Pittsburgh, D. S. Touretzky, et al., Eds., Morgan-Kaufman, (1988).

[15] S. E. Fahlman, Faster-learning variations on back-propagation: An empirical study, *Proc. 1988 Connectionist Models Summer School*, Pittsburgh, D. S. Touretzky, et al., Eds., Morgan-Kaufman, (1988).

[16] S. Y. Kung, J. Vlontos, and J. N. Hwang, VLSI array processors for neural network simulation, *Jour. Neural Network Computing*, 5–20 (1990).

[17] G. E. Hinton, Learning in parallel networks, *BYTE*, 265–273, (April 1985).

[18] E. Deprit, Implementing recurrent back-propagation on the connection machine, *Neural Networks*, 2, 295–314 (1989).

CHAPTER 5

How Slow Processes Can Think Fast in Concurrent Logic

F. KOZATO
G. A. RINGWOOD

5.1 INTRODUCTION

Introspection suggests that on time scales of minutes and spatial scales of meters human cognition is sequential and localized. On the scale of milliseconds and microns cognition is asynchronous and distributed. Ideograms (symbols) are indispensable for slow, high levels of thought processing such as formal logic, but they seem to be particularly weak at the faster, lower level tasks of perception, speech, and vision. As real neural networks already successfully implement speech and vision recognition systems, it is possible to speculate that artificial ones can do the same. Despite the inability of symbolic computer systems to deal adequately with perception, they are much more powerful than human symbolic processing. The combination of artificial neural networks and computer symbolic processing holds the promise of being better than the sum of its parts. As a first step toward investigating this thesis, a pedagogical implementation of neural networks in a *concurrent logic language* is presented. A concurrent logic language is chosen, first, because it is a logic language and so can represent knowledge expressed symbolically. Second, it has a computational model that subsumes that found in artificial neural networks. Thus, the language itself can provide a bridge between symbolic and subsymbolic processing.

Fast Learning and Invariant Object Recognition, By Branko Souček and the IRIS Group.
ISBN 0-471-57430-9 © 1992 John Wiley & Sons, Inc.

5.2 SELF-REPLICATING NEURAL NETWORKS

For the sake of definiteness, the network topology chosen for implementation is a binary tree. As will be illustrated such a neural network can be taught to recognize the parity of input bit vectors. RGDC (Reactive Guarded Definite Clauses) [1] is a concurrent logic language (CLL) descended from Parlog (Imperial College, UK) under the influence of FGHC (ICOT, Japan) and FCP (Weizmann Institute, Israel). RGDC is used here as representative of the class. Strand88, marketed by SSTL Ltd., is a commercial version of a predecessor of RGDC called Flat Parlog with Assignment. For a state-of-the-art review of concurrent logic languages the reader is referred to Ringwood [2, 3].

The syntax of RGDC is similar to, but sufficiently different, from Prolog to need some explanation. As in Prolog, an RGDC program consists of a set of clauses, but in RGDC a clause takes the form of a guard and a process behavior:

```
<clause> ::= <guard> <- <behaviour>.
```

The behavior is, logically, a conjunction of atoms with shared variables as in Prolog. The calls in the body of a clause are not hierarchical procedure calls as in Prolog but a set of communicating concurrent processes. Each goal in a behavior reduces independently of its conjuncts. For RGDC, process synchronization is specified by the guard condition:

```
<guard> ::= <head> <- <constraints>.
```

The < head > is the atom expected from Prolog but the constraints are a conjunction of primitives that only test the input arguments. The constraints are of the form of equations, inequations, comparisons, and type tests. The computational model of RGDC is very unlike Prolog; clause invocation in RGDC is not decided by the unifiability of the goal and head. Rather, the goal pattern must pattern match the head of a clause and satisfy the constraints, without incurring any binding of the input variables. This is condition synchronization as opposed to Prolog's control synchronization. Pattern matching and the constraints are used to check the advisability of a potential inference. That is, the deduction step is guarded and there is no backtracking; invocation of the body goals is irrevocable. (For the procedurally minded, the implication symbol between the guard and body can be compared with the Prolog cut. Unlike the cut, this mechanism is symmetric in the clauses it cuts off.)

This will, hopefully, become clearer with an example. A binary tree neural network, or pyramid, with three layers can be brought into existence by the RGDC process invocation:

```
<- pyramid(3, O, Is).
```

where the **pyramid** relation is defined by

```
/*pyramid(NumberOfLayers, OutputStream, ListOfInputStreams)*/
pyramid(1, A, Ss) <- true <-
   Ss = [S1, S2], protoNeuron(A, S1, S2).
pyramid(N, A, Ss) <- N > 1, N1 is N -1 <-
   protoNeuron(A, A1, A2),
   pyramid(N1, A1, S1s),
   pyramid(N1, A2, S2s),
   concatenate(S1s, S2s, Ss).
/*concatenate(List1, List2, JoinedList)*/
concatenate([], List, JoinedList) <- true <-
   JoinedList = List.
concatenate([Item | List1], List2, JoinedList) <- true <-
   JoinedList = [Item | List],
   concatenate(List1, List2, List).
```

The primitive *true* in the guards is the trivial constraint and is used here to indicate the mandatory presence of a guard for each clause. The directed (moded) nature of relations in RGDC, as opposed to Prolog, is revealed by the presence of equality primitives in the body of the clauses of **concatenate.** This is the only mechanism by which local bindings can be communicated to higher scopes.

A graphical trace of a parallel reduction of the initial process [4] is depicted in Figure 5.1; active (reducible) processes at each stage are shaded. The pyramid process evolves into a tree of generic neurons; the type of which is specified in the next section.

Unlike Prolog, which is a closed (transformational language), RGDC [5] is an open [6] (reactive [7]) programming language. Transformational systems begin with the input of data, transform the input, output the result, and terminate. This is just how an unintelligent machine would behave. It would input data wholesale, process it algorithmically, and output it. On the other hand, reactive systems can continuously interact with their environment. Their reason for being is not the output they produce on termination but, rather, their continuing interaction; sometimes reactive programs are effectively perpetual (they do not terminate). An intelligent machine would acquire knowledge as it needed, infer from it, and output reasonings as external situations demanded. Systems programs such as environments with multiple windowing systems, operating systems, and event driven real-time systems are more conventional forms of reactive applications. Reactive systems consist of conceptually parallel processes that communicate with each other and respond cooperatively to events that occur indeterminately in real time. RGDC processes are allowed to be perpetual. The resolvent at the end of the trace in Figure 5.1 is to be understood as a logical consequence of the initial process [5].

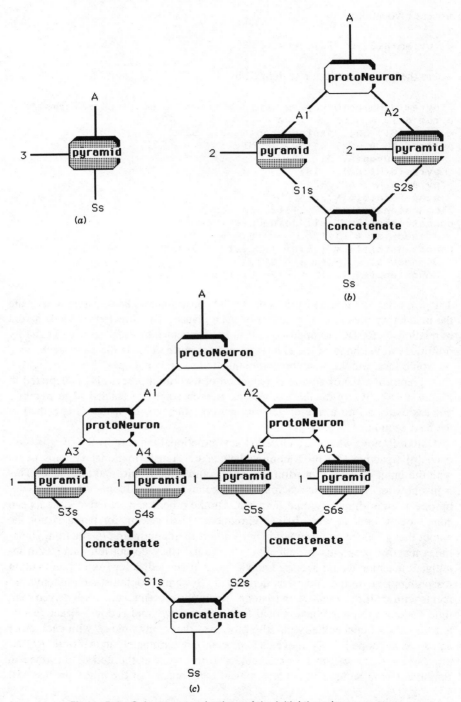

Figure 5.1   *Subsequent reductions of the initial three layer process.*

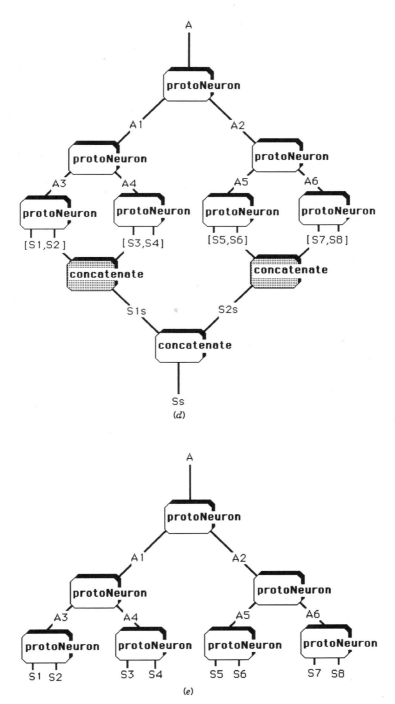

Figure 5.1 (Continued)

It is not the intention to refute the negation of the initial **pyramid** process, as would be the case with Prolog.

5.3 NEURON SPECIALIZATION

There are essentially two types of artificial neurons: the original McCulloch–Pitts model [8], logic gate models, which are motivated by computer hardware, and the later analogue, weighted sum, threshold activation models [9]. The logic gate models are, of course, ideally suited to implementation in conventional hardware. One such, a mutable form, the PLN, probabilistic logic neuron [10] was chosen for the present chapter for the sake of definiteness. Any other form of artificial neuron or network can be implemented by the same techniques used below.

The PLN is essentially a programmable, probabilistic, logic gate.

```
/*protoNeuron(Axon, Synapse1, Synapse2)*/
protoNeuron(A, S1, S2) <- true <-
    neuron(table(3, unknown, unknown, unknown, unknown) S1,
    S2, A).
```

Initially, the gate type is unspecified; see Figure 5.2. The constant unknown in the table is used to indicate that the neuron will produce an indeterminate response (0 or 1) to a binary input pattern. To produce this effect, the first parameter of table is used as the seed of a pseudorandom number generator. In this situation the PLN produces a 1 or 0 output with equal probability. This stochastic nature endows the PLN with indeterminate properties that biological neurons are speculated to possess [11]. (By changing the pyramid clauses it can be arranged that the different neurons do not have the same initial seed.)

As the neural network undergoes training, undetermined truth table entries become *learned* with respect to approved responses to controlled input (Fig. 5.3). The response behavior is captured by the RGDC process **neuron.**

```
/*neuron(State, InputStream1, InputStream2, OutputStream)*/
neuron(State, [o(S1) |S1s], [o(S2) | S2s], Output) <- true <-
    Output = [o(A) | S3s],
    gate((S1, S2), State, NewState,A),
    neuron(NewState, S1s,S2s,S3s).
```

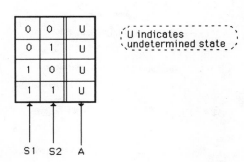

Figure 5.2 *Initial state of the PLN.*   S1 S2 A

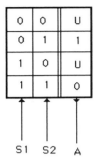

0	0	U
0	1	1
1	0	U
1	1	0

S1   S2   A

Figure 5.3 *Some partially learned state.*

The **neuron** process is defined recursively. Thus, while operationally a call to **neuron** is ephemeral, recursion imitates a perpetual process which can, as seen, change state. The functors "o" on the input and output indicate that a response in operational mode (as opposed to the training mode described in the next section) is required.

The response consists of truth table lookup. If the table value has been learned, this value is returned. If the table value is "unknown" a random number generator is used to produce an indeterminate response.

```
/*gate(InputPair, LookUpTable, Output)*/
gate((0, 0), table(Seed, learnt(T), U, V, W), NewState, A) <-
  true <- A = T, NewState = State.
gate((0, 0), table(Seed, unknown, U, V, W), NewState, A) <-
  NewSeed is if Seed < 0 then shiftleft(Seed) XOR 3 else
  shiftleft(Seed), B is NewSeed mod 2 <-
  A = B, NewState = table(NewSeed, unknown, U, V, W).
gate((0, 1), table(Seed, T, learnt(U), V, W), NewState, A) <-
  true <- A = U, NewState = State.
gate((0, 1), table(Seed, T, unknown, V, W), NewState, A) <-
  NewSeed is if Seed < 0 then shiftleft(Seed) XOR 3 else
  shiftleft(Seed), B is NewSeed mod 2 <-
  A = B, NewState = table(NewSeed, T, unknown, V, W).
gate((1, 0), table(Seed, T, U, learnt(V), W), NewState, A) <-
  true <- A = V, NewState = State.
gate((1, 0), table(Seed, T, U, unknown, W), NewState, A) <-
  NewSeed is if Seed < 0 then shiftleft(Seed) XOR 3 else
  shiftleft(Seed), B is NewSeed mod 2 <-
  A = B, NewState = table(NewSeed, T, U, unknown, W).
gate((1, 1), table(Seed, T, U, V, learnt(W)), NewState, A) <-
  true <- A = W, NewState = State.
gate((1, 1), table(Seed, T, U, V, unknown), NewState, A) <-
  NewSeed is if Seed < 0 then shiftleft(Seed) XOR 3 else
  shiftleft(Seed), B is NewSeed mod 2 <-
  A = B, NewState = table(NewSeed, T, U, V, unknown).
```

The algorithm for calculating random bits is taken from Knuth [12].

A trace of how inputs propagate in parallel through a PLN pyramid network is shown in Figure 5.4. (The word *propagate* does not really convey the sense of urgency associated with explosively parallel computation.)

5.4 THE TEACHER TEACHES AND THE PUPIL LEARNS

In artificial neural networks there is no conventionally stored database; there are no carefully worked out application-specific rules. The only principle that guides the system is that it incorporates some notion of a *right* and *wrong* response and

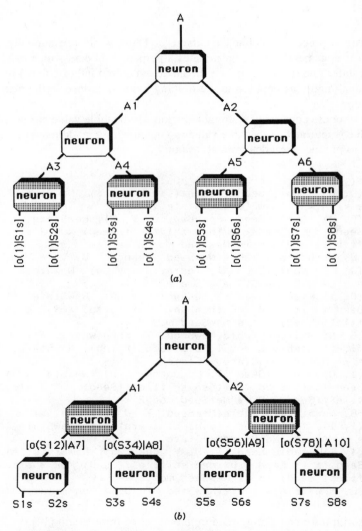

Figure 5.4   *Trace of virtual neurons firing in response to input.*

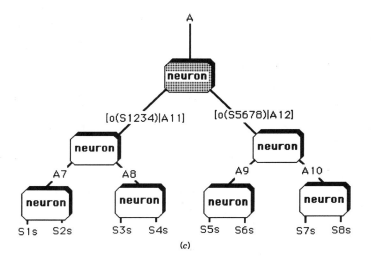

(c)

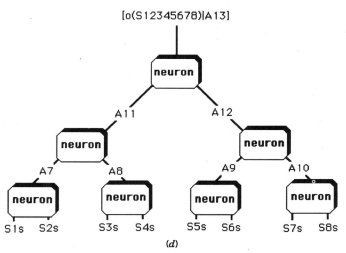

(d)

Figure 5.4   (Continued)

is constructed to strive for correctness. In this way the network can be self-taught: Each input produces an output; correct outputs are reinforcing; incorrect outputs cause internal adjustments. By modifying its internal state the network strives to achieve favorable responses. At first the response is by trial and error; later on, as the learning process continues, it becomes a mixture of trial, error, and experience. Eventually the machine behaves as if it ''knew'' exactly what it was the instructor was trying to tell it. When the neural machine has learned something, the instructor does not know at the conceptual level what is going on inside the machine—it is generally far too complex for that.

Training for a PLN neuron can be effected by a second clause for **neuron:** The functors ``t`` on the input are used to indicate that the training mode is operating.

```
/*neuron(State, InputStream1, InputStream2, OutputStream)*/
neuron(State, [t(S1, R1) | S1s], [t(S2, R2) | S2s], Output) <-
   true <- Output = [t(A, R) | S3s],
   gate((S1, S2), State, State1, A),
   training((A, R), State1, ((S1, R1), (S2, R2)), NewState),
   neuron(NewState, S1s, S2s, S3s).
```

Here, the recursive **neuron** clause simulates a perpetual process that changes state according to the **training** relation. Output response pairs (S1, R1), (S2, R2), and (A, R) are used to direct the responses from the proffered inputs back to the nodes responsible for them. This technique has been called *back communication* by adherents to concurrent logic languages, but it is nothing more than a partially instantiated term familiar to Prolog programmers. In essence, backcommunication is similar to the well publicized technique of error *back propagation* [13] used in training analogue neurons. The **training** process records the output and amends the look-up table as dictated by the response for the recursively reincarnated **neuron.**

It then remains to specify the training algorithm. The method chosen for the present work, is one of several possibilities [14]:

Step 1: Choose an input pattern from some training set and apply it to the input nodes.

Step 2: Allow values to propagate through all neurons in the network. (Each PLN responds according to the state of its truth table.)

Step 3: If the values on the output connections are the ones expected, then the output of each neuron becomes established (learned).

Step 4: Otherwise, return to Step 2 and try again (because the output of each neuron is stochastic the output will generally be different) until a correct output is generated or

Step 5: A ``sufficient`` number of errors has been made suggesting the possibility of succeeding is effectively zero. In this situation all nodes are returned to their initial indeterminate state.

Step 6: Repeat steps 1 to 5 until ``consistent`` success indicates that all patterns have been learned.

```
/*training(OutputResponsePair, OldLookUptable, InputResponse
   Pairs, NewLookUpTable)*/
training((A, confirmed), table(Seed,T, U, V, W), ((0, R1),
   (0, R2)), NewState) <- true <-
   NewState = table(Seed, learnt(A), U, V, W), R1 = confirmed,
   R2 = confirmed.
training((A, confirmed), table(Seed, T, U, V, W), ((0, R1),
```

```
(1, R2)), NewState) <- true <- NewState = table(Seed, T,
learnt(A), V, W), R1 = confirmed, R2 = confirmed.
training((A, confirmed), table(Seed, T, U, V, W), ((1, R1),
(0, R2)), NewState) <- true <- NewState = table(Seed, T, U,
learnt(A), W), R1 = confirmed, R2 = confirmed.
training((A, confirmed), table(Seed, T, U, V, W), ((1, R1),
(1, R2)), NewState) <- true <- NewState = table(Seed, T, U,
V, learnt(A)), R1 = confirmed, R2 = confirmed.
training((A, incorrect), State, ((X, R1), (Y, R2)), NewState) <-
true <- NewState = State, R1 = incorrect, R2 = incorrect.
training((A, reset), table(Seed, T, U, V, W), ((X, R1),
(Y, R2)), NewState) <- NewState = table(Seed, unknown,
unknown, unknown, unknown),
R1 = reset, R2 = reset.
```

Any other training scenario can be implemented in a similar way.

5.5 CONCLUSION

The implementation of a neural net described in this chapter has been successfully taught to recognize the parity of input bit vectors [15]. Clearly, this means that each PLN has learnt to behave as an EXCLUSIVE-OR gate. The implementation was carried out on a uniprocessor machine in Parlog86 [16] (RGDC is a subset of Parlog86), with the parallelism simulated by coroutining. The implementation was slow, not the least because of the overhead of process switching. The speed of process switching is of the order of the response rate of biological neurons, that is, microseconds. Organic neural nets illustrate how fast processing can be achieved even by such slow processing elements. This is due to the way in which parallelism is organized into small, equal sized portions without any synchronization problems. The feedforward network topology is amenable to the explosive computational parallelism of which organic brains are capable. With this topology of processes in RGDC there is only one producer and ideally many consumers, so there is no *binding conflict problem*. This is a problem in concurrent logic languages, a manifestation of mutual exclusion, that occurs when there is more than one producer [17]. As the number of processors is increased there will be less demand for context switching. In this regime the implementation of neurons by software processes could be a viable proposition. Still, to expand this model to a real application (which requires huge numbers of neurons) on multiprocessor systems, another factor, processor communication cost, must be considered. Since the communication is only an activation signal, this cannot be too expensive. Judicious partitioning of neurons across processes minimizes the cost and this will be particularly beneficial when there are highly interconnected clusters, with few connections between clusters. These virtual neurons can even be allowed to migrate between processors.

The choice of illustration, a pyramid network of PLN neurons, was purely for the sake of explanation and definiteness; the techniques presented here are capable of implementing any topology, any type of artificial neuron, and any training rules. It can be seen that the computational model of concurrent logic languages corresponds, to a large extent, with a connectionist one. Relations (processes) fire or not depending on their internal state and on data received from other processes via shared variables [5]. While shared variables do give potential synchronization problems in concurrent logic languages when there are multiple producers, a style of programming can be adopted, such as the feedforward network, where there are only single producers for shared variables [3].

There are some features of a neural network implementation in a concurrent logic language that are unusual. It is generally believed that neural nets should ultimately be built in hardware. Yet, experience has revealed many difficulties with this philosophy. For example, training a network is a very slow and painful business. For the network described above, learning proceeds by a process of trial and error. For each input–output pair, trials are made a predetermined number of times. This is the accepted regime because the intended implementation medium is hardware. When the implementation medium is software, as herein, the number of trials can be adjusted to reflect the number of *unknown* entries in the look-up tables. This is achieved by making the propagation signals carry information on the internal states of the neurons. This modification for the above implementation is simple but would be impractical, if not impossible, to achieve in a hardware implementation. Thus, for software implementations the learning phase can be dramatically shortened [14].

There is a growing belief that sophisticated cognitive systems can be built only from a suitable combination of neural networks and symbolic AI techniques [18]. From this point of view, the advantages of implementing neural nets in a programming language that is suitable for symbolic manipulation are clear. Furthermore, for hardware implementations, reconfiguring neural nets and adding new nodes to accommodate more concepts seems impossible without having great redundancy. In software, for languages like RGDC, this presents no difficulty. RGDC allows dynamic process creation, and this allows dynamic neuron creation. This is exemplified by Section 5.2 illustrating the dynamic construction of a neural net. Thus, in a learning situation, new neurons can be created as necessary. This increases the capacity of the system to learn new concepts. Because the language RGDC, by design [3] lends itself to partial evaluation, the training sessions could be viewed in this light. After a training session a virtual neural net will have acquired some knowledge. Viewed as partial evaluation, this is a new goal that has been specialized for the training data. Once a particular neural net has acquired some knowledge the resolvent can be saved as a partially evaluated goal. Such goals can be composed to give more complex nets with accumulated knowledge.

The implementation of neural nets in RGDC is not just a simulation. It offers an executable language for describing neural networks and opens up the possibility of dynamically evolving neural systems. Current research suggests a new direction for both neural network research and conventional symbolic AI with a view to their fusion.

REFERENCES

[1] D. Cohen, M. M. Huntbach, and G. A. Ringwood, "Logical Occam," in P. Kacsuk and M. Wise, Eds., *Distributed Prolog*, Wiley, New York, (to be pub.).

[2] G. A. Ringwood, Metalogic machines: A retrospective rationale for the Japanese fifth generation, *Knowledge Eng. Rev.*, 3, 303–320 (1989).

[3] G. A. Ringwood, A comparative exploration of concurrent logic languages, *Knowledge Eng. Rev.*, 4, 305–332 (1989).

[4] G. A. Ringwood, Predicates and pixels, *New Generation Computing*, 7, 59–80 (1987).

[5] G. A. Ringwood, "Pattern-Directed, Markovian, Linear, Guarded Definite Clause Resolution," Dept. Tech. Rep., Computing, Imperial College, London (1987).

[6] C. Hewitt, The challenge of open systems, *BYTE*, 10, 223–242 (April 1985).

[7] A. Harel and A. Pnueli, "On the Development of Reactive Systems," in K. R. Apt, Ed., *Logics and Models of Concurrent Systems*, Springer-Verlag, New York, 477–498, 1985.

[8] M. W. McCulloch and W. Pitts, A logical calculus of the ideas immanent in nervous activity, *Bull. Mathematical Biophysics*, 5, 115–188 (1943).

[9] W. H. Pitts and W. S. McCulloch, How we know universals: The perception of auditory visual forms, *Bull. Mathematical Biophysics*, 9, 127–147 (1947).

[10] I. Alexsander, "Logical Connectionist System," in R. Eckmiller and C. H. v. d.Malsburg, Eds., *Neural Computer*, Springer-Verlag, New York, 1988, pp. 189–197.

[11] T. J. Sejnowski, "Skeleton Filters in the Brain," in G. E. Hinton and J. A. Anderson, Eds., *Parallel Models of Associative Memory*, Lawrence Erlbaum Associates, Hillside, NJ., 1981, pp. 49–82.

[12] D. E. Knuth, *The Art of Computer Programming*, Vol. 2, Addison Wesley, Reading, Mass., 1969, p. 29.

[13] D. E. Rumelhart, G. Hinton, and R. J. Williams, "Learning Internal Representations by Error Propagation," in D. E. Rumelhart and J. L. McClelland, Eds., *Parallel Distributed Processing: Explorations in the Microstructures of Cognition*, Vol. 1: *Foundations*, MIT Press, Cambridge, Mass., 1986, pp. 318–362.

[14] C. Myers and I. Aleksander, "Learning Algorithms for Probabilistic Neural Nets," Tech. Rep., Dept. Computing, Imperial College, London (1988).

[15] F. Kozato, " Modelling Neural Networks in Parlog," M.Sc. thesis, Imperial College, London (1988).

[16] G. A. Ringwood, Parlog86 and the dining logicians, Communications of The Association of Computing Machinery, 31, 10–25 (1988).

[17] A. Burt and G. A. Ringwood, "The Binding Conflict Problem in Concurrent Logic Languages," Tech. Rep. Dept. Computing, Imperial College, London, (1988).

[18] J. A. Hendler, Marker-passing over microfeatures: Towards a hybrid symbolic-connectionist model, *Cognitive Sci.*, 13, 79–106 (1989).

BIBLIOGRAPHY

F. H. Crick and C. Asanuma, "Certain Aspects of the Anatomy and Physiology of the Cerebral Cortex," in D. E. Rumelhart and J. L. McClelland, Eds., Parallel Distributed Processing, Vol. 2, MIT Press, Cambridge, Mass., 1986, pp. 333–371.

S. E. Fahlman, *NETL: A System for Representing and Using Real-World Knowledge*, MIT Press, Cambridge, Mass., 1979.

J. J. Hopfield, Neural networks and physical systems with emergent collective computational abilities, *Proc. Natl. Acad. Sci. USA*, 79, 2554–2558 (1982).

M. Minsky and S. Papert, *Perceptrons: An Introduction to Computational Geometry*, MIT Press, Cambridge, Mass., 1969.

T. J. Sejnowski and C. R. Rosenberg, ''NETtalk: A Parallel Network that Learns to Read Aloud,'' Tech. Rep., Cognitive Neuropsychology Lab, Johns Hopkins University (1985).

CHAPTER 6

How to Deal with Multiple Possible Generalizers

DAVID H. WOLPERT

6.1 INTRODUCTION

For any real-world generalization problem, there are *always* many generalizers that could be applied to the problem. This chapter discusses some algorithmic techniques for dealing with this multiplicity of possible generalizers. All of these techniques rely on partitioning the provided learning set in two, many different times. The first technique discussed is cross-validation, which is a winner-takes-all strategy. (Based on the learning set, it picks one single generalizer from among the set of candidate generalizers, and tells you to train with that generalizer.) The second technique discussed is an extension of cross-validation called stacked generalization. As opposed to cross-validation's crude winner-takes-all strategy, stacked generalization uses the partitions of the learning set to combine the generalizers, in a nonlinear manner. This chapter presents experiments both demonstrating the efficacy of cross-validation and demonstrating that stacked generalization does even better. This chapter ends by discussing some of the theoretical aspects of stacked generalization, as well as the problem of removing all ad hocness, that is, the problem of avoiding the specification of an original set of candidate generalizers.

More specifically, this chapter concerns the problem of inferring a function from a subset of $\mathbf{R}^n$ to a subset of $\mathbf{R}^p$ (the *parent function*) given a set of m samples of that function (the *learning set*). The subset of $\mathbf{R}^n$ is the *input space*, and the subset of $\mathbf{R}^p$ is the *output space*. A *question* is an input space (vector) value. An algorithm that guesses what the parent function is, basing the guess only on a learning set of m $\mathbf{R}^{n+p}$ vectors read off of that parent function, is called a *generalizer*. A generalizer guesses an appropriate output for a question via the parent

Fast Learning and Invariant Object Recognition, By Branko Souček and the IRIS Group.
ISBN 0-471-57430-9 © 1992 John Wiley & Sons, Inc.

function it infers from the learning set. Colloquially, we say that the generalizer is "trained," or "taught," with the learning set and then "asked" a question.

Some examples of commonly used generalizers are back-propagated neural nets [1], Holland's classifier system [2], and various implementations of Rissanen's minimum description length principle [3, 4] (which, along with all other schemes that attempt to exploit Occam's razor, is analyzed in [5]). Other important examples are memory based reasoning schemes [6], regularization theory [7, 8], and similar schemes for overt surface fitting of a parent function to the learning set [9–13]. Conventional classifiers (e.g., ID3 [14], Bayesian classifiers like Schlimmer's Stagger system [15], and the classifiers discussed in [16]) are also generalizers, with the added handicap that classifiers are incapable of guessing a particular output value unless that value occurred in the learning set.

For simplicity, this chapter usually assumes little or no noise. This means that once we are provided with a learning set, we already know how best to guess for input space questions identical to the input space component of an element in the learning set. Building a system to guess properly for those elements—that is, "learning that learning set"—is trivial and can be achieved simply by building a look-up table. (Difficulties arise only when one insists that the look-up table be implemented in an odd way, e.g., as a feedforward neural net.) Phrased differently, it's a trivial exercise to build a generalizer that automatically reproduces any learning set on which it's trained. Accordingly, for the most part, this chapter concentrates on achieving good generalization for questions outside of the learning set.

For any real-world generalization problem there are always many possible generalizers one can use. One is *always* implicitly presented with the problem of how to address this multiplicity of possible generalizers. One possible strategy is to choose a generalizer according to subjective criteria. As an alternative, this chapter is a presentation of some objective (i.e., algorithmic) techniques for addressing the multiplicity of candidate generalizers.

Section 6.2 of this chapter discusses cross-validation, the most commonly used technique for dealing with multiple generalizers. Cross-validation is a way of choosing a single generalizer from among the set of candidate generalizers. It uses the learning set to make its decision; the idea is to let the data tell you what to do, rather than for you to impose some "reasonable" a priori criterion that always favors the same candidate generalizer. Readers familiar with cross-validation can skip directly to Section 6.3, which presents stacked generalization. Stacked generalization can be viewed as an extension of cross-validation. In particular, just like cross-validation, stacked generalization relies crucially on partitions of the learning set. The difference between cross-validation and stacked generalization is that instead of cross-validation's winner-takes-all strategy, stacked generalization combines the candidate generalizers in a nonlinear manner. Stacked generalization does this by means of another generalizer (hence the name "stacked generalization").* Section 6.4 presents both real-world and toy experiments confirming the

*As is shown in Section 6.3, cross-validation also implicitly makes use of an additional generalizer. In cross-validation's case however, this additional generalizer is fixed to a particularly crude one.

efficacy of stacked generalization. It then discusses some of the subtleties of stacked generalization. Finally, Section 6.5 investigates the problem of how to remove all ad hocness, that is, the problem of how to avoid specifying an original set of candidate generalizers.

6.2   CROSS-VALIDATION

This section first motivates and defines cross-validation. After this it presents a numerical experiment that demonstrates the efficacy of cross-validation.

6.2.1   Defining Cross-Validation

Consider the starfish parent function, with an associated learning set and question, all illustrated in Figure 6.1. As always, one has several generalizers one could use to try to answer the question. For the sake of argument, assume that those generalizers are all local, that is, assume their guess for what output goes with the question is strongly influenced by the elements of the learning set which lie near the question in input space. (This assumption is true to varying degrees for many generalizers, including memory based reasoners and back-propagated neural nets.) Since the four nearest neighbors of the question all have output 0.0, any such generalizer will guess an output less than 1.0 (in fact, most such generalizers would guess the output 0.0).

Now assume that instead of being local, one of our generalizers was designed to transform the learning set so that the input components were in polar coordinates, and then look for periodicities in the learning set. Such a generalizer would

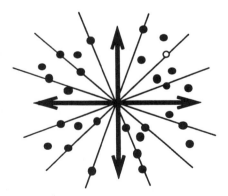

Figure 6.1   *The "starfish" parent function. The input space is two-dimensional, with axes indicated by the two large arrows. The output space is one-dimensional and should be thought of as coming out of the page. The parent function is defined by the following rule: Output = 1.0 if the polar angle of the input is an integer multiple of $\pi/8$ radians, 0 otherwise (i.e., the parent function looks like a 16-legged starfish). The learning set consists of samples of the parent function at the points indicated by the solid circles. A question, from outside of the learning set, is indicated by the open circle. The correct output guess for this question is 1.0.*

guess the parent function perfectly; in particular, it would guess the correct response, 1.0, to the indicated question.

What we need is a way of predicting—from the learning set alone—that for this problem the polar-coordinates generalizer is a better generalizer than any of the local generalizers. For this problem we could do this simply by seeing which generalizer has the least error in guessing part of the learning set when trained on the rest of it. If we teach any of the local generalizers with only part of the learning set, their guessing of the rest of the learning set will be far from perfect. However if we teach the polar-coordinates generalizer with part of the learning set, it will still have sufficient information to infer the exact starfish input–output surface for the parent function, and therefore it will guess perfectly the rest of the learning set. In other words, for this problem and these generalizers, there is a correlation between {the generalization error when training occurs with the full learning set and the question lies outside of the learning set} and {the error at guessing part of the learning set when trained with the rest of it}.

Cross-validation [17–20] is a formalization of this concept. Let θ be a learning set, containing m input–output pairs. From θ construct the set of partitions of θ $\{\theta_{ij}\}$, $1 \leq i \leq m$, $1 \leq j \leq 2$. For fixed i, θ_{i2} consists of a single input–output pair from θ, and θ_{i1} consists of the rest of the pairs from θ. The input component of θ_{i2} is written as "in(θ_{i2})," and the output component is written as "out(θ_{i2})." Varying i varies which input–output pair constitutes θ_{i2}; since there are m pairs in θ, there are m values of i.

Let G be a particular generalizer. If ω is a learning set and q is a question, then G's guess for what output corresponds to q, given the training evidence in ω, is written as $G(\omega; q)$. The *cross-validation error* of G with respect to θ is defined as the average over i of $[G(\theta_{i1}; \text{in}(\theta_{i2})) - \text{out}(\theta_{i2})]^2$. It measures G's average squared error at guessing one pair from θ when trained on the rest of θ. Given a learning set and a set of candidate generalizers, the technique of cross-validation simply says to generalize from the learning set using whichever generalizer has lowest cross-validation error with respect to that learning set.

6.2.2 Using the NETtalk Data Set to Test Cross-Validation

The assumption implicit in cross-validation works just as well for problems more complicated than the starfish problem. As an example, consider the problem of generalizing how to read aloud, that is, the problem of being given some examples of text and associated phonemes, and from those examples inferring how to translate arbitrary text to the proper corresponding phonemes. This problem was first addressed by Sejnowski and Rosenberg [21], by using back propagation to create the feedforward neural net NETtalk. NETtalk's input space is (an encoding of) seven contiguous letters. The output corresponds to the phoneme an English speaker would voice for the middle of the seven letters if the speaker encountered the letters while reading aloud some text. More precisely, the output of the neural net is interpreted as a vector of real-valued numbers, each such number indicating a degree of emphasis on a different articulatory feature. To convert such a vector to a phoneme, one finds the phoneme whose articulatory vector makes the smallest angle with the vector output by the neural net. This phoneme is then taken as the output of NETtalk as a whole.

The efficacy of cross-validation for the problem of generalizing how to read aloud was investigated in [10]. The investigation began by constructing a parameterized set of generalizers. To do this first a parameterized metric in the seven-dimensional input space was defined. The most obvious metric was a weighted Hamming distance in the seven letter input field, so the distance between any two sets of seven letters was the (weighted) sum counting the number of the seven slots in which the two sets have different letters. Given such a metric and given a question (i.e., given a seven-dimensional input vector), the guessed articulatory vector was given by the "center of mass" of the four elements of the learning set whose input lies nearest to the question (nearness being determined using the metric just specified). The "mass" of each element of the learning set is the reciprocal of its input–space distance to the question, and the "position" of each element is its output space vector:

$$G(\theta; \mathbf{q}) = \left\{ \sum_{i=1}^{4} \left[\frac{y(\mathbf{x}_i)}{d(\mathbf{q}, \mathbf{x}_i)} \right] \right\} \bigg/ \left\{ \sum_{i=1}^{4} \left[\frac{1}{d(\mathbf{q}, \mathbf{x}_i)} \right] \right\}, \qquad (6.1)$$

where the metric

$$d(\mathbf{a}, \mathbf{b}) \equiv \sum_{\alpha=1}^{7} \left[\rho_\alpha (1 - \delta(\mathbf{a}_\alpha, \mathbf{b}_\alpha)) \right]$$

[$\delta(. , .)$ being the Kronecker delta function]. Letters in bold are (input space) vectors; roman subscripts distinguish different input space vectors from one another, and Greek subscripts run over the input components of a particular input space vector; $\mathbf{q}$ is the question, the $\mathbf{x}_i$ are the input vectors of the elements of the learning set θ which lie closest to $\mathbf{q}$, and the $y(\mathbf{x}_i)$ are the associated (articulatory vector) outputs. The ρ_α are a set of seven real-valued constants; they are the weights that define the input space metric. The usual Hamming metric has all the $\rho_\alpha = 1$. The number 4 is arbitrary.

Generalizers of the type given in Eq. (6.1) have a number of nice properties. Primary among these are their speed, their ease of use and analysis, the fact that they always guess correctly for questions contained in the learning set (assuming no noise),* and the fact that learning set points further away from the question contribute proportionally less to the guess for what output goes with that question [9–11].

Different sets of ρ_α give different guesses for the same learning set and question, that is, they give different generalizers. Therefore we can apply cross-validation: Vary the ρ_α, measure the resultant cross-validation error for the learning set, and find the ρ_α with the lowest such error. We then use the generalizer induced by this optimal set of ρ_α to generalize from the entire learning set.

---

*If a question lies on top of an element of the learning set, that learning set element has infinite "mass," and by itself fixes the guessed output.

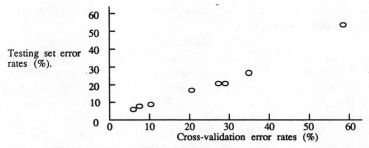

Figure 6.2 *The horizontal axis gives the cross-validation error rate of eight different generalizers for guessing 2189 elements of the (reading aloud) learning set when taught with the rest of the learning set. The vertical axis gives the error rates for guessing the 2189 elements of a testing set when taught with the full learning set (see reference [10] for details). The correlation between the two errors is clear.*

The results of this strategy for eight different sets of ρ_α are depicted in Figure 6.2. The cross-validation error for each set of ρ_α was approximated by training the generalizer on a single fixed subset of the learning set and then examining its behavior on the remainder of the learning set—said remainder, containing 2189 input–output pairs. The generalization error was calculated by training on the entire learning set and then examining guessing behavior on a distinct testing set consisting of 2189 elements. The learning and testing sets used are (a normalized version of) the same ones used by Sejnowski and Rosenberg [22].

Using the technique of cross-validation, we would choose the generalizer corresponding to the leftmost circle in Figure 6.2. The efficacy of cross-validation lies in the fact that this leftmost generalizer has the lowest error rate on the testing set (an error rate less than a third of that of NETtalk!) of all the generalizers considered.

There are many more sophisticated ways than cross-validation to use the basic idea of choosing one of the generalizers by means of partitions of the learning set. A number of them correspond to different choices of the partition set, θ_{ij}. For example, the bootstrap [20] technique can be loosely thought of as cross-validation modified by using an i.i.d. partition set rather than the cross-validation partition set (CVPS) defined above. Other interesting variations of cross-validation are generalized cross-validation [23], and using cross-validation as an aid to horizontal generalization [24]. (Most conventional generalizers are vertical generalizers, and work by searching for vertical patterns, from inputs to outputs. Horizontal generalizers instead search for horizontal patterns, from one part of the parent function to another.)

6.3 STACKED GENERALIZATION

This section starts by motivating stacked generalization and presenting a simple example of it. After this, some variations of stacked generalization are synopsized.

6.3.1 Combining Generalizers

Cross-validation is a winner-takes-all strategy. As such, it is rather simple minded; one would prefer to *combine* the generalizers rather than choose just one of them. Interestingly, this goal of combining generalizers can be achieved using the same idea of exploiting partition sets which is employed by cross-validation and its variations. To see how, consider the situation depicted in Figure 6.3. We have a learning set θ, and a set of two candidate generalizers G_1 and G_2. We want to infer (!) an answer to the following question: If G_1 guesses g_1 and G_2 guesses g_2, what is the correct guess?

To answer this question we make the same basic assumption underlying cross-validation: Generalizing behavior when trained with proper subsets of the full learning set correlates with generalizing behavior when trained with the full learning set. To exploit this assumption, the first thing one must do is choose a partition set θ_{ij} of the full learning set θ. For convenience, choose the CVPS. Now pick any partition i from θ_{ij}. Train both G_1 and G_2 on θ_{i1}, and ask them both the question, in(θ_{i2}). They will make the pair of guesses g_1 and g_2. In general, since the generalizers weren't trained with the input–output pair θ_{i2}, neither g_1 nor g_2 will equal the correct output, out(θ_{i2}). Therefore, we have just learned something: When G_1 guesses g_1 and G_2 guesses g_2, the *correct* guess is out(θ_{i2}).

From such information we want to be able to infer what the correct guess is when both G_1 and G_2 are trained on the full learning set and asked a question q.

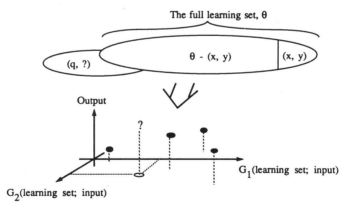

Figure 6.3   *A stylized depiction of how to combine the two generalizers G_1 and G_2 via stacked generalization. A learning set θ is symbolically depicted by the full ellipse. We want to guess what output corresponds to the question q. To do this, we create a CVPS of θ; one of these partitions is shown, splitting θ into {(x, y)} and {θ − (x, y)}. By training both G_1 and G_2 on {θ − (x, y)}, asking both of them the question x, and then comparing their guesses to the correct guess y, we construct a single input–output pair (indicated above by one of the small solid ellipses) of a <u>new</u> learning set L. This input–output pair gives us information about how to go from guesses made by the two generalizers to a correct output. The remaining partitions of θ give us more of such information; they give us the remaining elements of L. We now train a generalizer on L and ask it the two-dimensional question {$G_1(\theta; q)$, $G_2(\theta; q)$}. The answer is our final guess for what output corresponds to q.*

The most natural way to carry out such inference is via a generalizer. To do this, first cast the information gleaned from the partition *i* as an input–output pair in a new space (the new space's input being the guesses of G_1 and G_2, and the new space's output being the correct guess). Repeat this procedure for all partitions in the partition set. Different partitions gives us different input–output pairs in the new input–output space; collect all these input–output pairs, and view them as a learning set in the new space.

This new learning set tells us all we can infer (using the partition set at hand) about the relationship between the guesses of G_1 and G_2 and the correct output. We can now use this new learning set to "generalize how to generalize"; we train a generalizer on this new learning set, and ask it the two-dimensional question $\{G_1(\theta; q), G_2(\theta;q)\}$. The resultant guess serves as our final guess for what output corresponds to the question *q*, given the training information θ. Using this procedure, we have inferred the biases of the generalizers with respect to the provided learning set, and then collectively corrected for those biases to get a final guess.

Procedures of this sort where one feeds generalizers with other generalizers are known as "stacked generalization." [25]. The original learning set, question, and

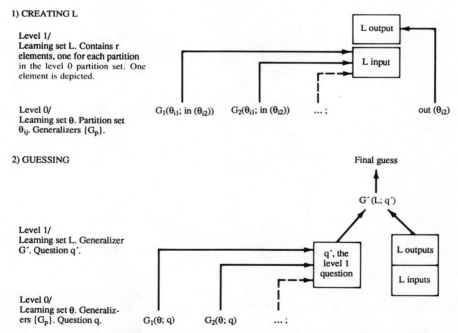

Figure 6.4 *A stylized depiction of the two stages involved in the most straightforward implementation of stacked generalization. In the first stage, the level 1 learning set L is created from the level 0 partition set θ_{ij} and the set of level 0 generalizers $\{G_p\}$. In the second stage, the exact same architecture used to create L is used to create a level 1 question from a level 0 question. After this the final guess is found by training the level 1 generalizer on L and then asking it the newfound level 1 question. Note that this entire procedure is twice parallelizable; once over the partitions and once over the level 0 generalizers.*

generalizers are known as the "level 0" learning set, question, and generalizers. The new learning set, new question, and generalizer used for this new learning set and new question are known as the "level 1" learning set, question, and generalizer (see Fig. 6.4).

6.3.2 Variations of Stacked Generalization

There are many variations of the basic version of stacked generalization outlined above. (See [25] for a detailed discussion of some of them.) One variation is to have the level 1 input space contain information other than the outputs of the level 0 generalizers. For example, if one thinks that there is a strong correlation between {the guesses of the level 0 generalizers, together with the level 0 question} and {the correct output}, then one might add another dimension to the level 1 input space for the value of the level 0 question.

Another useful variation is to have the level 1 output space be an estimate for the error of the guess of one of the generalizers rather than a direct estimate for the correct guess. In this version of stacked generalization the level 1 learning set has its outputs set to the error of one of the generalizers rather than to the correct output. When the level 1 generalizer is trained on this learning set and makes its guess, that guess is interpreted as an error estimate; that guess is subtracted from the guess of the appropriate level 0 generalizer to get the final guess for what output corresponds to the question.

There are some particularly nice features of this error estimating version of stacked generalization. One is that it can be used even if one has only a single generalizer, that is, it can be used to improve any single generalizer's guessing. (This use of stacked generalization, with a level 1 input space consisting of more than just the guess of the level 0 generalizer, is illustrated in Fig. 6.5.) Another nice feature of having the level 1 output be an error estimate is that this estimate can be multiplied by a real valued constant before being subtracted from the appropriate level 0 generalizer's guess. When this constant is 0, the guessing of the entire system reduces to simply using that level 0 generalizer by itself. As the constant grows, the guessing of the entire system becomes less and less the guess of that level 0 generalizer by itself and more and more the guess of a full stacked generalization architecture; that constant provides us with a knob determining how conservative we wish to be in our use of stacked generalization. Yet another nice feature of having the level 1 output space be an error estimate for one of the level 0 generalizers is that with such an architecture the guess of that level 0 generalizer often no longer needs to be in the level 1 input space, since its information is already being incorporated into the final guess automatically (when one does the subtraction). In this way one can reduce the dimensionality of the level 1 input space by one.

Another obvious variation of the basic idea of stacked generalization is to stack on yet another level; rather than directly generalizing from the level 1 learning set, use a level 2 space made from the level 1 values and generalize there. Yet another variation is to use a partition set different from the CVPS. For example, some

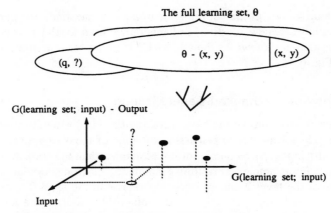

Figure 6.5 *A stylized depiction of how to improve the performance of a single generalizer G via stacked generalization A learning set θ is symbolically depicted by the full ellipse. We want to guess what outputs correspond to the question q. To do this we create a CVPS of θ; one of these partitions is shown, splitting θ into {(x, y)} and {θ − (x, y)}. By training G on {θ − (x, y)}, asking it the question x, and then subtracting the correct output y from its guess, we construct a single input–output pair (indicated above by one of the small solid ellipses) of a new learning set L. This pair gives us information about how to go from {guess made by the generalizer, together with the question's value} to {the error of that guess}. The remaining partitions of θ give us more of such information; they give us the remaining elements of L. We now train a generalizer on L and ask it the two-dimensional question {G(θ; q), q}. The answer is our guess for the error of G when trained on θ and asked the question q; to get our final guess for what output corresponds to q, we subtract this error estimate from G's guess.*

implementations of GMDH [26] are equivalent to stacked generalization with a special partition set. As another example, we can choose partition sets in which the partition elements are not disjoint, that is, sets θ_{ij} where $\theta_{i1} \cap \theta_{i2} \neq 0$, in general. For example, schemes like hierarchical neural nets [27] and the work of Zhang [28] using a level 1 generalizer to combine memory based reasoners, backpropagation, and ID3 are simply instances of stacked generalization, where the partition set has the same θ_{i2} as in the CVPS, but for all i $\theta_{i1} = \theta$.*

Another interesting variation is cross-validation itself; cross-validation is simply a special case of stacked generalization (and therefore so is any scheme like fan generalizers [24] or nonlinear time-series analysis, which exploits cross-validation). This is essentially because a winner-takes-all strategy is simply a special case of "combining" a set of generalizers, where the "combining" is particularly

---

*It should be noted that there are some major disadvantages to this partition set. For example, if this partition set is used when there is no noise, and if one of the level 0 generalizers guesses perfectly for questions on which it has been trained, then, *as far as the level 1 generalizer can tell*, that level 0 generalizer always guesses perfectly for all questions. Accordingly, any reasonable level 1 generalizer will simply say that one should use that level 0 generalizer directly and ignore any other level 0 information. In general, when using this partition set one is not "generalizing how to generalize"; the level 1 space contains information on how well the level 0 generalizers *learn*, not on how well they *generalize*.

crude. To see this, examine the behavior of stacked generalization with the architecture illustrated in Figures 6.3 and 6.4 and with the following level 1 generalizer: "Fit the learning set with one of the input–output hyperplanes {output = kth component of the input}. Choose which such hyperplane according to which one is a best root-mean-square fit to the learning set." Clearly this level 1 generalizer is exceptionally crude, and better performance would be expected from using a more sophisticated level 1 generalizer. Nonetheless, cross-validation is exactly equivalent to using this level 1 generalizer in the architecture of Figures 6.3 and 6.4.

6.4 DISCUSSION OF STACKED GENERALIZATION

This section first presents a toy experiment demonstrating the efficacy of stacked generalization. It then discusses some subtleties that arise with stacked generalization.

6.4.1 A Test of Stacked Generalization

As an illustrative example of stacked generalization, it is helpful to consider the following toy experiment (first reported in [25]). This experiment is designed to test the ability of stacked generalization to combine generalizers, all of which have thrown out (different) information present in the input space, in such a way as to recover all of that information.

The experiment was based on the NETtalk "reading aloud" problem. As in Section 6.2, the parent function for this problem has seven (suitably encoded) letters as input, and the output of the parent function is the phoneme that would be voiced by an English speaker upon encountering the middle letter if all seven letters had occurred in the midst of some text that the speaker was reading aloud. The data set used for the experiment was standard Carterette and Jones [22], modified (as in [10]) to force consistency among the several speakers recorded.

Three separate generalizers were combined. Each such level 0 generalizer was of the form given in Eq. (6.1). Each of these level 0 generalizers looked exclusively at only one of the seven input letter slots, that is, for each of them ρ_α had all of its components but one set to 0. (Effectively, this means that each of the level 0 generalizers had a one-dimensional input space rather than a seven-dimensional one, since only variations in one of the slots had any effect). The level 0 generalizers differed from each other in which letter slot they looked at; that is, they differed in which component of ρ_α they set to 1.

The first level 0 generalizer looked exclusively at the third letter slot of the seven letter input field, the second looked exclusively at the fourth letter slot, and the third looked exclusively at the fifth letter slot. As in the examples in Figures 6.3 and 6.4, the CVPS was used, the guesses of the level 0 generalizers formed the inputs of the level 1 space, and the outputs of the level 0 and level 1 spaces were identical (i.e., the level 1 output space wasn't an error space). For simplicity the full level 0 generalizers were used; each level 1 input component consisted of a single integer representing the closest legal phoneme to the real valued output articulatory vector of the corresponding level 0 generalizer (see Section 6.2). In other words, level 1 inputs were symbolic. Like the level 0 generalizers, the level 1 generalizer was also of the form given in Eq. (6.1). The level 1 generalizer used a full Hamming metric however, over all components of the three-dimensional level 1 input space. Level 1 outputs were articulatory vectors, which were converted in the usual way to phonemes.

The (level 0) learning set was made by looking at successive seven-letter windows of the first 1024 words of Carterette and Jones; that is, it consisted of $(1024 \times 5) - 6 = 5114$ elements. The testing set was constructed from the successive seven-letter windows of the next 439 words of Carterette and Jones, that is, it consisted of $(439 \times 5) - 6 = 2189$ elements. The three level 0 generalizers got a total of 507, 1520, and 540 of the testing set questions correct, respectively. Since each individual guess was either correct or incorrect, these three numbers suffice to determine exactly the expected error in the associated estimates of average guessing accuracies: Generalizer 1 had an average generalizing accuracy of $23\% \pm .90\%$, generalizer 2 had an average generalizing accuracy of $69\% \pm .98\%$, and generalizer 3 had an average accuracy of $25\% \pm .92\%$. As one would expect, generalizer 2, looking at the middle letter of the input field, guesses best what phoneme should correspond to that middle letter.

The stacked generalizer got 1926 correct, for an average accuracy of $88\% \pm .69\%$. Cross-validation (i.e., a level 1 generalizer that worked by globally fitting a surface of the form {output = one of the inputs}) chose generalizer 2. Therefore, the improvement over cross-validation that resulted from using a better level 1 generalizer was approximately 20 (of generalizer 2's) standard deviations.

The purpose of this text-to-phoneme experiment wasn't to beat the performance (reported in [10]) of a generalizer having access to all seven input letters, nor even to beat the performance of back propagation (i.e., NETtalk) on this data. Rather it was to test stacked generalization and, in particular, to test whether stacked generalization can be used to combine separate pieces of incomplete input information. Presumably one could construct a stacked generalizer for the text-to-phoneme problem that performed better than the one presented here. Such a generalizer could be found by varying the parameters of the stacked generalizer architecture, perhaps using a different level 1 generalizer, and so on.

In addition to working well for toy experiments like the one reported here, there is a good deal of evidence that stacked generalization also works well for real-world problems. For example, Gustafson et al. have reported that (what amounts to) stacked generalization beats back propagation on some hydrodynamics problems [29]. Similarly, a number of researchers have reported on the efficacy of simply averaging a set of generalizers, for example, for aspects of the problem of predicting protein structure [30]. He Xiandong has reported on the efficacy of (what amounts to) using stacked generalization with a GMDH partition set together with radial basis function generalizers for time-series predictions [26]. This is all in addition to the large body of research reporting on the efficacy of hierarchical neural nets and cross-validation.

6.4.2 Subtleties of Stacked Generalization

Consider the use of stacked generalization presented in Figures 6.3 and 6.4. Note that it's possible for the level 1 learning set to be multivalued, that is, the level 1 learning set might contain a pair of points with identical input components but different output components. This is because there might be two (or more) partitions in the partition set that result in the same guesses by all of the $\{G_p\}$, even though they have different θ_{i2}'s. In practice this occurs very rarely, especially if the data takes on a continuum of values. Moreover, unless the level 1 generalizer tries so hard to reproduce its learning set that it can't deal gracefully with such multivaluedness, this multivaluedness is not, of itself, a reason for concern. Also, even if the level 1 generalizer does have a marked lack of grace under such conditions, if the level 1 input space is enlarged to include the level 0 input value, then the level 1 learning set will now be single-valued and no problems will arise.

The whole process outlined in Figures 6.3 and 6.4 is itself a generalizer; it takes (level 0) learning sets and (level 0) questions and maps them to guesses. Therefore, it's sensible to ask how well the whole process meets the properties that are often desired in conventional generalization using a single (level 0) generalizer. One such property is reproduction of the level 0 learning set. Many conventional generalizers either always reproduce their learning set or strive to do so. However this isn't necessarily the case with the whole process of stacked generalization (viewed as a generalizer of the level 0 learning set), regardless of whether or not the constituent level 0 and level 1 generalizers necessarily reproduce *their* learning sets. This lack of reproducing the level 0 learning set might not be a problem. For example, when one has noisy data, one often wishes to avoid "fitting the noise" so that exact reproduction of the learning set is not desirable.* And for nonnoisy data, it should often be the case that if the learning set is large enough, then the learning set *is* reproduced, to a good approximation.

Nonetheless, there are many cases where one would like to enforce exact reproduction of the learning set. There are several ways to achieve this. The most obvious is to simply place a filter on the questions being fed to the stacked generalizer: if a level 0 question already exists in the (level 0) learning set, bypass the generalizers and answer that question directly from the learning set. (After all, the purpose of stacked generalization is to improve guessing for questions outside of the learning set, not to provide a complicated means of implementing the look-up-table, "If the question is in the input projection of the learning set, guess the corresponding output.")

A more elegant scheme has been devised by Gustafson et al. [29]: Require that the level 1 surface guessed by the level 1 generalizer contains the line $\alpha\mathbf{e}$, where α runs over the reals and $\mathbf{e}$ is a diagonal vector, that is, a vector in $\mathbf{R}^{k+1}$ all $k + 1$ of whose coordinate projections are identical and nonzero (k being the dimensionality of the level 1 input space). Under this scheme, so long as the level 0 generalizers all reproduce the level 0 learning set, then so will the entire stacked generalizer. The reason is that if the level 0 question is contained in the level 0

*Indeed, the behavior of a stacked generalizer when one has large learning sets can sometimes be used as means of determining whether or not one's data is noisy.

learning set, then all the level 0 generalizers will make the same guess (namely, the output component of the corresponding element of the level 0 learning set), and then this level 1 generalizer will also make that guess.

There are other ways to ensure reproduction of the learning set that don't restrict the level 1 generalizer. For example, one could *teach* the level 1 generalizer to reproduce the level 0 learning set, so to speak. To do this, for every set θ_{i1} don't simply create the single element of the level 1 learning set corresponding to $\theta_{i2} = \theta - \theta_{i1}$. Rather, for each θ_{i1} create m points in the level 1 space, one for all m possible values of θ_{i2} (i.e., allow θ_{i2} to range over all θ rather than just over $\theta - \theta_{i1}$). Modulo any issues of multivaluedness of the level 1 learning set, as long as the individual level 0 and level 1 generalizers reproduce their learning sets, then under this scheme so will the entire stacked generalizer.

There are a number of other subtle aspects of stacked generalization. For example, it is usually the case that special care is needed when using stacked generalization with the CVPS to try to improve the guessing of a single purely local generalizer. As another example, when combining several generalizers, best results usually occur when the level 1 generalizer is relatively global, nonvolatile and smooth, and not overly concerned with exact reproduction of the level 1 learning set (an extreme example of such a level 1 generalizer being the one used in cross-validation). It is also usually preferable if the level 0 generalizers "span the space of generalizers" and are "mutually orthogonal," loosely speaking. A complete discussion of these issues is beyond the scope of this chapter; see [25] for a detailed discussion.

6.5 REMOVING AD HOCNESS

Although stacked generalization is less ad hoc than simply choosing a single generalizer according to subjective criteria, it still contains a lot of "ad hocness." There are two separate places where this ad hocness occurs. The first is in the specification of the set of candidate generalizers. The second is in the specification of the architecture of the stacked generalization (what the level 1 space is, what the level 1 generalizer is, etc.)

It is possible to perform a rigorous mathematical analysis of any particular implementation of stacked generalization (and of cross-validation in particular) [31]. Such an analysis results in equations telling us under what circumstances any particular implementation of stacked generalization will result in improved generalization, and under what circumstances it will result in worse generalization. Given such a mathematics, the conventional way to "remove ad hocness" is to make an assumption about the physical universe (e.g., an assumption about the prior distribution of parent functions) and then use that assumption in concert with the provided mathematics to determine what implementation of the generalizing system should be used.* In essence however, such a procedure simply translates be-

*This is the approach advocated by so-called *Bayesians*.

tween ad hoc assumptions concerning the details of the generalizing system and "prior" assumptions concerning the universe. Using such a procedure doesn't change the fact that assumptions—almost always justified by simply stating that they're "reasonable"—are still being made. The only difference is that the assumptions are being expressed differently.

An alternative approach that can sometimes remove some ad hocness is to simply see if one can modify the generalizing system to avoid making some of those ad hoc assumptions. The rest of this section is an investigation of one way of trying to do this with cross-validation. The goal is to modify cross-validation so that we don't need to specify a set of candidate generalizers in an ad hoc manner. We want a procedure that takes in a learning set and then produces a generalizer that has zero cross-validation error on that learning set (the number zero being about as non-ad-hoc as you can get). Furthermore, we want the details of the procedure to be as non-ad-hoc as possible.

As an example, one might hope that there exists some special and unique generalizer that always has zero cross-validation error on any learning set. If such a generalizer existed, then a non-ad-hoc version of cross-validation would be to always use that generalizer. Unfortunately, no single generalizer has zero cross-validation error for all learning sets. For example, let θ be a learning set consisting of the three input–output pairs $\{(x_1, y_1), (x_2, y_2), (x_3, y_3)\}$, and similarly let $\theta' \equiv \{(x_1, y_1), (x_2, y_2), (x_3, y_4)\}$, where $y_3 \neq y_4$. Then any generalizer with zero cross-validation error for θ must guess y_3 when asked the question x_3 after training on the learning set $\{(x_1, y_1), (x_2, y_2)\}$. However any generalizer with zero cross-validation error for θ' must guess y_4 when provided with the same learning set and question; no generalizer can have zero cross-validation error for both learning sets.

This means that the generalizer chosen by any non-ad-hoc variant of cross-validation must depend on the learning set. Unfortunately, for any single learning set θ, question q, and guess y, it is trivial to construct by hand a generalizer G with zero cross-validation error over θ such that $G(\theta; q) = y$. In other words, once the generalizer chosen is allowed to vary with the learning set, the restriction of zero cross-validation error, by itself, doesn't result in unique generalization. Therefore we must impose some extra restrictions.

The most reasonable way to do this is to limit the set of candidate generalizers. Yet we still wish to have as little ad hocness as possible. One way around this impasse is to limit the set of candidate generalizers by using restrictions that are based directly on generalizing behavior, rather than on any aspect of how the generalizer is implemented.

An example of a restriction on how a generalizer is implemented is a restriction on the allowed network architecture in a feedforward neural net. An example of a restriction on generalizing behavior is to limit the set of candidate generalizers to those generalizers that are invariant under (some of) the symmetry operations of Euclidean space. For example, a generalizer obeys Euclidean scale invariance in the input space if whenever all of the input components of the elements of the learning set are scaled by an identical nonzero factor k, and the question is scaled by the same amount, the guess remains unchanged. For a generalizer obeying such an invariance, the generalizing behavior is the same no matter what units are used to express input values. Under the restriction of meeting the Euclidean symmetries, only those generalizers that obey input space scaling invariance can be in the set of candidate generalizers.* In addition to input scaling invariance, there are other restrictions implied by the requirement of meeting the Euclidean symmetries. For example, translation invariance in the input space means that if all the input components of the elements of the learning set are translated by an identical input space vector **t,** and the question is as well, then the guess is unchanged. Invariances in the output space are defined similarly: output space scaling invariance means that if all the output components of the elements of the learning set are scaled by a constant K, then so is the guess of the full generalizer; output space translation invariance means that if all the output components of the elements of the learning set are incremented by a constant T, then so is the guess of the full generalizer. To limit the set of candidate generalizers to those meeting the Euclidean symmetries means we don't allow any generalizer that doesn't obey these invariances. In general, local generalizers often obey the Euclidean invariances, whereas most global generalizers do not. (See [11] for a more detailed discussion of such invariances and what kinds of generalizers obey them.)

To continue with this example, one might hope that if we restrict the set of candidate generalizers to those generalizers that obey the Euclidean invariances, then for any given learning set one and only one of the candidate generalizers will have zero cross-validation error. Unfortunately, there exist learning sets for which there exists no generalizer that both has zero cross-validation error and obeys the invariances of Euclidean space. For example, consider the learning set $\{(1, 1), (2, 2), (3, 4)\}$. If a generalizer G obeying the invariances of Euclidean space had zero cross-validation error for this learning set, then $G(\{(1, 1), (2, 2)\}; 3) = 4$. The Euclidean invariances then force the following set of mappings by G: translation invariance in the input space mean $G(\{(-0.5, 1), (0.5, 2)\}; 1.5) = 4$; scaling invariance in the input space then means that $G(\{(0.5, 1), (-0.5, 2)\}; -1.5) = 4$; input translation again gives $G(\{2, 2), (3, 1)\}; 1) = 4)$; output translation now gives $G(\{(2, .5), (3, -0.5)\}; 1) = 2.5$; output scaling gives $G(\{(2, -1), (3, 1)\}; 1) = -5$; output translating, this turns into $G(\{(2, 2), (3, 4)\}; 1) = -2$. However, the original learning set was $\{(1, 1), (2, 2), (3, 4)\}$, for which zero cross-validation error would require that $G(\{(2, 3), (3, 4)\}; 1) = 1$; we arrive at a contradiction.

To summarize, with no restrictions on the set of candidate generalizers, requiring perfect cross-validation isn't strong enough to pick a single generalizer. However for at least one set of restrictions on the set of candidate generalizers, requiring perfect cross-validation can sometimes be *too* strong; for some learning sets,

---

*Note that requiring scaling invariance is *not* the same as requiring that the guess is the same for all questions related to each other by a rescaling. The distinction is between requiring that $G(\{(x_1, y_1), (x_2, y_2)\}; q) = G(\{(k \times x_1, y_1), (k \times x_2, y_2)\}; k \times q)$ and requiring that $G(\{(x_1, y_1), (x_2, y_2)\}; q) = G(\{(x_1, y_1), (x_2, y_2)\}; k \times q)$.

no generalizer from the set of candidate generalizers has zero cross-validation error. One can investigate stronger versions of cross-validation* and the same behavior occurs. So the question arises: Given a particular version of cross-validation, is there *any* set of candidate generalizers, even one specified in an ad hoc manner, such that requiring zero cross-validation error will always pick out one and only one of those generalizers?

Unfortunately, for all versions of cross-validation for which there is a known answer to this question, the answer is *no*. (See [32], in which zero cross-validation error is referred to as ''self-guessing,'' for a proof). Accordingly, it appears that we cannot remove the ad hocness in cross-validation, and in general we have three choices:

1. Overrestrict the set of candidate generalizers, and search for which one has minimal cross-validation error on the provided learning set. (Note that for some learning sets, the resultant cross-validation error might be zero; there will be some other learning sets, however, for which the minimal cross-validation error is not zero.)
2. Underrestrict the set of candidate generalizers, but define some bijective mapping taking each candidate generalizer to a ''goodness''-measuring real number. Search among the set of candidate generalizers with zero cross-validation error on the provided learning set for the one with maximal goodness.
3. Overrestrict the set of candidate generalizers and define some bijective mapping taking each candidate generalizer to a ''goodness''-measuring real number. Search among the set of candidate generalizers for the one with both minimal cross-validation error on the provided learning set and maximal goodness. (As an example, one might search for the generalizer with minimal sum of cross-validation error and (the negative of) goodness.)

Note that for both choices (2) and (3) one has to define the goodness mapping. Specifying such a mapping is no more ad hoc than specifying an overrestricted set of generalizers (the ad hocness one must make to use choice (1).) Indeed, one can view choice (1) as a special case of choice (3), where the goodness mapping maps a few of the candidate generalizers to huge values, while mapping all the other generalizers to small values. Nonetheless, in practice it's usually easiest to pick a set of candidate generalizers rather than worry explicitly about goodness mappings. This is why essentially all research to date involving cross-validation has been in the guise of choice (1).

---

*One example of such a strengthened version of cross-validation is finding a generalizer such that the points at which a parent function is sampled for training is irrelevant: Have a learning set θ. Define a set of functions parameterized by generalizers: $f_G(q) \equiv G(\theta; q)$, i.e., $f_G(.)$ is the parent function guessed by generalizer G after training on learning set θ. Our goal is to find a generalizer G such that for *any* learning set θ' of samples of $f_G(.)$, the generalizer always guesses the same parent function $f_G(.)$, that is, such that $G(\theta'; q) = f_G(q) \ \forall \ \theta'$ chosen by sampling $f_G(.)$.

ACKNOWLEDGMENTS

This article was prepared under the auspices of the Department of Energy.

REFERENCES

[1] D. Rumelhart and J. McClelland, *Explorations in the Microstructure of Cognition*, 2 vols., MIT Press, Cambridge, Mass., 1986.

[2] J. Holland, *Adaptation in Natural and Artificial Systems*, University of Michigan Press, Ann Arbor, Mich., 1975.

[3] J. Rissanen, Stochastic complexity and modeling, *Annals Statistics*, 14, 1080–1100 (1986).

[4] J. Rissanen, A universal prior for integers and estimation by minimum description length, *Annals Statistics*, 11, 416–431 (1983).

[5] D. Wolpert, (1990). The relationship between Occam's razor and convergent guess, *Complex Syst.*, 4, 319–368 (1990).

[6] C. Stanfill and D. Waltz, Toward memory-based reasoning, *Communications ACM*, 29, 1213–1228 (1986).

[7] T. Poggio and MIT AI Lab staff, ''MIT Progress in Understanding Images,'' in L. Bauman, Ed., *Proc. Image Understanding Workshop*, Morgan-Kaufman, San Mateo, California, (1988).

[8] V. Morozov, *Methods for Solving Incorrectly Posed Problems*, Springer-Verlag, 1984.

[9] D. Wolpert, A benchmark for how well neural nets generalize, *Biological Cybernetics*, 61, 303–313 (1989).

[10] D. Wolpert, Constructing a generalizer superior to NETtalk via a mathematical theory of generalization, *Neural Networks*, 3, 445–452 (1990).

[11] D. Wolpert, A mathematical theory of generalization: Part I, *Complex Systems*, 4, 151–200 (1990).

[12] J. Farmer and J. Sidorowich, ''Exploiting Chaos to Predict the Future and Reduce Noise,'' Los Alamos Rep. LA-UR-88-901 (1988).

[13] S. Omohundro, ''Efficient Algorithms with Neural Network Behavior,'' Rep. UIUCSCS-R-87-1331 Computer Science Dept., University of Illinois, Urbana-Champaign, (1987).

[14] J. Quinlan, Induction of decision trees, *Machine Learning*, 1, 81–106 (1986).

[15] T. Dietterich, Machine learning, *Annual Rev. Computer Sci.*, 4, 255–306 (1990).

[16] R. Duda and P. Hart, *Pattern Classification and Scene Analysis*. Wiley, New York, 1973.

[17] M. Stone, An asymptotic equivalence of choice of model by cross-validation and Akaike's criterion, *J. Roy. Statistic. Soc. B*, 39, 44–47 (1977).

[18] M. Stone, Asymptotics for and against cross-validation, *Biometrika*, 64, 29–35 (1977).

[19] M. Stone, Cross-validatory choice and assessment of statistical predictions, *J. Roy. Statistic. Soc. B*, 36, 111–120 (1974).

[20] B. Efron, (1979). Computers and the theory of statistics: Thinking the unthinkable, *SIAM Review*, 21, 460–480 (1979).

[21] T. J. Sejnowski and C. R. Rosenberg, "NETtalk: A Parallel Network That Learns to Read Aloud," Elec. Eng. Computer Sci. Tech. Rep. JHU/EECS-86/01, Johns Hopkins University (1988).

[22] E. C. Carterette and M. H. Jones, Informal speech, UCAL Press, Los Angeles (1974).

[23] Ker-Chau Li, From Stein's unbiased risk estimates to the method of generalized cross-validation, *Annals Statistics*, 13, 1352–1377 (1985).

[24] D. Wolpert, "Improving the Performance of Generalizers by Time-Series-like Preprocessing of the Learning Set," Rep. LA-UR-91-350, Los Alamos Laboratory (1991).

[25] D. Wolpert, "Stacked Generalization," *Neural Networks* (in press).

[26] He Xiangdong and Zhu Zhaoxuan, "Nonlinear Time Series Modeling by Self-Organizing Methods," Department of Mechanics Rep., Peking University, Beijing, PRC (1990).

[27] J. Deppisch et al., "Hierarchical Training of Neural Networks and Prediction of Chaotic Time Series," Institut fur Theoretische Physik und SFB Nicktlineare Dynamik, Universitat Frankfurt, Germany Rep., (1990).

[28] Xiru Zhang, Private communication concerning stacked generalization and protein folding.

[29] S. Gustafson, G. Little, and D. Simon, "Neural Network for Interpolation and Extrapolation," Rep. 1294-40, Research Institute, University of Dayton, Dayton, Oh. (1990).

[30] G. Schulz et al., Comparison of predicted and experimentally determined secondary structure of adenyl kinase, *Nature*, 250, 140–142 (1974).

[31] D. Wolpert, "On the Connection Between In-Sample Testing and Generalization Error," *Complex Systems* (in press).

[32] D. Wolpert, A mathematical theory of generalization: Part II, *Complex Systems*, 4, 201–249 (1990). (Cross-validation is a special case of the technique of "self-guessing" discussed here.)

CHAPTER 7 ⸻⸻⸻⸻⸻⸻⸻

Infinitesimal versus Discrete Methods in Neural Network Synthesis

ANDREAS ALBRECHT

7.1 INTRODUCTION

The design and analysis of artificial neural networks is one of the major fields in current AI research. Stimulating work has been done in statistical physics [1, 2], where various modifications of neural networks have been proposed as architectures for learning procedures [3].

The dominating mathematical tools in neural network design are taken from mathematical analysis and statistics; that is explicable from the source statistical physics and applications of neural networks in pattern recognition and signal processing. These methods are applied to networks, that means to systems of superpositions, in order to show convergence properties of learning strategies.

However, little is known about the superposition of continuous functions representing, for example, the output of neural networks, where the inputs are continuous variables and nodes represent simple continuous functions from a given basis. That explains, in our opinion, the fact that propositions about the convergence of learning procedures like back propagation are restricted to networks with a small depth.

The representation of continuous functions by superpositions of simple functions is closely connected to one of the famous problems formulated by D. Hilbert in 1900 (problem No. 13). The solution of this problem was given by A. N. Kolmogorov and V. I. Arnol'd in the middle of the 1950s [4, 5], initiating a systematic investigation of superpositions by subsequent papers [6-9].

Fast Learning and Invariant Object Recognition, By Branko Souček and the IRIS Group.
ISBN 0-471-57430-9 © 1992 John Wiley & Sons, Inc.

The theorem of Kolmogorov states that

for each continuous function $f(x_1, x_2, \ldots, x_n)$ defined on $[0, 1]^n$ there exist continuous functions $\psi^{a,b}(y)$ and $\phi^b(z)$ such that

$$f(x_1, x_2, \ldots, x_n) = \sum_{b=1}^{2n+1} \phi^b \left[\sum_{a=1}^{n} \phi^{a,b}(x_a) \right] \qquad (7.1)$$

That means, given the basis $B_f = \{x + y, \phi^1, \ldots, \phi^{2n+1}, \psi^{1,1}, \ldots, \psi^{n,2n+1}\}$, each continuous function can be realized by a network of depth log (n) + log $(2n + 1)$ with bounded fan-in, or a network with depth-four and unbounded (linear) fan-in. However, the functions $\psi^{a,b}$, ϕ^b might be quite difficult in terms of simple continuous functions like addition, multiplication, and constants.

In the paper [6] the authors introduced the so-called ϵ-entropy as a complexity measure for continuous functions. Given a set of functions $\mathcal{F}$, the minimal number of elements in ϵ-nets for $\mathcal{F}$ is denoted by N_ϵ. Kolmogorov/Tichomirov called the value $H_\epsilon(\mathcal{F}) := \log N_\epsilon$ the ϵ-entropy of $\mathcal{F}$. In [6] they performed the calculation of $H_\epsilon(\mathcal{F})$ for several classes $\mathcal{F}$.

For Lipschitz-functions defined on $\Delta = [a, b]$, where

$$|f(x) - f(x + \delta)| \le p \cdot \delta$$

and p is a constant, the authors in [6] obtained

$$H_\epsilon(\mathcal{LIP}) = \frac{|\Delta| \cdot p}{\epsilon} - 1$$

The corresponding value for the class $\mathcal{F}_{2\pi}^h$ of analytic functions with the period 2π and $|Im(z)| \le h$ is

$$H_\epsilon(\mathcal{F}_{2\pi}^h) = 2 \left(\log \frac{1}{\epsilon} \right)^2 / (h \cdot \log e) + O \left(\log \frac{1}{\epsilon} \log \log \frac{1}{\epsilon} \right)$$

The aim of our paper is to report some results concerning the complexity of approximate representations of continuous functions by (simple) basic functions, where the methods are derived from Boolean circuit synthesis, an area of discrete mathematics. Therefore, we try to illustrate the significance of discrete methods and propositions on Boolean circuit complexity for the synthesis of neural networks.

Concerning the existence (not the complexity) of representations as in (7.1), there is an interesting paper on differentiable functions by S. S. Marchenkov [7] based on Boolean circuit synthesis. In particular, Marchenkov proved that

for each m and q there exist q-times differentiable functions $f(x_1, x_2, \ldots, x_n)$ where a representation by superpositions of p-times differentiable functions depending on k variables is impossible if only $k/p < m/q$.

The proof is based on Lupanov's asymptotically optimal method for the synthesis of Boolean functions.

The present paper is an extended version of [10].

7.2 CIRCUITS REALIZING CONTINUOUS FUNCTIONS

In [11] Gashkov points out that circuit synthesis of continuous functions might be important for the analysis of artificial neural systems modeling the human brain. But, to our knowledge, up to now there does not exist any "feedback" from these results to actual neural network design as described, for example, in [12].

Nevertheless, we think that results from circuit synthesis of continuous functions are applicable to propositions about the performance of neural networks with certain size and depth. That is, in particular, the case if the representation of relatively large classes of functions (patterns, signals) by a unique network is required.

Let I denote any subset from the set of real numbers $\mathbf{R}$ and $C(I^n)$ the set of continuous functions $f: I^n \to \mathbf{R}$. Given $K \subset C(I^n)$, we define $J_\epsilon := H_\epsilon(K)/\log(H_\epsilon(K))$, where $H_\epsilon(K)$ denotes the ϵ-entropy of K. We assume, that $H_\epsilon(K)$ tends to infinity for $\epsilon \to 0$.

As usually, a circuit on n inputs over the basis B is an acyclic graph, where the nodes represent functions from B. The fan-in of nodes corresponds to the number of variables of the represented function $g(x_1, x_2, \ldots, x_m) \in B$.

Let $s(S)$ denote the number of nodes in the circuit S, and f_S the function realized by S. For $g(x_1, x_2, \ldots, x_m) \in B$ we define $\rho_B(g) := 1/(m-1)$ and denote $\rho_B := \min_{g \in B} \rho_B(g)$. Furthermore, we define

$$s(f, \epsilon) := \min_{|f_S - f| \le \epsilon} s(S)$$

$$s(K, \epsilon) := \max_{f \in K} s(f, \epsilon)$$

Using the methods developed for Boolean circuit synthesis, Gashkov [13] proved the following lower bound for finite basic systems $B \subset C(I^n)$:

$$s_B(K, \epsilon) \ge \rho_B \cdot J_\epsilon(K) \tag{7.2}$$

We see that only structural properties of basic functions influence the lower bound. This bound is tight for some classes of functions, for example, for bounded Lipschitz-functions [14]:

$$s_B(W_{pq}) \le \rho_B \cdot J_\epsilon(W_{pq}) \cdot (1 + o(J_\epsilon)) \tag{7.3}$$

where

$$B := \{x - y, x \cdot y, |x|, \tfrac{1}{2}\}$$

and

$$W_{pq} := \{ f : | f(x) - f(x + \delta)| \leq p \cdot \delta, \, -q \leq f(x) \leq +q\}$$

A set of basic functions B is called quasifinite if $\mathbf{R} \subset B$ and $B \backslash \mathbf{R}$ is finite. For circuits over quasifinite basis systems consisting of polynomials Gashkov proved [13]:

$$S_B(K, \epsilon) \geq c_B \cdot \min \{M_{2\epsilon}, \sqrt{H_{2\epsilon}(K)}\} \qquad (7.4)$$

where

$$M_\epsilon(K) := H_\epsilon(K)/\log (1/\epsilon)$$

and c_B is a constant not depending on K and ϵ. In the same paper an upper bound $O\{\sqrt{H_{2\epsilon}}\}$ is shown for analytic functions of a certain type.

The basic methods to obtain upper and lower bounds mentioned above are approximate representations known from mathematical analysis together with synthesis methods from Boolean circuit theory for the coefficients depending on the individual function to be represented.

From the point of view of neural network synthesis the complexity of circuits over the basis $B := \{x + y, x \cdot y, 1/(1 + e^{-x})\} \cup \mathbf{R}$ is of special interest, because the lower bound (7.4) was proved only for basic systems built by polynomials. That means, one has to analyze approximate representations of continuous functions where $1/(1 + e^{-x})$ is among the basic functions. On the other hand we think that the model of Boolean threshold functions is powerful enough in order to reflect the main computational problems in neural network synthesis.

7.3 BOOLEAN THRESHOLD CIRCUITS

With the renewed interest in models for the human brain one can observe a growing number of theoretical investigations concerning Boolean threshold circuits, for example, [15–20]. Early results on threshold circuits are due to R. O. Winder, E. I. Neciporuk, and O. B. Lupanov [21, 22, 23].

For the synthesis of arbitrary $n$ary functions over the basis B_{th} built by all $n$ary Boolean threshold functions, Neciporuk [22] proved that (for almost all $f(x_1, x_2, \ldots, x_n)$)

$$s(f) \geq 2 \cdot \sqrt{2^n/n} \qquad (7.5)$$

where $s(f)$ is the minimal number of threshold functions (gates) needed for f. Lupanov [23] obtained the same main value for the upper bound

$$s(f) \leq 2 \cdot \sqrt{2^n/n} \cdot \{1 + o(2^{n/2}/n)\} \qquad (7.6)$$

It is important to note that the gate number $O(\sqrt{2^n/n})$ can be reached by threshold circuits over B_{th} with the constant depth 4, see [23]. That means, roughly speaking, four layers of threshold elements with unbounded fan-in are enough in artificial neural networks.

At present, threshold circuits with constant depth and polynomial size $n^{O(1)}$ are in the center of interest. Especially, the relation to other complexity classes is investigated, for example, to $\mathfrak{NC}^1$—the family of Boolean circuits with bounded fan-in, gate number $n^{O(1)}$, and depth $O(\log(n))$ $(= \log^1(n))$. There are competing conjectures concerning the relationship between $\mathfrak{TC}^o$—the family of functions realized by polynomial-sized threshold circuits with unbounded fan-in and constant depth—and $\mathfrak{NC}^1$. Immermann/Landau [17] have conjectured that $\mathfrak{TC}^o = \mathfrak{NC}^1$, while Yao [20] discusses a conjecture that $\mathfrak{TC}^o \neq \mathfrak{NC}^1$.

For a deeper analysis of $\mathfrak{NC}^1$ the class $\mathfrak{AC}$ was introduced, representing circuits (or accepted languages of binary strings) of polynomial size and unbounded fan-in AND and OR gates. The depth of $\mathfrak{AC}$ circuits "counts" the number of changes of AND and OR gates. The subclass of circuits with constant depth $O(1)$ is denoted by $\mathfrak{AC}^o$.

Furst/Saxe/Sipser [24] proved that parity cannot be computed by circuits from $\mathfrak{AC}^o$. As a consequence one obtains that bounded-depth circuits for multiplying integers or taking the transitive closure of graphs require more than a polynomial number of AND and OR gates.

Hajnal et al. [16] separated subclasses from $\mathfrak{TC}^o$ of small depth; in particular, they showed that the inner product mod 2 of two binary vectors of length n, the function $f(\mathbf{x}, \mathbf{y}) = x_1y_1 \oplus x_2y_2 \oplus \cdots \oplus x_ny_n$, belongs to depth-three circuits from $\mathfrak{TC}^o$, but not to depth-two circuits.

In [20] Yao has shown that languages accepted by *monotone* depth $(k-1)$ threshold circuits require exponential size for depth k $\mathfrak{AC}^o$ circuits. Allender proved in [15] that any language accepted by depth k $\mathfrak{AC}^o$ circuits is accepted by depth-three threshold circuits of size $n^{O(\log^k n)}$.

In [25] Paturi/Saks have shown a lower bound $\Omega(n^2/\log^2 n)$ on the number of edges in depth-two threshold circuits for parity whose weights are bounded by a polynomial in n. They obtained a sharper lower bound $\Omega(n^2)$ if the weights w_i are limited by $|w_i| \leq 1$. The th-circuit for parity from [16] has $(n+1)$ gates and $n(n+1)$ edges.

Reif [19] investigated the relationship of threshold circuits to circuits with unbounded fan-in over finite fields $\mathbf{Z}_{p(n)}$, where each node computes either multiple sums or products of integers modulo a prime number $p(n)$. In particular, he proved that any analytic function with convergent rational polynomial power series (such as integer reciprocal, sine, cosine, exponentiation), can be computed with an accuracy of 2^{-n^c} for any constant c by threshold circuits from $\mathfrak{TC}^o$. These results show that circuits from $\mathfrak{TC}^o$ can compute high accuracy approximations to a large class of multivariate rational polynomials and, furthermore, can interpolate rational polynomials with a constant number of variables. But even learning by algebraic interpolation appears to be appropriate in certain constrained cases of pattern recognition [19].

Stimulated by Valiant's definition of learnability [26, 27] the notion of learning threshold circuits was introduced in [28]. A learning threshold circuit is a pair of threshold circuits, one called the representation circuit RC and the other the computation circuit CC. In the learning mode, the purpose of the RC is to represent and evaluate the current hypothesis, while the purpose of CC is to modify the current hypothesis as needed. Let $s(S_{th})$ denote the number of nodes in the threshold circuit S_{th}. Given a sequence of learning circuits $\mathcal{LC} := \{[RC_n, CC_n]\}$ for concepts $\mathcal{C} := \{C_n\}$, we are interested in lower bounds for $s(S_{th})$ depending on $|C_n|$.

For a threshold function $\phi(x_1, x_2, \ldots, x_n)$ we denote by $N(\phi, t)$ the set of all functions

$$\psi(x_1, x_2, \ldots, x_n) = \phi(f_1(x_1, x_2, \ldots, x_n), f_2(x_1, x_2, \ldots, x_n), \ldots,$$

$$f_t(x_1, x_2, \ldots, x_n))$$

where the f_i are arbitrary $n$ary Boolean functions. For the number of elements $|N(\phi, t)|$, Neciporuk has shown [22]:

$$|N(\phi, t)| \leq 2 + 2^t \cdot \binom{2^{n+1} + 2t}{t} \tag{7.7}$$

We assume that $n^3/\log(|C_n|)$ tends to zero. Using some standard representations of threshold circuits [23] one obtains from (7.7) by counting arguments the following lower bound [29]:

$$s(RC_n) \geq \Omega(\sqrt{\log |C_n|/n}) \tag{7.8}$$

In terms of the Vapnik–Chervonenkis dimension [30] a similar lower bound is proved in [18].

St. Judd [31] formalized a notion of loading information into connectionist networks that characterizes the training of feedforward neural networks. He proved that the problem

> Given a network and a set of training examples, do there exist node functions that allow the network to produce outputs consistent with the examples?

is $\mathcal{NP}$-complete.

In [32] it was shown that even in the case of simple 2-layer, 3-node, and n-input neural networks the learning problem remains intractable. The authors consider a network where each of the n inputs (first layer) is connected to the two nodes of the second layer, and the single node of the third layer has two inputs. The network is given a set of $O(n)$ training examples and the learning algorithm has to find three threshold functions for the nodes such that the network produces outputs consistent with the linear number of examples. The $\mathfrak{N}\mathcal{P}$-complete set splitting problem is reduced to this learning task. These results show that a precise analysis of individual learning problems is required.

It was mentioned that the sum mod 2 can be realized by a depth-two circuit from $\mathfrak{IC}^o$ although this function requires $O(\log{(n)}/\varphi{(n)})$ changes of AND and OR gates in the bounded fan-in model of $\mathfrak{NC}^1$. This number of AND and OR changes results from the difficulty to break up the variable dependencies in neighboring levels of the hypercube.

Given a Boolean function $f(\tilde{x})$ we consider the different levels of the hypercube together with the corresponding values of $f(\tilde{x})$:

$$L_u := \{[\tilde{\sigma}, f(\tilde{\sigma})] \mid \tilde{\sigma} \in \{0,\ 1\}^n \text{ and } \|\tilde{\sigma}\| = u\}$$

where

$$\|\tilde{\sigma}\| = \sum_{i=1}^{n} \sigma_i.$$

For the parity function

$$\text{exor}(\tilde{x}) = \oplus_{i=1}^{n} x_i$$

neighboring levels L_u, L_{u-1} are labeled by alternating values.

The function $f(\tilde{x})$ depends on the variable x_i between the levels L_u, L_{u-1} if there exist $\tilde{\sigma} \in L_u$, $\tilde{\eta} \in L_{u-1}$ such that $\|\tilde{\sigma} - \tilde{\eta}\| = 1$ and $f(\tilde{\sigma}) \neq f(\tilde{\eta})$, where $\tilde{\sigma} - \tilde{\eta} = \Sigma_{i=1}^{n} \sigma_i \oplus \eta_i$. The function $\text{exor}(\tilde{x})$ depends for each $\tilde{\sigma} \in L_{n/2}$ on $n/2$ variables ($n/2$ odd). During the decomposition of $\text{exor}(\tilde{x})$ by an $\mathcal{GC}$ circuit, in the OR step a part of the nodes from $L_{n/2}$ changes the label from one to zero while in the following AND step a part of the nodes from $L_{n/2-1}$ changes the label from zero to one. This procedure is finished if only dependencies on a single variable remain in the corresponding branches of the circuit.

We consider an intermediate stage of the decomposition: Given the pair of levels $[L_u, L_{u-1}]$ we denote by $G(p;\ s,\ t)$ bipartite subgraphs of the graph built by the edges of the hypercube, where

all s nodes from $M_1 \subseteq L_u$ are labeled by the value one
all t nodes from $M_2 \subseteq L_{u-1}$ are labeled by the value zero
for the number of edges from $E(M_1, M_2)$ it holds $|E|/\frac{1}{2}(s + t) \geq p$

After an AND or OR step from $G(p;\ s,\ t)$ remains at least an

$$O(\sqrt{\tfrac{1}{2}(s + t)})$$

bipartite subgraph with an average number of $(p - \epsilon)$ dependencies on variables. Thus, for $O(\sqrt{m})$ nodes within the graph G the dependencies on different variables are hard to remove by the logical operations AND and OR. But including the arithmetical operation "counting" by the help of threshold functions, the $\text{exor}(\tilde{x})$ is realized in two steps.

Learning algorithms for functions $f(x_1, \ldots, x_n) \in \mathfrak{NC}^1$ have to establish the necessary connections from the n inputs (or the $2n$ literals $x_1, \ldots, x_n, \bar{x}_1, \ldots, \bar{x}_n$) to the $n^c = 2^{2l}$ inputs of the corresponding complete binary tree T_f^a with alternating AND and OR nodes. The tree T_f^a is obtained from C_f of depth $c \cdot \log(n)$ by introducing additional gates for each input to gates from C_f. Therefore, the learning task is to find a $[2n, n^c]$ bipartite graph for the input distribution with n^c edges; the "circuit part" has a standardized form. We distinguish between the inputs $\tilde{\sigma}$ to the whole circuit C_f^a and the inputs $\tilde{\eta}_{\tilde{\sigma}}$ to the binary tree T_f^a. We note that for $C_f^a(\tilde{\sigma}) = 1$ we have the necessary condition $\|\tilde{\eta}_{\tilde{\sigma}}\| \geq 2^l$, $n^c = 2^{2l}$.

We propose the following structure for experiments on learning functions $f(\tilde{x}) \in \mathfrak{NC}^1$ by threshold circuits of bounded depth:

1. The input structure is fixed (in difference to C_f^a); $2n$ literals are the input to the first circuit part.
2. The threshold circuit tc_1 transforms the input to tuples $\tilde{\eta}$ of length 2^{2l} with $\|\tilde{\eta}\| = 2^l$; in this part the learning task for the input structure of C_f^a is "hidden."
3. The threshold circuit tc_2 "simulates" the binary tree T_f^a for inputs $\tilde{\eta}$ with $\|\tilde{\eta}\| = 2^l$.

The circuit tc_2 performs for all subtrees of T_f^a of depth $2d$, $d = 1, \ldots, l$, the test, whether there is the necessary number of ones at the corresponding inputs or not. This can be done in parallel by $\Sigma_{d=1}^{l} 2^{2l}/4^d$ threshold gates with polynomial bounded fan-in. For subtrees of depth $2d$ we need 2^{l-d} positive outputs from the threshold gates. The outputs of threshold gates corresponding to subtrees of depth $2d$ are weighted by the value $2^{(l-1)(l-d)}$; thus, we operate with hyperpolynomial weights $n^{c_1 \cdot \log(n)}$, the binary representation is of length $\log^{O(1)} n$: The output gate of tc_2 has the threshold $\Sigma_{d=1}^{l} 2^{l-d} 2^{(l-1)(l-d)}$. Positive examples of $f(\tilde{x})$ are forced by tc_1 to tuples $\tilde{\eta}$ with $\|\tilde{\eta}\| = 2^l$, negative examples to a bounded number of fixed tuples. For the synthesis of tc_1 one can combine the strategies for learning the input structure of C_f^a and the evaluation of tuples with $\|\tilde{\eta}\| \geq 2^l$ performed by T_f^a.

7.4   FINAL REMARKS

We think that further progress in understanding the computational power of (probabilistic) threshold circuits will lead to new learning strategies and structural paradigms in neural network synthesis.

The proposed experimental structure from the previous section can be analyzed only for small values of the constant in n^c. The critical point is that the structure is derived from $\mathcal{RC}$ circuits while the essential idea of threshold circuits is "to count" and "to classify" a large number of features of the given input. The second part of the proposed structure makes use of this viewpoint on processing the input information. But the threshold complexity (with respect to the circuit depth) of functions seems to be determined by the operations performed by the subcircuit tc_1.

It would also be interesting to know more about constraint threshold circuits from $\mathcal{TC}^o$, where the restrictions are similar to the fractal-like structure of the human brain: four main levels, each of them substructured like the whole system.

The author would like to thank Edgar Körner for valuable discussions on neural network research.

REFERENCES

[1] D. H. Ackley, G. H. Hinton, and T. J. Sejnowski, A learning algorithm for Boltzmann machines, *Cognitive Sci.*, 9, 147–169 (1985).

[2] J. J. Hopfield, Neural networks and physical systems with an emergent collective computational power, *Proc. Nat. Acad. Sci.*, 79, 2554–2558 (1982).

[3] G. E. Hinton, "Connectionist Learning Procedures," Tech. Rep. CS-TR-87-115, Carnegie-Mellon University, (1987).

[4] A. N. Kolmogorov, On the representation of multivariate continuous functions by superpositions of continuous functions depending on one variable and addition (in Russian), *Dokl. Acad. Nauk SSSR*, 11(5), 953–956 (1957).

[5] V. I. Arnold, On the representation of continous functions depending on three variables by superpositions of continous functions depending on two variables (in Russian), *Dokl. Acad. Nauk SSSR*, 114(4), 679–681 (1957).

[6] A. N. Kolmogorov and B. M. Tichomirov, ϵ-entropy and ϵ-capacity, *Usp. Mathem. Nauk*, 14(2), 3–86 (1959).

[7] S. S. Marchenkov, On an analysis method for superpositions of continous functions (in Russian), *Probl. Kibernet.*, 37, 5–18 (1980).

[8] A. G. Vitushkin, Linear superpositions of functions, *Usp. Mathem. Nauk*, 22(1), 77–124 (1967).

[9] A. G. Vitushkin, On the representation of functions by means of superpositions and related topics, *L'Enseignement Mathematique*, XXIII(3/4), 50–93 (1977).

[10] A. Albrecht, Infinitesimal vs. discrete methods in neural network synthesis, in *Proc. 5th Internat. Workshop on Parallel Processing by Cellular Automata and Arrays*, 15–24 (1990).

[11] S. B. Gashkov, On the circuit and formula complexity of boolean functions realized over basic systems built by continous functions (in Russian), *Probl. Kibernet.*, 37, 57–118 (1980).

[12] Ph. Treleaven, "Neurocomputers," Tech. Rep. CS-RN-89-8, University College, London (1989).

[13] S. B. Gashkov, On the complexity of approximate realizations of analytic functions by circuits and formulae (in Russian), *Vestnik Mosc. Univ., Ser. Math. i Mech.*, (4), 36–42 (1983).

[14] S. B. Gashkov, On the complexity of approximate realizations of certain classes of differentiable functions depending on one variable by circuits (in Russian), *Vestnik Mosc. Univ., Ser. Math. i Mech.*, (3), 35–40 (1984).

[15] E. Allender, "A Note on the Power of Threshold Circuits," Tech. Rep. TR-5, Inst. of Informatics, University of Wuerzburg (July 1989).

[16] A. Hajnal, W. Maass, P. Pudlak, M. Szegedy, and G. Turan, Threshold functions of bounded depth, in *Proc. 28th IEEE Symp. on Foundations of Computer Sci.*, 99–110 (1987).

[17] N. Immermann and S. Landau, The complexity of iterated multiplication, *Proc. 4th IEEE Structure in Complexity Theory Conf.*, 104–111 (1989).

[18] J.-H. Lin and J. S. Vitter, Complexity issues in learning by neural nets, *Proc. 2nd Workshop on Computational Learning Theory*, 118–133 (1989).

[19] J. Reif, On threshold circuits and polynomial computation, *Proc. 2nd IEEE Structure in Complexity Theory Conf.* (1987).

[20] A. C. Yao, Circuits and local computation, *Proc. 21st ACM Symp. on Theory of Computing*, 186–196 (1989).

[21] R. O. Winder, Bounds on threshold gate realizability, *IEEE Trans. EC*, 12(5), 561–564 (1963).

[22] E. I. Neciporuk, On the synthesis of threshold circuits (in Russian), *Probl. Kibernet.*, 11, 49–110 (1964).

[23] O. B. Lupanov, On the synthesis of threshold circuits (in Russian), *Probl. Kibernet.*, 26, 109–140 (1973).

[24] M. Furst, J. B. Saxe, and M. Sipser, Parity, circuits, and the polynomial-time hierarchy, *Proc. 22nd IEEE Symp. on Foundations of Computer Science*, 260–270 (1981).

[25] R. Paturi and M. E. Saks, On threshold circuits for parity, *Proc. 31st IEEE Symp. on Foundations of Computer Sci.* (1990).

[26] L. G. Valiant, A theory of the learnable, *Comm. ACM*, 27(11), 1134–1142 (1984).

[27] M. J. Kearns and L. G. Valiant, "Learning Boolean Formulae Is as Hard as Factoring," Tech. Rep. TR-14-88, Aiken Comp. Lab., Harvard University, Cambridge, Mass. (1988).

[28] P. Raghavan, Learning in threshold networks: A computational model and applications, *Proc. 1st Workshop on Computational Learning Theory*, 15–23 (1988).

[29] A. Albrecht, On the complexity of learning circuits, *Proc. Internat. Workshop on Neural Informatics*, 29–35, Academy of Sci. Pub., (1989).

[30] A. Blumer, A. Ehrenfeucht, D. Haussler, and W. K. Warmuth, "Learnability and the Vapnik-Chervonenkis Dimension," Tech. Rep. UCSC-CRL-87-20, University of California at Santa Cruz (1987).

[31] St. Judd, Learning in neural networks, *Proc. 1st Workshop on Computational Learning Theory*, 1–7 (1988).

[32] A. Blum and R. L. Rivest, Training a 3-node neural network is $\mathcal{NP}$-complete, *Proc. 1st Workshop on Computational Learning Theory*, 8–14 (1988).

BIBLIOGRAPHY

J. Alspector and R. B. Allen, A neuromorphic VLSI learning system, *Proc. Stanford VLSI Conf.*, 313–349, MIT Press, Cambridge, Mass. (1987).

S. B. Gashkov, On the complexity of approximate "circuit and formula" realizations of continous functions and on the continous analogy of the "Shannon effect" (in Russian), *Vestnik Mosc. Univ., Ser. Math. i Mech.*, (6), 25–33 (1986).

S. A. Goldman, M. J. Kearns, and R. E. Schapire, Exact identification of circuits using fixed points of amplification functions, *Proc. 31st IEEE Symp. on Foundations of Computer Sci.* (1990).

CHAPTER 8 ⸻

Systolic Array Implementations of Neural Networks

JAI-HOON CHUNG
HYUNSOO YOON
SEUNG RYOUL MAENG

8.1 INTRODUCTION

In recent years, artificial neural networks have become a subject of a very extensive research, since they are envisioned as an alternative to the problems such as pattern recognition, vision, and speech recognition that artificial intelligence had been unable to solve [1]. However, as simulations of large neural networks on a sequential computer frequently require days and even weeks of computations, and the long computational time had been a critical obstacle for progress in neural network researches, extensive efforts are being devoted to the parallel implementation of neural networks.

A systolic array [2] is one of the best solutions to the parallel implementation of neural networks. It can overcome the communication problems generated by the highly interconnected neurons, and can exploit the massive parallelism inherent in the problem. Moreover, since the computation of neural networks can be represented by a series of matrix-by-vector multiplications, the classical systolic algorithms can be used to implement them.

There have been several research efforts on systolic algorithms and systolic array structures to implement the neural networks. The approaches can be classified into two groups. One is mapping the systolic algorithms for neural networks onto parallel computers such as Warp, MasPar MP-1, and Transputer arrays [3–10], and the other is designing a VLSI systolic array dedicated to one or two specific models [11–18].

The major design issues of the mapping approaches are designing systolic al-

Fast Learning and Invariant Object Recognition, By Branko Souček and the IRIS Group.
ISBN 0-471-57430-9 © 1992 John Wiley & Sons, Inc.

gorithms that can be partitioned and mapped efficiently onto the parallel computers and mapping the algorithms efficiently onto the fixed interconnection structures of the parallel computers minimizing the communication/synchronization overhead. The major design issues of the VLSI approaches are designing the basic cell architectures to be used as modular building blocks to implement large neural networks and designing the array structures to exploit the model-specific parallelisms to maximize the performance. Systolic ring arrays and two-dimensional mesh arrays have been suggested as the resultant array structures.

In this chapter, we investigate the systolic approaches to implement neural networks. In Section 8.2, we introduce the basic neural network models and their characteristics. The basic systolic algorithms and the systolic array structures to implement the neural networks and the issues of exploiting the parallelisms inherent in the neural networks are presented in Section 8.3. In Section 8.4, the various systolic approaches are studied separately in each subsection. A VLSI systolic array for multilayer neural networks is presented in Section 8.5 as a case study of systolic array design. A summary and future research areas for systolic array implementations of neural networks are given in Section 8.6.

8.2 OVERVIEW OF NEURAL NETWORKS

Artificial neural networks, or simply neural networks, are biologically inspired; that is, they are composed of elements that perform in a manner that is analogous to the most elementary functions of the biological neuron. These elements are then organized in a way that may be related to the anatomy of the brain [19].

In this section, we briefly describe the representative neural network models and their characteristics.

8.2.1 Basic Characteristics of Neural Networks

Neural networks consist of many simple, neuronlike processing elements called *neurons* that interact using weighted connections. The neuron was designed to mimic the characteristics of the biological neuron. A set of inputs are applied, each representing the output of another neuron. Each input is multiplied by a corresponding weight, analogous to a synaptic strength, and all of the weighted inputs are then summed to determine the *state* or *active level* of the neuron.

Neural networks are characterized by a few key properties: The *network topology*, which is specified by the interconnection pattern of the neurons; the *recall procedure*, which is specified by the output function of the neuron according to the input; and the *training/learning procedure*, which establishes the values of the weights.

In an artificial neural network, neurons are generally configured in regular and highly interconnected topologies. For example, in Hopfield model [20], the neurons form a fully connected topology, and the output from each neuron feeds back to all of its neighbors. In the back-propagation model [21] and Boltzmann machine [22], the network consists of one or more layers between the input and output neurons, and typically the output from each neuron of a layer feeds to all of the neurons in its adjacent layer. In the self-organizing feature map [23], the network connects a vector of input neurons to a two-dimensional grid of output neurons. Table 8.1 summarizes the representative neural network models and their characteristics [24, 25].

8.2.2 Training/Learning Procedures

A neural network is learned so that the application of a set of inputs produces the desired (or at least consistent) set of outputs. Learning is accomplished by sequentially applying input patterns while adjusting network weights according to a predetermined procedure. During training, the network weights gradually converge to values such that each input pattern produces the desired output pattern.

There are mainly two classes of learning algorithms: *supervised* learning and *unsupervised* learning. In supervised learning the system submits a training pair—consisting of an input pattern and the desired output—to the network. The network adjusts weights based on the neuron's error value so that the difference diminishes with each cycle. Unsupervised learning procedures classify input patterns without requiring information on target output. In such procedures, the network must detect the regularities of the patterns and the grouping for each applied input to produce a consistent output. The back-propagation model, the Hopfield network, and the Boltzmann machine are typical examples of the supervised learning procedure. A major example of an unsupervised learning procedure is the self-organizing feature map.

8.2.3 Updating the Weights

Two different strategies are in common use for updating the weights in the network. In the first approach, the weights are updated every cycle of the entire set of training patterns presentation. This update cycle is called an *epoch*. With this method we can always get the true gradient descent of the composite error function in weight-space. This approach is called the *batch* or *periodic* updating [26], or *true gradient* method [27]. If there is no closed training set, some arbitrary update cycle is chosen [26].

In the second approach, the network weights are updated continuously after each training pattern is presented. This approach is called the *online* or *continuous* updating [26], or *stochastic gradient* method [27]. This method might become trapped for a few atypical training patterns, but the advantage is that it eliminates the need to accumulate the error over a number of patterns presented and allows a network to learn a given task more quickly, if there is a lot of redundant information in the training patterns. A disadvantage is that it requires more weight update steps. The issue of weight updating time has been controversial with contention among researchers.

TABLE 8.1 Representative Neural Network Models and Their Characteristics

Neural Model	Year Introduced	Primary Applications	Strengths	Limitations
Perceptron	1957	Typed character recognition	Oldest neural network	No recognition of complex patterns; sensitive to changes
Back-Propagation	1974–85	Speech synthesis from text; adaptive control of robot arms; scoring of bank loan applications	Most popular network today; works well, simple to learn	Supervised training only; correct input–output examples must be abundant
Self-Organizing Feature Map	1980	Mapping one geometrical region onto another	More effective than many algorithmic techniques	Require extensive training
Hopfield	1982	Retrieval of complete data or images from fragments	Large-scale implementation	No learning; weights must be set in advance
Boltzmann	1985–86	Pattern recognition for images, sonar radar	Simple network that uses noise function to reach global minimum	Long training time

8.3 SYSTOLIC ALGORITHMS FOR NEURAL NETWORK IMPLEMENTATIONS

In this section, the similar features between neural networks and systolic arrays and the systolic algorithms for neural network implementations are briefly described. The massive parallelism inherent in neural networks is classified and the issues of exploiting the parallelism are presented.

8.3.1 Systolic Arrays and Neural Networks

The systolic array design differs from the conventional von Neumann computer in its highly pipelined computation [28]. Once a data item is brought out from the memory it can be used effectively at each cell it passes while being pumped from cell to cell along the array. This is especially appealing for a wide class of compute–bound computations, where multiple operations are performed on each data item in a repetitive manner. This avoids the classic memory access bottleneck problem commonly incurred in von Neumann machines [28].

A systolic array has a spatial locality and a temporal locality. It manifests a locally communicative interconnection structure, and there is at least one unit-time delay allocated so that signal transactions from one processing element to the next can be completed. When a large number of processors work together, communication becomes a significant problem. Therefore, regular and local communication in systolic arrays is advantageous.

A systolic array is one of the best solutions to the parallel implementation of neural networks. Since it consists of modular processing units with regular interconnections, it can overcome the communication problems generated by the highly interconnected neurons. Moreover, by using a regular and simple design and exploiting the VLSI technology, great savings in design cost can be achieved.

The neural networks and the systolic arrays have many similar features. The communication only between neighbor neurons and no global computation in neural networks are similar to the spatial/temporal locality of systolic arrays. The highly interconnected structures of neural networks can be mapped onto the regular structure of systolic array, and the massive parallelism can be exploited by the large number of processing elements of systolic arrays. The propagation of each neuron's state to the neighbor neurons corresponds to the pipelined computation/communication. Since the operations required in neural network computation are simple and primitive and the results of the operations are propagated through the network, the computation can be executed synchronously. Moreover, the fact that the training patterns are presented from outside the world of neural network and the input and output are performed only at the array boundaries is another resemblance between them. In Table 8.2, the similar features between neural networks and systolic arrays are summarized.

8.3.2 Systolic Algorithms for Neural Networks

The computation of artificial neural networks can be represented by a series of matrix-by-vector multiplications interleaved with the nonlinear activation func-

TABLE 8.2   Similar Features between Neural Networks and Systolic Arrays

Neural Network	Systolic Array
Communication between neighbor neurons	Spatially local communication
No global computation	Temporally local computation
Massive parallelism	Large number of processing elements
Highly interconnected neurons	Mapping onto regular structures
Propagation of each neuron's state	Pipelined computation/communication
Simple, primitive operations	Synchronous computation/communication
Pattern presentation from the outside world	Input/output only at array boundary

tions. The matrix represents the weights associated to the connections, and the vector represents the input patterns or the activation levels of neurons as shown in Figure 8.1. The resultant vector of a matrix-by-vector multiplication is applied to the nonlinear activation function.

The classical systolic algorithms for matrix-by-vector multiplications can be used to implement neural networks. The systolic algorithms for the multiplication of a 4×4 matrix and a 4×1 vector are shown in Figure 8.2. Figure 8.2*a* and Figure 8.2*b* show the one-dimensional algorithms and the corresponding linear systolic arrays, and Figure 8.2*c* and Figure 8.2*d* show the two-dimensional systolic algorithms and the corresponding systolic arrays. In the one-dimensional arrays, the elements of the matrix are fed into the array in which each cell contains each element of the vector, as shown in Figure 8.2*b*, or the elements of the vector are also fed into the cells as shown in Figure 8.2*a*. On the other hand, in the two-

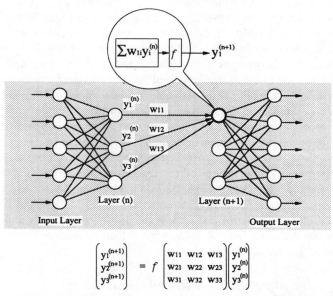

Figure 8.1 *Multilayer neural network: The computation is represented by a series of matrix-by-vector multiplications interleaved with the nonlinear activation functions.*

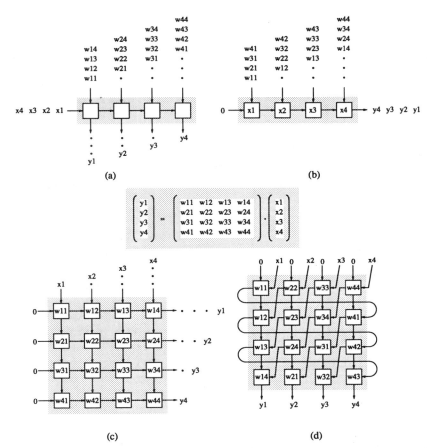

Figure 8.2 Systolic algorithms for matrix-by-vector multiplication and their corresponding systolic array: (a), (b) one-dimensional systolic arrays; (c), (d) two-dimensional systolic arrays.

dimensional arrays, each cell contains each element of the matrix and the vectors are fed into the array.

In the systolic array in the form of Figure 8.2c, the matrix elements are set into the two dimensional systolic array *basic cells* and the vector elements propagate vertically from the top cell to the bottom cell step by step through the array. Each basic cell is a computational element that performs the multiplication $x_i \cdot w_{ji}$, adds it to the partial sum received from the left cell, and sends the result to the right cell.

The systolic algorithm in the form of Figure 8.1d is presented by S.Y. Kung and J.N. Hwang [29], in which the data flow can be simplified by reordering the weight elements so that the outputs of each layer are aligned with the inputs of the next layer. This has an advantage that the load of each processor can be balanced when it is partitioned vertically and mapped onto a linear array. They proposed a mapping of the algorithm onto a linear array, and the similar approach has been studied in [7]. However since the numbers of neurons of the adjacent layers in many practical multilayer neural networks are much different, the application of this algorithm to such networks is inefficient when we are going to organize a physically two-dimensional systolic array.

8.3.3   Exploiting the Inherent Parallelism of Neural Networks

The massive parallelism inherent in neural networks may be classified into three types and can be exploited in systolic array implementations.

Spatial Parallelism.   This type of parallelism is exploited by executing the operations required in each layer on multiple processors. In the spatial parallelism, there are three levels of parallelism exploitation:

S1. Partitioning the neurons of each layer into groups.
S2. Partitioning the operations of each neuron into sum of products operations and the nonlinear function.
S3. Partitioning the sum of products operations into several groups.

The parallelism S1 is called *network partitioning* [10], and exploited in most of parallel implementations of neural networks [30]. These abovementioned partitioned operations can be executed on different processors in parallel. Most of neural network simulators implemented on MIMD computers exploit parallelism S1 and S2, but parallelism S3 is not exploited much because of the communication overhead.

Training Set Parallelism.   This type of parallelism is also called *data partitioning* [10] and can be exploited by partitioning the training patterns and executing on multiple processors independently. This derives from the fact that the back propagation and similar algorithms provide for the linear combination of the individual contributions made by each pattern to the adjustment of the network's weight. The weights in each processor are updated periodically by all-to-all broadcasting of the weight increments for the subset of the entire training pattern set allocated in each processor. The training set parallelism is exploited in [8, 9, 10, 31].

Pattern Pipelined Parallelism.   This type of parallelism can be exploited by multiple input pattern pipelining, in which processors that completed the parts of operations required for a pattern start execution for the next pattern while the other processors are processing for the previously presented training patterns. This parallelism can be applied not only to the training patterns in the learning phase, but also to the input patterns in the recalling phase:

P1. Pipelining of input patterns in the recalling phase.
P2. Pipelining of training patterns in the learning phase.

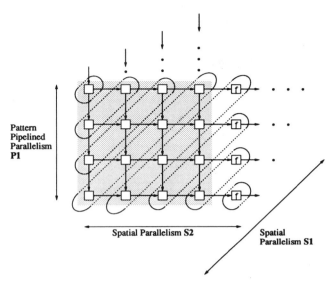

Figure 8.3 *Exploitation of spatial parallelism and pattern pipelined parallelism in systolic array implementations.*

The depth of pipelining is proportional to the number of neurons in the network, and the exploitation of this parallelism is effective when the size of the training set is much larger than the number of neurons in the network.

Exploiting the Parallelisms in Systolic Arrays. The exploitation of the training set parallelism is trivial. We need duplicated copies of a systolic array and a broadcast network, and the training set is partitioned so that every systolic array processes a subset of them. This is useful when the number of the training patterns is too large. In [9], a toroidal mesh array is proposed to exploit the training set parallelism by connecting each ring systolic array that has a duplicated copy of the weights.

The spatial parallelism and the pattern pipelined parallelism can be exploited in systolic array implementations as shown in Figure 8.3. The spatial parallelism S3 is too fine-grained to be exploited in the systolic arrays shown in Figure 8.2. It is exploited in MasPar MP-1, a massively parallel SIMD computer [3]. The exploitation of the pattern pipelined parallelism P2 is presented in Section 8.5.

8.4 SYSTOLIC APPROACHES TO NEURAL NETWORK IMPLEMENTATIONS

There have been several research efforts on systolic algorithms and systolic array structures to implement the neural networks. The approaches can be classified into two groups. One is mapping the systolic algorithms for neural networks onto parallel computers, and the other is designing a VLSI systolic array dedicated to specific models.

In this section, we first present the design issues of each classification, and investigate each approach focused on the main design philosophy, characteristics, and systolic algorithms and systolic array structures.

8.4.1 Mapping Systolic Algorithms onto Parallel Computers

Most of the implementations of neural networks to date were done entirely in software, which were executed on general-purpose, sequential computers. Although these approaches are very flexible, they are highly inefficient for large networks. The implementations of neural networks on parallel computers offer a good compromise between high performance over sequential computers and flexibility over dedicated VLSI approaches.

The critical issue in these implementations is efficient mapping of neural network structures onto the networks of processors of the parallel computers, and there have been several heuristic mapping approaches onto parallel computers. These heuristic mapping approaches were generated by means of an ad hoc method by the researchers intimately familiar with the machines and experienced in mapping algorithms onto them [34].

The systolic mapping is a systematic technique to map the problems efficiently onto parallel computers. The major design issues of the these systolic mapping approaches are designing systolic algorithms that can be partitioned and mapped efficiently onto the parallel computers, and mapping the algorithms efficiently onto the fixed interconnection structures of the parallel computers.

Kung and Hwang's Work. S. Y. Kung and J. N. Hwang [49] suggested systolic algorithms and mapping methods for a single layer neural network such as the Hopfield model, and multilayer neural networks. In their design, the operations of neural networks are expressed in terms of recursive matrix operations, the matrix operations are expressed in dependence graphs, and the dependence graphs are mapped onto systolic arrays.

In Figure 8.4, the dependence graph for a Hopfield neural network and its mapping onto ring systolic array are shown. The consecutive matrix-by-vector multiplication array architecture design can be derived from a cascaded data dependence graph. To facilitate a systolic design with smooth data movements, the data ordering of the w_{ji} elements is arranged so that the direction of input $y_i^{(n)}$ in the dependence graph becomes aligned with that of output $y_i^{(n+1)}$.

The systolic array for multilayer neural networks is shown in Figure 8.5. The ring systolic arrays for single layer networks are assigned to each of the layers and cascaded to form a mesh array. If the size of the hidden layers is fixed to be equal to that of the input/output layers then the ring systolic arrays can be perfectly cascaded.

Transputer Arrays. J. R. Millán and P. Bofill [9] proposed a systolic algorithm and its transputer implementation for a generalized back-propagation neural net-

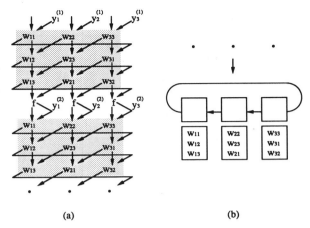

(a)   (b)

Figure 8.4 *Systolic algorithm and the resultant ring systolic array for a Hopfield neural network:* (a) *cascaded dependence graph for consecutive matrix-by-vector multiplication;* (b) *mapping onto ring systolic array.*

work. Their algorithm is based on the systolic algorithm shown in Figure 8.4a and a spatial mapping onto transputer arrays; the ordering of the operations within each PEs and the data storage management schemes according to the characteristics of the transputer family are suggested. In Figure 8.6, the resultant ring systolic array of transputers and the information flow are shown.

Sandy/8 at Fujitsu.   Sandy/8 [7] is a 456-PE prototype neurocomputer under development at Fujitsu Laboratory. Each PE consists of a floating point DSP, TMS340C30, and a local memory of 148 kbytes. The machine cycle of the DSP is 60 nsec, in which one multiplication and one addition operation of two floating point numbers can be done. They are connected in a ring topology with one tray per PE, as shown in Figure 8.7. Each tray functions as a container, and a router

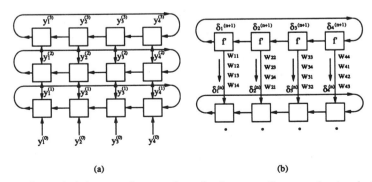

(a)   (b)

Figure 8.5 *Cascaded ring systolic array for a back-propagation neural network:* (a) *for a multilayer neural network;* (b) *for back-propagation learning.*

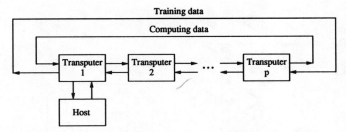

Figure 8.6 *Information flow in a ring array of transputers.*

that is connected to its neighbors thus forms a ring systolic array. The neurons at the same column in each layer are mapped onto the corresponding PE as shown in Figure 8.7, and a systolic algorithm similar to that explained in the subsection on Kung and Hwang's work is used.

The Warp Systolic Computer. The Warp [33] is a systolic array computer of linearly connected cells developed at CMU, each of which is a programmable processor capable of performing 10 million floating-point operations per second. Data flow through the Warp array on two communication channels in the same or in the opposite directions are shown in Figure 8.8. There are two cluster proces-

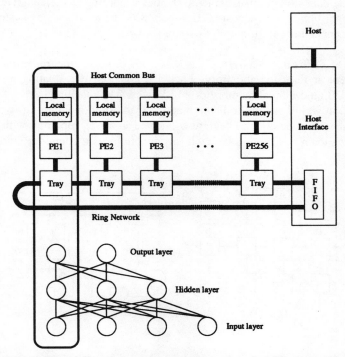

Figure 8.7 *The Sandy/8 prototype system and mapping of multilayer neural network.*

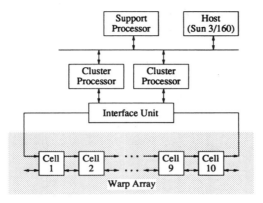

Figure 8.8   *The Warp architecture.*

sors, an interface unit, and a support processor between the host and the Warp array to provide efficient I/O and the large cluster memory.

The neural network models studied on the Warp are the multilayer back-propagation model [10] and the Kohonen's self-organizing feature map [8]. In [10], a network partitioning method for exploiting the spatial parallelism and a data partitioning method for exploiting the training set parallelism are implemented, as shown in Figure 8.9a. In Figure 8.9b, the first nine cells process each subset of the partitioned training pattern set, while the tenth cell is reserved for computing weight updates. Weights are no longer partitioned among the cell's local memories; instead they are pumped through the array from the cluster memory. This scheme is automatically load balanced for any arbitrarily connected network, and since the cells store only the activation levels of the neurons, simulations of much larger networks are possible.

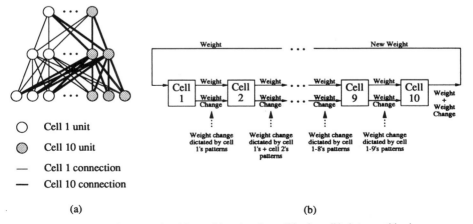

Figure 8.9   *Mapping algorithms: (a)* network partitioning; *(b)* data partitioning.

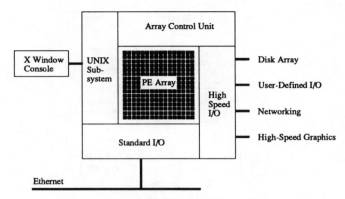

Figure 8.10 The MasPar MP-1 system block diagram.

MasPar MP-1. The MasPar MP-1 [34] is a massively parallel SIMD computer that can contain up to 16K processor elements. The MP-1 consists of the PE array, Array Control Unit (ACU), and a host as shown in Figure 8.10. Each PE is register based with approximately 1 k bits of register memory and 16 k bytes of general storage. On-chip support of integer and floating point operations is provided with a maximum speed of 30,000 MIPS and 1.4 GigaFLOPS when the system is fully configured with 16 k PEs. There are three types of interprocessor communication mechanisms: ACU-PE array communications, X-network nearest-neighbor communications, and the global router communications. The implementation of a 2-D systolic algorithm for neural networks onto the MasPar MP-1 is a direct mapping of Kung and Hwang's dependence graph onto the PE array [3, 4]. An adder tree operation is used to compute all summations to exploit the spatial parallelism S3 as mentioned in the subsection on spatial parallelism. The X-network's nearest-neighbor communication supports facilitate the 2-D systolic array implementation on MasPar MP-1.

GCN at Sony. The GCN (Ciga CoNnection) [5, 6] is a systolic array of mesh-connected processor elements, each of which consists of an Intel i860 processor, a large local memory, and high bandwidth FIFO devices that are used for communication between adjacent PEs as shown in Figure 8.11. A mapping algorithm for the neural network onto GCN, named net-data partition, has been suggested. In the net-data partition, the data partitioning for exploiting the training set parallelism is used in each column of the mesh, while the network partitioning for exploiting the spatial parallelism is used in each row of the mesh. The multilayer back-propagation model, Kohonen feature map, and the Boltzmann machine have been studied.

8.4.2 VLSI Systolic Arrays

The major objective of the VLSI implementation of neural networks is to produce a very high performance system. To optimize parallelism and performance in these

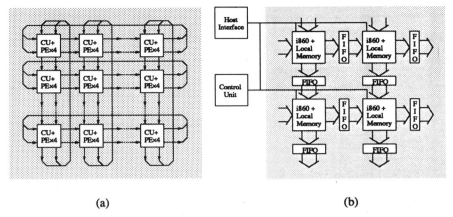

(a)   (b)

Figure 8.11   *The GCN organization:* (a) system organization; (b) node organization.

approaches, and to meet the constraints of VLSI designs, a VLSI neurocomputer must have the following architectural properties. The design must be simple and modular, and it must have the regularity of the communication structure and the expansibility and design scalability [25].

The systolic array is one of the best choices that satisfies the requirements of the VLSI neurocomputers. The major design issues of the VLSI systolic array approaches are designing the basic cell architectures to be used as modular building blocks to implement large neural networks, and designing the array structures to exploit the model-specific parallelisms to maximize the performance. Two-dimensional systolic mesh arrays have been suggested as the resultant array structures to maximize the spatial parallelism.

VLSI Systolic Array for Hopfield Model.   F. Blayo and P. Hurat [11] designed a VLSI systolic array, named APLYSIE, dedicated to pattern recognition based on the Hopfield neural network. Since the neurons are fully connected in the Hopfield neural network, they present an array structure that implements an N neuron network as a systolic square array made up of N^2 cells. Their algorithm is based on the systolic one shown in Figure 8.2c, and their array structure is shown in Figure 8.12. In Figure 8.12, the X components of each input patterns are located in diagonal cells after initialization. These components propagate vertically from cell to cell, first to the north, and they are fed back into the array when they reach the topmost or bottommost cell. After $2N$ steps, the new X components reach diagonal cells where the vector X components are updated to continue the recurrences. A cell architecture for a 16×16 cell VLSI chip implementation and a 128-neuron board by assembling 64 chips performing 200 million neuron updatings per second have been proposed.

Systolic Array for Hopfield Model and Kohonen Feature Maps.   F. Blayo and C. Lehmann [12, 15] designed a systolic array, named GENES (GENeric

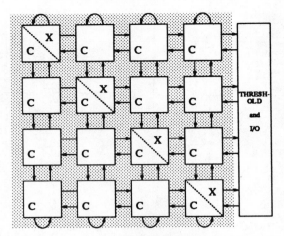

Figure 8.12 *Systolic array for Hopfield neural network.*

Element Synthesis), for both the Hopfield model and the Kohonen' self-organizing feature map based on the operational and structural analyses that underline the common computational requirements between several neural network models. While APLYSIE was completely dedicated to the Hopfield model, the GENES is intended to be used as a generic building block for different models. The GENES organization for the Kohonen network is shown in Figure 8.13. A chip architecture of the elementary cell and an evaluation of the final silicon area have been presented.

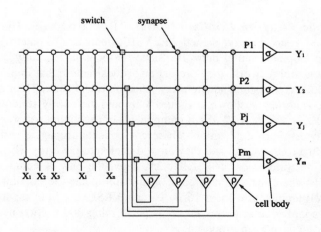

Figure 8.13 *GENES organization for Kohonen feature maps.*

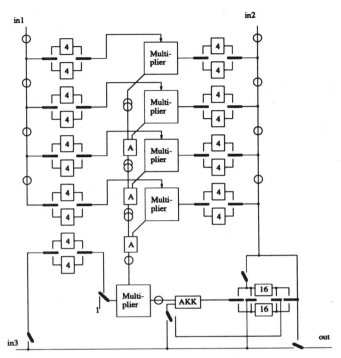

Figure 8.14 Elementary chain module for recalling and learning.

Systolic Neuro-Emulator.   U. Ramacher et al. [16, 17, 18] proposed a programmable systolic array to emulate all the neural network models. They analyzed today's neural paradigms to find the computer intensive algorithmic strings that are shared by all neural models, and proposed an elementary structure to systolically emulate the neural algorithms. Figure 8.14 shows the elementary functional block of a chain that is reconfigurable for recalling, learning, and update. A neurochip architecture to implement four chain modules and a two-dimensional array structure of the neurochips for the systolic neuro-emulators have been suggested.

Combined Array for Recalling and Learning.   H. Kwan and P. C. Tsang [14] proposed a systolic array design for the back-propagation neural network. The arrays for feedforward execution and for back-propagation learning are designed respectively, and the two arrays are combined into one array, in which switches are added to cope with the differences between the two phases. The resultant array accepts the input pattern and calculates the output of the network, and after all the outputs are obtained, target output pattern is fed into the network to calculate the errors at the output layer. In their design, the pattern pipelined parallelism can be exploited in each pass, respectively.

8.5 VLSI SYSTOLIC ARRAY FOR MULTILAYER NEURAL NETWORK: A CASE STUDY

As a case study on the systolic array implementation of neural networks, we present a systolic array for a multilayer neural network with a back-propagation learning algorithm (see Figure 8.15). It is based on the spatial parallelisms that can be exploited in systolic arrays, and it exploits the pattern pipelined parallelisms inherent in the networks.

In this section, the back-propagation learning algorithm is first introduced, and a systolic array that exploits the inherent parallelisms of a back-propagation neural network is presented, then the potential performance of this design is evaluated and compared with various high performance neurocomputers.

8.5.1 The Back-Propagation Learning Algorithm

The back-propagation neural network [21] is the most popular network today [24], and has been widely used in pattern classification, speech recognition, machine vision, sonar, radar, robotics, and signal processing applications [1].

The operations of the back-propagation learning algorithm are represented by following equations. Consider an L-layer (layer 1 to layer L) network consisting of N_k neurons at the kth layer. Layer 1 is the input layer, layer L is the output layer, and layers 2 to $L - 1$ are the hidden layers. The neurons between the adjacent layers are fully connected.

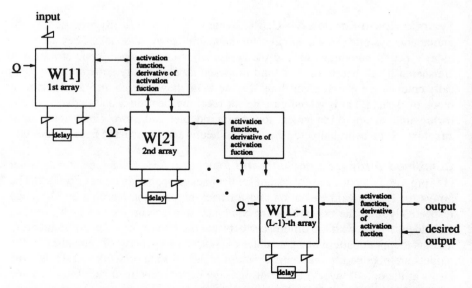

Figure 8.15 Systolic array for a back-propagation neural network: combined design for the forward and backward passes.

The Forward Pass.   The forward pass of such a network can be described by Eqs. (8.1, 8.2, 8.3):

$$y_{pj}^{(n)} = x_{pj}^{(n)} = i_{pj}, \quad (n = 1) \tag{8.1}$$

$$x_{pj}^{(n)} = \sum_{i=1}^{N_{n-1}} y_{pi}^{(n-1)} \cdot w_{ji}^{(n)}(t) - \theta_j, \quad (2 \le n \le L) \tag{8.2}$$

$$y_{pj}^{(n)} = f(x_{pj}^{(n)}) = \frac{1}{1 + e^{-x_{pj}^{(n)}}}, \quad (2 \le n \le L) \tag{8.3}$$

where $x_{pj}^{(n)}$ is the net input to neuron j in layer n for pattern p and i_{pj} is the input to neuron j in input layer for pattern p. The $w_{ji}^{(n)}(t)$ is the value of a weight associated to the connection from neuron i in layer $n - 1$ to neuron j in layer n after weight updates of t times, and θ_j is the threshold of neuron j. The $y_{pj}^{(n)}$ is the state output from neuron j in layer n for pattern p.

The Backward Pass.   The backward pass of the network operations can be described by Eqs. (8.4, 8.5, 8.6):

$$\beta_{pj}^{(n)} = y_{pj}^{(n)} - d_{pj}, \quad (n = L) \tag{8.4}$$

$$\beta_{pj}^{(n)} = \sum_{k=1}^{N_{n+1}} \delta_{pk}^{(n+1)} \cdot w_{kj}^{(n+1)}(t), \quad (2 \le n \le L - 1) \tag{8.5}$$

$$\delta_{pj}^{(n)} = \beta_{pj}^{(n)} \cdot y_{pj}^{(n)} \cdot (1 - y_{pj}^{(n)}) = g(\beta_{pj}^{(n)}), \quad (2 \le n \le L) \tag{8.6}$$

where $\beta_{pj}^{(n)}$ is the net error input to neuron j in layer n for pattern p and d_{pj} is the desired output of neuron j in output layer for pattern p. $\delta_{pj}^{(n)}$ is the error output from neuron j in layer n to neurons in layer $n - 1$ for pattern p. Because the weights associated with the errors in the output layer after the forward pass should be adjusted, the t must be the same as that in the forward pass.

The Weight Increment Update.   After presentation of the training patterns, weights are updated according to Eqs. (8.7, 8.8):

$$\Delta w_{ji}^{(n)}(u + 1) = \Delta w_{ji}^{(n)}(u) + \delta_{pj}^{(n)} \cdot y_{pi}^{(n-1)}, \quad (2 \le n \le L) \tag{8.7}$$

$$w_{ji}^{(n)}(t + 1) = w_{ji}^{(n)}(t) + \epsilon \Delta w_{ji}^{(n)}, \quad (2 \le n \le L) \tag{8.8}$$

where u is the number of training patterns presented, t is the number of weight updates, and ϵ is the learning rate (typically 1.0). To reduce the average error for all the training patterns, the error output must be averaged over all the training patterns before updating the weights. In practice, however, it is sufficient to average over several inputs before updating weights [35]. If the weights are updated after presentation of p patterns, the relation $u = p \cdot t$ is satisfied.

Terminating Conditions.   The learning phase is terminated when the total error is sufficiently small [36]:

$$E = \sum_p E_p = \sum_p \sum_{i=1}^{N_L} (y_{pi}^{(L)} - d_{pi})^2 < \alpha \qquad (8.9)$$

where the index p ranges over the set of training input patterns, i ranges over the set of output units, and E_p represents the error on pattern p. Note that α is the user-defined sufficiently small value.

8.5.2 Exploiting the Pattern Pipelined Parallelism

To exploit the pattern pipelined parallelism in the learning phase, the forward and backward passes should be executed in parallel sharing the weights. In this design, we use the systolic algorithms in the form of Figure 8.2c. In Figure 8.16, the systolic array organizations between two adjacent layers are shown. One layer consists of five neurons and the other layer consists of three neurons. Figure 8.16a is for the forward pass, Figure 8.16b is for the backward pass.

Each basic cell w_{ji} is a computational element that contains the weight value and the weight increment associated to the connection between neuron i of a layer and neuron j of the next layer. In Figure 8.16a, each basic cell in a row of the array receives the input patterns or the activations propagated from the previous array and computes the sum-of-products operations shown in Eq. (8.2). These sum-of-products are fed into next array after being applied the activation function. This systolic algorithm can be equally adopted to the backward pass. In Figure 8.16b, which represents an array for layer $n + 1$ to layer n of a network, each row of the array receives the errors propagated from the previous array and computes the sum-of-products operations shown in Eq. (8.5). These sum-of-products are fed into the next array after being applied the derivative of the activation function.

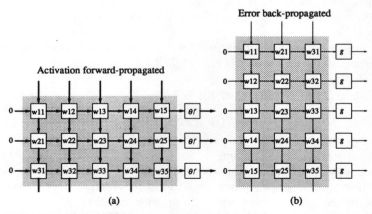

Figure 8.16 Systolic array exploiting the pattern pipelined parallelism: (a) for forward pass; (b) for backward pass.

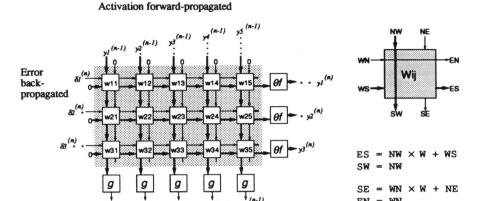

Figure 8.17 *Systolic array organization between two adjacent layers of multilayer neural networks: (a) combined design for forward and backward passes; (b) basic cell operations.*

The arrays in Figure 8.16a and b can be combined into an array as shown in Figure 8.17a. The weight matrix is shared between the forward and backward passes, and the data paths of the activations forward-propagated and the errors back-propagated are disjoint. Each basic cell executes the sum-of-products operations shown in Eq. (8.2, 8.5) and weight updating operations shown in Eqs. (8.7, 8.8). The θf unit executes the thresholding and the activation function shown in Eqs. (8.2, 8.3), and the g unit executes the derivative of the activation function shown in Eq. (8.6). The g unit has a FIFO queue to contain the outputs of a neuron, that are fed back to the basic cells to compute the weight updates in the backward pass. The operations of the basic cell that can be executed in parallel are shown in Figure 8.17b.

8.5.3   Systolic Array Organization

In Figure 8.18, an example of a systolic array organization for a (5-3-2) three-layer network is shown. The elements of two weight matrix are set into the two-dimensional arrays, the 3 × 5 weight matrix represents the weights associated with the connections between the input layer and the hidden layer, and the 2 × 3 weight matrix represents the weights associated with the connections between the hidden layer and the output layer. The second matrix is transposed in the figure.

In the forward pass, the data flow is denoted by the bold lines. The elements of input patterns are fed into the first array step by step from the leftmost basic cell to the rightmost basic cell, and propagated vertically from the top cell to the bottommost cell. In the first array, each cell w_{ji} performs the product operation with w_{ji} and the input from the above cell, adds it to the subtotal received from

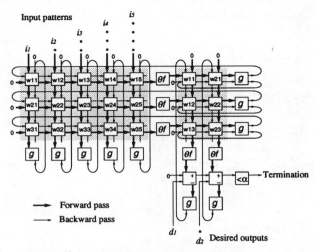

Figure 8.18   *Example of a systolic array organization for a three-layer neural network.*

the left cell, and then sends it to the right cell. After the total sum is calculated in the rightmost basic cells of the first array, each value is fed into the θf unit to be applied to the thresholding and the activation function, and fed into the second array. In the second array, each cell w_{ji} performs the product operation with w_{ji} and the input from the left cell, adds it to the subtotal received from the above cell, and then sends it to the below cell. After the total sum is calculated in the bottommost basic cells of the second array, each value is fed into the θf unit.

In the output of the network, the difference between the actual output and the desired output, as shown in Eq. (8.4), is computed for a pattern presented. The differences are accumulated to get the total error, as shown in Eq. (8.9). If the value is sufficiently small, the learning phase ends. If not, in the output of the network, the backward pass starts. The data flow of backward pass is denoted as thin lines. Each error value is applied to the derivative of the activation function and fed into the second array from the above through the wraparound connection.

Each cell w_{ji} in the second array performs the product operation with w_{ji} and the input from the above cell, adds it to the partial sum received from the left cell, and then sends it to the right cell. After the total sum is calculated, it is fed into the g unit, applied the derivative of the activation function, and fed into the first array from the left. In the first array the error output needs not be calculated. The error inputs from the second array are propagated to the right cells and used to update the weight value.

All of these operations are pipelined. So the continuously generated output values of a neuron must be stored to be fed back to update the weight. In this design, these values are stored in the g units. As mentioned in Section 8.2.3, the weights are updated over several training patterns. While the weights are updated, the feeding of training patterns are stopped, and the pipeline is stalled.

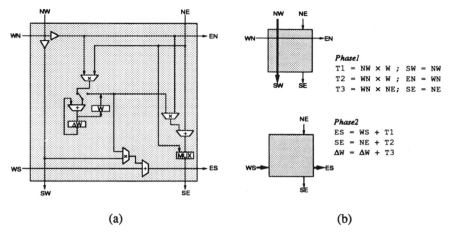

(a)   (b)

Figure 8.19 *The basic cell architecture: (a)* the internal data path; *(b)* the basic cell operations.

8.5.4   Basic Cell Architecture

The internal data path of the basic cell is shown in Figure 8.19*a*. It consists of three multipliers, three adders, and two registers for weight value and weight increment. The basic cell operations are divided into two phases, and at each phase, three multiplications and three additions are executed in parallel, as shown in Figure 8.19*b*.

8.5.5   Performance Evaluation

Let us consider an *L*-layer network consisting of N_k neurons at the *k*th layer. The required cycles *C*, for forward and backward passes of this design, are denoted by Eqs. (8.10, 8.11):

$$C_{\text{forward}} = \sum_{i=1}^{L} N_i + L - 2 \tag{8.10}$$

$$C_{\text{backward}} = \sum_{i=1}^{L} N_i + L - 1 \tag{8.11}$$

When the forward and backward passes are pipelined, the required cycles for a single training pattern are denoted by Eq. (8.12):

$$C_{\text{single}} = (C_{\text{forward}} + C_{\text{backward}}) - N_L + 1 \tag{8.12}$$

Equation (8.12) shows only the effects of the spatial parallelism and the forward/backward pipelining. The effects of the forward/backward pipelining on performance is not great even though N_L is much greater than 1. However, it makes the pipelining of multiple training patterns possible. When multiple patterns are pipelined, the required cycles for learning p training patterns are denoted by Eq. (8.13):

$$C_p = C_{\text{single}} + (p - 1) \tag{8.13}$$

The *speedup* S_p, by the pipelining of multiple training patterns is denoted by Eq. (8.14). When $p \gg C_{\text{single}}$, the speedup can be approximated to C_{single} that is the depth of the pipelining and dependent only on the network size.

$$S_p = \frac{p \cdot C_{\text{single}}}{C_p} = \frac{p \cdot C_{\text{single}}}{C_{\text{single}} + (p - 1)} \tag{8.14}$$

For updating the weights, the cycles that feeding of training patterns is stopped are denoted by Eq. (8.15):

$$C_{\text{update}} = C_{\text{single}} - (N_1 + N_2 - 2) = 2 \sum_{i=1}^{L} N_i + 2L - (N_1 + N_2 + N_L) \tag{8.15}$$

When we update the weight t times during presentation of p patterns, the total required cycles are denoted by Eq. (8.16):

$$C_{\text{total}} = \begin{cases} C_p + C_{\text{update}} \times t, & (p > t) \\ C_{\text{single}} \times p, & (p = t) \end{cases} \tag{8.16}$$

The performance of neurocomputers is measured in *millions of connection updates per second* (MCUPS). Let N be the number of connections of the target neural network, then the MCUPS is calculated by Eq. (8.17):

$$\text{MCUPS} = \frac{\text{total connections calculated}}{\text{total elapsed time in } \mu\text{sec}} = \frac{N \times p}{C_{\text{total}} \times \text{cycle time}} \tag{8.17}$$

In this design, the cycle time is determined as the maximum time among the time required by one multiplication and one addition, the time for thresholding and activation function (table look-up), and the time required to feed the input patterns continuously.

Speed measurements of several high performance neural network implementations have been performed for NETtalk [35] as a benchmark [7, 10, 37, 38, 39]. NETtalk learns to transform written English text into a phonetic representation. The network consists of (203-60-26) three layers, and the total number of connections is 13,826 including 86 connections to the true unit for thresholds. Assuming we implement this design with 100 nsec of cycle time for computation and 50 nsec for communication, the performance comparison with high performance neurocomputers is shown in Table 8.3. The potentially high performance of this design

TABLE 8.3 Performance Comparison of Neurocomputers

Machine	No. of PEs	No. of Training Patterns	MCUPS for NETtalk (203-60-26)	MCUPS for (128-128-128) network	MCUPS for (256-128-256) network	Ref.
Cray-2	1	1	7			[37]
VACA	4 k	1	51.4			[38]
Sandy/8	256	1	116			[7]
CMU Warp	10	1	17			[10]
	20	1	32			[38]
CMU iWarp	10	1	36			[40]
DAP-610	4 k					[39]
(8 bits)		1	160			
(16 bits)		1	40			
CM-1	16 k	1	2.6			[10]
	64 k	1	13			[37]
CM-2	64 k	1			40	[41]
	64 k	64 k		1,300		[31]
This design	13 k	1	248			
	32 k	64 k		324,000		
	64 k	1			637	

shows that the array structure that can exploit the massive parallelism of neural networks plays an important role in VLSI systolic array designs.

8.6 SUMMARY AND FUTURE RESEARCH AREAS

8.6.1 Summary

Since a systolic array can overcome the communication problems generated by the highly interconnected neurons, and can exploit the massive parallelism inherent in the problem, there have been several research efforts on systolic algorithms and systolic array structures to implement the neural networks. The approaches can be classified into a mapping approach, in which the systolic algorithms are partitioned and mapped onto the parallel computers, and a VLSI approach, in which VLSI systolic arrays dedicated to specific models are designed. In Table 8.4, these approaches are summarized.

8.6.2 Future Research Areas

An algorithmic mapping technique that does not require any constraints about the regularity of a neural network such as fully interconnected layers, local interconnections of a specific range, limited number of layers, or uniform size of layer is required. The mapping constitutes a fundamental step on the way to evaluation of existing parallel machines for various neural network models. It also provides us with some indication as to which aspects of the models are responsible for inefficiencies in implementation, thus directing the study of neural network models toward these aspects.

TABLE 8.4 Systolic Approaches to Neural Networks

Approach	Dimension	Researchers (System)	Models Studied	Parallelisms Exploited	Ref.
Mapping	1-D Systolic Array	Kung & Hwang (Ring Systolic)	Hopfield	Spatial S1	[29]
		Pomerleau, et al. (Warp)	Back-Propagation	Spatail S1, S2 Training	[10]
		Mann & Haykin (Warp)	Kohonen	Training	[8]
		Millán & Bofill (Transputers)	Back-Propagation	Spatial S1 Training	[9]
		Kato et al. (Sandy/8)	Back-Propagation	Spatial S1	[7]
	2-D Systolic Array	Kung & Hwang (Cascaded Ring)	Back-Propagation	Saptial S1 Pattern P1	[29]
		Chinn et al. (MasPar MP-1)	Back-Propagation	Spatial S1, S2, S3	[3]
		Hiraiwa et al. (GCN)	Back-Prop. Kohonen Boltzmann	Spatial S1 Training	[6]
VLSI	2-D Systolic Array	Blayo & Hurat (APLYSIE)	Hopfield	Spatial S1, S2 Pattern P1	[11]
		Blayo & Lehmann (GENES H8)	Hopfield Kohonen	Spatial S1, S2 Pattern P1	[12]
		Ramacher et al. (Neuro-Emulator)	General Model	Spatial S1, S2 Pattern P1	[18]
		Kwan & Tsang (Combined Array)	Back-Propagation	Spatial S1, S2 Pattern P1	[14]
		Chung, Yoon, & Maeng (Pipelined Array)	Back-Propagation	Spatial S1, S2 Pattern P1, P2	[13]

Algorithmic partitioning is essential since the size of a neural network problem is inherently larger than the size of the VLSI array. The size of the VLSI arrays is constrained by technical factors. A natural solution to the I/O problem, as well as to overcome the limited size of the array, is to divide the computational problem into smaller problems.

From the hardware implementation point of view, an extendable and reconfigurable architecture design to be used as a generic building block for neural network implementation is in demand. Even with the future 0.3-μm technology, single chip direct implementation of a complete neural network is difficult since the applications may require quantities of neurons and the size of neural networks required in the application field becomes larger.

REFERENCES

[1] DARPA, *Neural Network Study*, AFCEA International Press, 1988.

[2] H. T. Kung, Why systolic architectures? *IEEE Computer*, Vol. 15, No. 1, 37–46 (January 1982).

[3] G. Chinn, K. A. Grajski, C. Chen, C. Kuszmaul, and S. Tomboulian, Systolic array implementations of neural nets on the MasPar MP-1 massively parallel processor, *Proc. Internat. Joint Conf. on Neural Networks*, Vol. II, 169–173 (June 1990).

[4] K. A. Grajski, G. Chinn, C. Chen, C. Kuszmaul, and S. Tomboulian, Neural network simulation on the MasPar MP-1 massively parallel processor,'' *Proc. Internat. Neural Network Conf.*, Vol. II, 673 (July 1990).

[5] A. Hiraiwa, M. Fujita, S. Kurosu, S. Arisawa, and M. Inoue, A two level pipeline RISC processor array for ANN, *Proc. Internat. Joint Conf. on Neural Networks*, Vol. II, 137–140 (January 1990).

[6] A. Hiraiwa, M. Fujita, S. Kurosu, S. Arisawa, and M. Inoue, Implementation of ANN on RISC processor array, *Proc. Internat. Conf. on Application Specific Array Processors* 677–688 (September 1990).

[7] H. Kato, H. Yoshizawa, H. Iciki, and K. Asakawa, A parallel neurocomputer architecture towards billion connection updates per second, *Proc. Internat. Joint Conf. on Neural Networks*, Vol. II, 51–54 (January 1990).

[8] R. Mann and S. Haykin, A parallel implementation of Kohonen feature maps on the warp systolic computer, *Proc. Internat. Joint Conf. on Neural Networks*, Vol. II, 84–87 (January 1990).

[9] J. R. Millán and P. Bofill, Learning by back-propagation: A systolic algorithm and its transputer implementation, *Neural Networks*, 119–137 (July 1989).

[10] D. A. Pomerleau, G. L. Gusciora, D. S. Touretzky, and H. T. Kung, Neural network simulation at warp speed: How we got 17 million connections per second, *Proc. IEEE Internat. Conf. on Neural Networks*, Vol. II, 143–150 (July 1988).

[11] F. Blayo and P. Hurat, A VLSI Systolic Array Dedicated to Hopfield Neural Network, in J. G. Delgado-Frias and W. G. Moore, Eds., *VLSI for Artificial Intelligence*, Kluwer Academic Publishers, Boston, 1989, pp. 255–264.

[12] F. Blayo and C. Lehmann, A systolic implementation of the self organization algorithm, *Proc. Internat. Neural Network Conf.*, Vol. II, 600 (July 1990).

[13] J. H. Chung, H. Yoon, and S. R. Maeng, A systolic array exploiting the inherent parallelisms of artificial neural networks, *Proc. Internat. Conf. on Parallel Processing*, Vol. I, 652–653 (August 1991).

[14] H. K. Kwan and P. C. Tsang, Systolic implementation of multi-layer feed-forward neural network with back-propagation learning scheme, *Proc. Internat. Joint Conf. on Neural Networks*, Vol. II, 84–87 (January 1990).

[15] C. Lehmann and F. Blayo, A VLSI implementation of a generic systolic synaptic building block for neural networks, *Proc. Internat. Workshop on VLSI for Artificial Intelligence*, 115–122 (October 1990).

[16] U. Ramacher and J. Beichter, Architecture of a systolic neuro-emulator, *Proc. Internat. Joint Conf. on Neural Networks*, Vol. II, 59–63 (January 1990).

[17] U. Ramacher and J. Beichter, Systolic synthesis of neural networks, *Proc. Internat. Neural Network Conf.*, Vol. II, 572–576 (July 1990).

[18] U. Ramacher and W. Raab, Fine-grain system architectures for systolic emulation of neural algorithms, *Proc. Internat. Conf. on Application Specific Array Processors* 554–566 (September 1990).

[19] P. D. Wasserman, *Neural Computing: Theory and Practice*, Van Nostrand Reinhold, New York, 1989.

[20] J. J. Hopfield, Neural networks and physical systems with emergent collective computational abilities, *Proc. National Acad. Sci. USA*, 79, 2554–2558 (1982).

[21] D. E. Rumelhart, G. E. Hinton, and R. J. Williams, "Learning Internal Representations by Error Propagation," in D. E. Rumelhart and J. L. McClelland, Eds., *Parallel Distributed Processing: Explorations in the Microstructures of Cognition*, Vol. 1: *Foundations*, MIT Press, Cambridge, Mass., 1986, pp. 318–362.

[22] E. H. L. Aarts and J. H. M. Korst, Computations in massively parallel networks based on the Boltzmann machine: A review, *Parallel Computing*, 129–145 (1989).

[23] T. Kohonen, *Self-Organization and Associative Memory*, 2nd ed., Springer-Verlag, 1987.

[24] R. Hecht-Nielsen, Neurocomputing: Picking the human brain, *IEEE Spectrum*, Vol. 25, No. 3, 36–41 (March 1988).

[25] P. Treleaven, M. Pacheco, and M. Vellasco, VLSI architectures for neural networks, *IEEE Micro*, 8–27 (December 1989).

[26] S. E. Fahlman, Faster-learning variations on back-propagation: An empirical study, *Proc. 1988 Connectionist Models Summer School*, 38–51 (June 1988).

[27] A. Petrowski, L. Personnaz, G. Dreyfus, and C. Girault, "Parallel Implementations of Neural Network Simulations," in *Hypercube and Distributed Computers*, North-Holland, New York, 1989, pp. 205–218.

[28] S. Y. Kung, *VLSI Array Processors*, Prentice Hall, Englewood Cliffs, N.J., 1988.

[29] S. Y. Kung and J. N. Hwang, Parallel architectures for artificial neural nets, *Proc. IEEE Internat. Conf. on Neural Networks*, Vol. II, 165–172 (July 1988).

[30] H. Yoon, J. H. Nang, and S. R. Maeng, "Neural Networks on Parallel Computers," in B. Souček, Ed., *Neural and Intelligent Systems Integration*, Wiley, New York, 1991, pp. 235–279.

[31] A. Singer, Exploiting the inherent parallelism of artificial neural networks to achieve 1300 million interconnects per second, *Proc. Internat. Neural Network Conf.*, Vol. II, 656–660 (July 1990).

[32] V. K. P. Kumar and K. W. Przytula, Algorithmic mapping of neural network models onto parallel SIMD machines, *Proc. Internat. Conf. on Application Specific Array Processors*, 259–271 (September 1990).

[33] M. Annaratone, E. Arnould, T. Gross, H. T. Kung, M. Lam, O. Menzilcioglu, and J. A. Webb, The Warp computer: Architecture, implementation, and performance, *IEEE Trans. on Computers*, C-36(12), 1523–1538 (December 1987).

[34] MasPar MP-1 family data-parallel computers brochures, MasPar Computer Corp., Sunnyvale, Calif., Order No. PL006.0490, 1990.

[35] T. J. Sejnowski and C. R. Rosenberg, Parallel networks that learn to pronounce English text, *Complex Systems*, 145–168 (1987).

[36] J. L. McClelland and D. E. Rumelhart, *Explorations in Parallel Distributed Processing: A Handbook of Models Programs, and Exercises*, MIT Press, Cambridge, Mass., 1988, pp. 121–159.

[37] G. Blelloch and C. R. Rosenberg, Network learning on the connection machine, *Proc. 10th Internat. Joint Conf. on Artificial Intelligence (IJCAI '87)*, 323–326 (August 1987).

[38] B. Faure and G. Mazare, Implementation of back-propagation on a VLSI asynchronous cellular architecture, *Proc. Internat. Neural Network Conf.*, Vol. II, 631–634 (July 1990).

[39] F. J. Núñez and J. A. B. Fortes, ''Performance of Connectionist Learning Algorithms on 2-D SIMD Processor Arrays,'' in D. S. Touretzky, Ed., *Advances in Neural Information Processing Systems*, Morgan Kaufmann Publishers, San Mateo, Calif., 1989, pp. 810–817.

[40] S. Borkar et al., iWarp: An integrated solution to high-speed parallel computing, *Proc. Supercomputing '88*, 330–339 (November 1988).

[41] X. Zhang, M. Mckenna, J. P. Mesirov, and D. L. Waltz, ''An Efficient Implementation of the Back-Propagation Algorithm on the Connection Machine CM-2,'' in D. S. Touretzky, Ed., *Advances in Neural Information Processing Systems*, Morgan Kaufmann Publishers, San Mateo, Calif., 1989, pp. 801–809.

PART II _____

INVARIANT OBJECT RECOGNITION

CHAPTER 9 ———————————————

Translation Invariant Neural Networks

STEPHEN S. WILSON

9.1 INTRODUCTION

In most network architectures designed for image applications, the first step in the procedure for recognizing or classifying objects in an image involves isolating each object by a segmentation operation that locates the positions and boundaries of the objects. Next, a set of features is derived from each object and is transferred to the inputs of the network. Sometimes the features are the actual gray level values of the pixels. In many network designs, the input to the network is a window of a specific size, and objects are scaled in size to fit exactly in that window. Finally the full power of the network is applied to these inputs in order to classify or identify the objects, one at a time. In short, signals from an image region covering a potential object are moved to a stationary network with a fixed configuration of connections. The architecture of this type of network is shown in Figure 9.1.

In principle this procedure works in most commercial applications of machine vision, because objects do not significantly change appearance if they are moved in the field of view, with the result that the processing model is uniform throughout the entire image. The networks for these applications where processing is invariant with respect to spatial translations of an object are called translation invariant neural networks.

For rotation and scale independent object recognition, some work has successfully been done by first transforming the image to polar coordinates [1, 2]. In this case it is imperative that the desired object be correctly segmented from the rest

Fast Learning and Invariant Object Recognition, By Branko Souček and the IRIS Group.
ISBN 0-471-57430-9 © 1992 John Wiley & Sons, Inc.

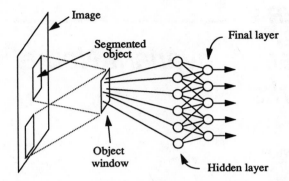

Figure 9.1 A common network architecture for image applications.

of the scene, because the origin of the polar coordinate system must be centered on a unique point of the object in order for recognition to take place. Successful recognition is very sensitive to a displacement of that origin. In this method the input image is in rectangular coordinates and the object window in Figure 9.1 is in polar coordinates.

In industrial applications, there is often too much noise or background confusion in the image, so that potential objects of interest cannot be segmented in a simple manner. Some patterns such as the surface of an integrated circuit chip cannot be segmented because the pattern of interest is connected to a larger surrounding pattern that fills the image. A reliable segmentation operation may be impossible or so complex that the only recourse is to apply the full force of a multilayer network at every position in the image where the object may possibly appear. A concept different than that illustrated in Figure 9.1 must be used.

Rather than using a network where the number of inputs correspond to the size of the object, there must be as many inputs as there are pixels in the image, so that the network covers the entire image, rather than just a single object. In this case, the network to analyze an image must have built-in translation invariant properties. In Section 9.2, it is shown that the assumption of translation invariance for a single layer leads to the result that the relative neighborhood connection topology and weights of inputs are identical for every cell. A definition of a convolution on a matrix of images leads to a compact representation of multilayered translation invariant networks. Translation invariant networks in image processing and machine vision have special properties that allow unique procedures in training network connections and in running the network at high speeds after training. There can be many neurons at each image pixel site with connections to cells in a surrounding neighborhood. Typical applications require hundreds of thousands of neural cells with millions of connections. Not all computer systems designed for network computations can handle the speeds for real-time vision applications that require translation invariant networks.

A large number of neural chips and neural hardware systems have been developed by various corporations and institutions. A summary of some of the most important state-of-the-art systems and applications are discussed by Souček [3, 4]. Systems have been designed using popular chips such as the Transputer [4], the TRW Mark IV [4] and the ANZA system [4] with a Motorola MC 68020 microprocessor and MC 68881 floating point coprocessor. Some systems are based on custom neural chips such as that developed by Texas Instruments [5], the Σ-chip [6], and an associative memory chip [7]. Other systems involving special chip sets work well with neural networks, such as the Active Memory chip [4] from Oxford Computer, the Distributed Array Processor (DAP) from Active Memory Technology [8], and the PIXIE [9], Centipede [9], and Firefly [10] chips from Applied Intelligent Systems, Inc.

Many of these systems are not used in large scale, high speed commercial machine vision applications because they are research tools, and are either too expensive, or too slow for real-time applications. Fine grained massively parallel systems using a single instruction, multiple data (SIMD) architecture are very efficient and fast for translation invariant neural networks. A number of SIMD array processor architectures has been surveyed by Fountain [11]. The applications in this chapter will focus on the Applied Intelligent Systems, Inc. (AISI) family of fine grain parallel array processors that are designed for low cost real-time applications and have from 64 processing elements (AIS-3000) to 1024 processing elements (AIS-5000). Although the number of processing elements in the AISI computers is not impressive compared with other massively parallel systems, the speed is impressive. Based on the Abingdon Cross benchmark [12], the AISI computers compare very favorably with other more massive systems because the processing elements are more complex and can do most operations in much fewer clock cycles. Computers in the AISI family are able to process simple layers with 8×8 neighborhood sizes and 512×512 images at a rate near 1000 million binary connections per second with weights that are ± 1. More complex networks with ± 1 weights and soft limited outputs can operate at a rate of around 270 million connections per second. Section 9.3 presents network models and computational methods that are efficient on SIMD systems. Larger neighborhood sizes can be used at a slight reduction in performance.

Training translation invariant networks is a unique problem because there is a vast number of neurons in the image defined by a relatively small set of weights and connections that are replicated throughout the image. The major development in this chapter is in Section 9.4, which deals with the problem of training hidden layers with unsupervised learning, where neurons in various hidden layers are in competition to define image features. The result of training is that an orthogonal set of feature layers is defined and provides a complete description of image features to serve as inputs to the final layer. Simulated annealing [13, 14] and Hebbian learning [15, 16] were found to be successful methods for training the final output layer and are briefly reviewed in Section 9.5. An example of an application that requires translation invariant networks is presented in Section 9.6, where it is shown that two hidden layers can be successfully trained to recognize a specific area on an integrated circuit chip where a large degree of rotation and scale variation can be tolerated.

9.2 TRANSLATION INVARIANT NETWORKS

In applications, where objects cannot be segmented from the surrounding background, the full nonsegmented image must be used in the network. There must be as many input signals as there are pixels in the image, so that the network covers the entire image, rather than just a single object.

In this type of network, where identical neural processing is applied to every pixels site, translation invariance should be fundamental part of the structure of the network to provide maximum computing efficiency. A translation invariant network, where there is a mapping of neurons to image pixels, is called an *iconic* network [17]. The output y_j of a simple feedforward cell is a nonlinear output function f of a weighted sum of input signals s_i:

$$y_j = f\left(\sum_i w_{ij} s_i \right) \tag{9.1}$$

In the simplest iconic network, there is one neural cell at each pixel site. It is more appropriate to index the cells according to the position of each cell in the image:

$$Y(\mathbf{u}') = f\left(\sum_{\mathbf{v}'} W'(\mathbf{v}', \mathbf{u}') S(\mathbf{v}') \right)$$

where $\mathbf{v}' = (v_x, v_y)$, and $\mathbf{u}' = (u_x, u_y)$ are position vectors. Capital letters represent input or output images. There are $n \times m$ neural cells corresponding to the full size of the image.

Suppose an object is moved so that the input signals in the image are shifted by some arbitrary vector $\mathbf{r}$. Then translation invariance means that the output signals will be unchanged except for a shift by the same vector $\mathbf{r}$. Translation invariance is put into the structure of a network by explicitly writing the relationship between the input and output signals when translated by vector $\mathbf{r}$:

$$Y(\mathbf{u}' + \mathbf{r}) = f\left(\sum_{\mathbf{v}'} W'(\mathbf{v}', \mathbf{u}') S(\mathbf{v}' + \mathbf{r}) \right)$$

Since $\mathbf{u}'$ and $\mathbf{r}$ are arbitrary in the domain of the image, let $\mathbf{u}' = 0$ and $\mathbf{r} = \mathbf{u}$. Then

$$Y(\mathbf{u}) = f\left(\sum_{\mathbf{v}'} W'(\mathbf{v}', 0) S(\mathbf{v}' + \mathbf{u}) \right)$$

The weights in this form are dependent only on $\mathbf{v}'$. It is more convenient to let $\mathbf{v}' = -\mathbf{v}$, reverse the order of the sum, express the weights reflected about the origin, and retain only the dependence of W on $\mathbf{v}$. Thus, let $W'(-\mathbf{v}', 0) = W(\mathbf{v})$, and the translation invariant form of a network becomes

$$Y(\mathbf{u}) = f\left(\sum_{\mathbf{v}} W(\mathbf{v})S(\mathbf{u} - \mathbf{v}) \right) = f(W * S) \qquad (9.2)$$

The fundamental result of Eq. (9.2) is that a translation invariant feedforward neural network layer on images is nothing more than a nonlinear function f, applied to a two-dimensional discrete convolution, where the weights define a convolution kernel. Figure 9.2 is a diagram of this type of network where only a few interconnections are shown. An enlarged view of a single cell shows the relation of the iconic network to a convolution.

A difficulty with this derived form of the network is that all neurons are made uniform and lose the independence and distinction of connections from one neural cell to another. There is only one feature type defined over a large number of locations rather than a large number of features defined by different cells in the network. This loss of generality in the structure of an iconic network can be retrieved by putting a full layer as shown in Figure 9.1 at each pixel site in the image, as shown in Figure 9.3. In applications there would be a much larger num-

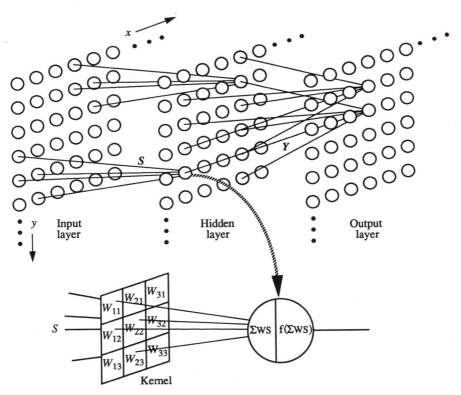

Figure 9.2 *Translation invariant, or iconic, neural network.*

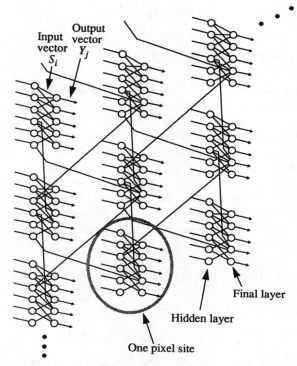

Figure 9.3 *Iconic network with multiple features at each pixel site.*

ber of connections across pixel boundaries than the example shown in Figure 9.3. In the usual network, shown in Figure 9.1 and expressed by Eq. (9.1), the input and output are often defined as vectors. In an iconic network, the input and output images become vector spaces, where there are as many components in the vector as there are neural cells at each pixel. The concept of a convolution must be extended. A closeup view of an example of a network at one pixel site is shown in Figure 9.4. The s components of the image vector space $\mathbf{S}$ are input to layer $\mathbf{Y}$ where there are y neural cells that provide the y components of the output vector image.

As seen in Figure 9.4, at cell Y_4, for example, there are weighted sums of signals coming from a number of S components. The contribution to the sum from a component, for example S_3, is a convolution with some kernel W_{34} on input image S_3. Let the kernels W be indexed by the image input and output components $i = 1, \ldots, s$ and $j = 1, \ldots, y$ respectively. The total sum of contributions for this example is

$$Y_4(\mathbf{u}) = f(W_{34}(0)S_3(\mathbf{u} - 0) + W_{34}(\mathbf{v}_a)S_3(\mathbf{u} - \mathbf{v}_a) + W_{34}(\mathbf{v}_b)S_3(\mathbf{u} - \mathbf{v}_b)$$

$$+ W_{44}(0)S_4(\mathbf{u} - 0) + W_{64}(0)S_6(\mathbf{u} - 0) + W_{64}(\mathbf{v}_c)S_6(\mathbf{u} - \mathbf{v}_c))$$

$$= f(W_{34} * S_3 + W_{44} * S_4 + W_{64} * S_6)$$

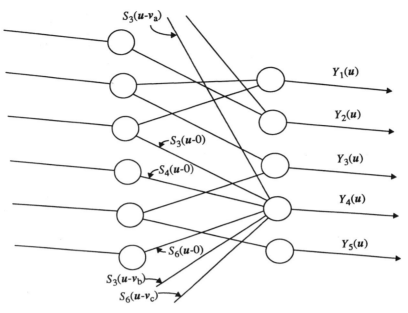

Figure 9.4 Cells at a single pixel site.

From this example it is seen that in general the total weighted sum for cells $Y_j(\mathbf{u})$ is the sum of all convolutions with the various input components of image S by various kernels.

$$Y_j(\mathbf{u}) = f\left(\sum_{i=1}^{S} \sum_{\mathbf{v}} W_{ij}(\mathbf{v}) S_i(\mathbf{u} - \mathbf{v}) \right) \qquad (9.3)$$

A single component $Y_j(\mathbf{u})$ over all $\mathbf{u}$ will be called a *component sublayer*, or just *sublayer*.

The sum over convolution kernels can be represented by a convolution where images and kernels are matrix spaces [18]. A matrix convolution is written as

$$\mathbf{Y} = Y_{mj}(\mathbf{u}) = \sum_{i} \int_{\mathbf{v}} S_{mi}(\mathbf{u} - \mathbf{v}) W_{ij}(\mathbf{v}) \, d\mathbf{v} = \sum_{i} S_{mi} * W_{ij} \equiv \mathbf{S} * \mathbf{W} \qquad (9.4)$$

where vector $\mathbf{v}$ spans the domain of the kernel space, and $\mathbf{u}$ spans the domain of the image. The order of S and W are reversed so that the sum over index i defines a matrix multiplication using the usual matrix notation. The convolution of two image matrices can be written with bold faced symbols which indicate matrices. The convolution in Eq. (9.3) is shown in the discrete form, where Eq. (9.4) is shown in terms of an integral to emphasize the difference between the matrix sum and the spatial sum. Furthermore, Eq. (9.4) illustrates that in this model there can be a continuum of neurons in principle. In most applications the images are (row) vector spaces and the m index on Y and S is dropped. The weights are rectangular image matrices. Using a matrix convolution, the equation for the iconic layer in Figure 9.4 can be compactly written as

$$\mathbf{Y} = f(S * \mathbf{W})$$

If the images in Eq. (9.3) were only one pixel square, then $\mathbf{v} = \mathbf{u} = (0, 0)$, the sum over $\mathbf{v}$ is unnecessary, and Eq. (9.3) degenerates to Eq. (9.1). Thus, the usual definition of a network is a trivial subspace of an iconic network.

9.3 THE BASIC NETWORK CELL

The uniformity over the image of an iconic network allows the efficient use of fine grain massively parallel processors. The Applied Intelligent Systems, Inc. parallel computers consist of arrays of simple processing elements, where there is nominally one processor for each column in the image. During operation, a controller broadcasts the same instructions to a large number of simple, identical processing units. The array contains a large number of simple bit-serial arithmetic units and look-up tables that handle 4 bits in and 1 bit out. In general, each of the four inputs are connected to cells of different hidden layers in arbitrary neighborhoods, and serves as a definition of a simple neural cell. More complex cells are easily constructed from these, that have more than four inputs, and integer, rather than binary outputs. Details of the processors can be found in the references [9].

The processing units can efficiently compute a weighted sum and the nonlinear output function. Because of the large number of cells and connections in an iconic network, the architecture of the network must be as simple as possible for real-time applications. The weights used in training the applications to be discussed here are ± 1, corresponding to excitation and inhibition. The number of connections range from four to around forty. The output signals are either hard or soft limited.

9.3.1 Hardware

Associated with each processing element is a column of memory that stores one or more columns of images. A block diagram of the system is shown in Figure 9.5. There are three separate linear chains of components in the system: processing elements (PE), image I/O chips, and external memory chips. During operation of the system, a single instruction is sent from the controller and broadcast to all the processing elements and then the controller cycles through memory addresses so that entire rows in an image are read into the processing elements, one row at a time. As each row is processed, the results are read back into the memory, one row at a time. The entire image is processed in n cycles where n is proportional to the image height only. Then the controller broadcasts another instruction to the

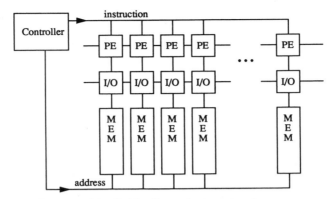

Figure 9.5 *Diagram of Applied Intelligent Systems, Inc. linear array processor.*

processing elements, and the cycles are repeated. A small amount of the controller overhead is used in sending instructions, while most of the time is spent in cycling memory addresses.

The idea of processing the entire image memory after each new instruction reduces the instruction overload and looping overhead, but sometimes leads to a requirement for more image memory for storage of intermediate results. In massively parallel array processors the number of processing elements is generally much smaller than the image size, but library functions give a seamless programming model, where there is one virtual processor per pixel, so that programming is independent of the actual number of processing elements. The processing elements are pipelined so that the processing of each row of data occurs simultaneously with memory accesses, with the result that the memories are never idle and have no wait states during the processing phase.

In the above fine grained architecture, the two most important instructions in general network computations are image translations and the addition function. If the weight at a point $\mathbf{v}$ in the kernel of the convolution in Eq. (9.3) is positive, then the image $S(\mathbf{u} - \mathbf{v})$ is translated by $\mathbf{v}$ and multiplied by the weight and summed to an accumulator. There are a number of different components S_i that are translated and summed. For negative weights, images are shifted, multiplied, and subtracted from the accumulator. A translation corresponds to the relative offset of a connection to a neural cell. Thus, image translations provide a mechanism for the connectivity of an iconic network.

The weight to be multiplied is a constant over the whole image and can be provided by a sequence of adds. The number of adds corresponds to the number of 1 bits in the weight expressed as a binary number. A weight multiplication is very simple for signals that are either 0 or ± 1. A weight that is a power of 2 requires the least time and is equivalent to the time needed to process weights that are ± 1. As seen in Figure 9.5, in a linear array architecture, the vertical component of a translation requires no processing overhead because there is no vertical movement of data. An address displacement in the controller allows any vertical image row displacement to occur naturally during a memory read or write operation. The horizontal component of an image translation does require data movement and consists of one read and write cycle per row through the nearest-neighbor connections for each unit of horizontal displacement. A sequence of horizontal shifts along with one vertical address displacement will cause an image to be translated in any direction.

9.3.2   Hard Limiting

The four-input look-up table contained by each processing element is shown in Figure 9.6. Four arbitrary image rows can be read into shift registers R1 through R4, where the inputs are transformed by the look-up table and the results are written back to memory. The output of a neural cell with only four binary connections can be directly computed using the look-up table (LUT). The parallel operations are schematically shown in Figure 9.7, where four bit planes corresponding to the four input connections are first shifted, then the look-up table is applied. Although only one LUT is shown, there are as many virtual LUT circuits as there are pixels in the image. The actual number of LUTs depends on the machine. After shifting, the images are directly sent to the truth tables so that the outputs can be computed, one row at a time. Weight multiplications and summing operations are not necessary because truth tables are universal. The table values can be adjusted to correspond to all possible weights and binary output functions for the four binary input signals. With binary output cells a hard limiting function shown Figure 9.8a is used often at a maximum threshold.

For the simple cell definition shown in Figure 9.7, an average of 16 clock cycles are needed to translate each row of the four images if the relative connection displacement vector is in a 8×8 window. Four read cycles and one write cycle are needed for the truth table operation. The total of 21 cycles requires 2.1 microseconds. For a system with an array of 512 processing elements, there are 4×512 connections in 2.1 microseconds, or close to 1000 million connections per second.

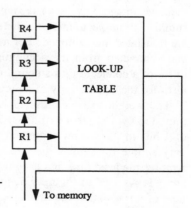

Figure 9.6   *Four-input look-up table in each processing element.*

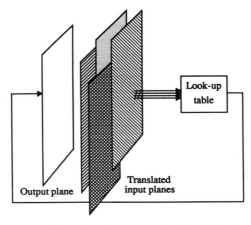

Figure 9.7 *Operation of an array of cells with four inputs.*

9.3.3 Soft Limiting

If the number of inputs is greater than four, the 4-bit truth tables cannot directly be applied, and an alternate scheme must be used. One method for neural computations in a system with ± 1 weights would be to translate the input planes, one at a time, according to the relative locations of the connections. After each translation, that bit plane is added or subtracted, depending on the weight, to an accumulator to form a weighted sum. A soft limited output function would then be applied, as shown in Figure 9.8b.

For ± 1 weights, the soft limiting function shown in Figure 9.8c is much more efficient and can be computed at the same time that the convolution is computed. Rather than accumulating a large number in the weighted sum and then applying soft limiting, a more efficient scheme is to initially set all accumulators at the maximum value, and then decrement that value depending on the input. The output need only be encoded in three bits. The accumulators are initially set to the value 7 (equal to binary 111) and are decremented by 1 only under two conditions: (1) a signal is 0 at a $+1$ weighted connection, or (2) a signal is 1 at a -1 weighted connection. If an accumulator is decremented to 0, then it will stay clamped to 0.

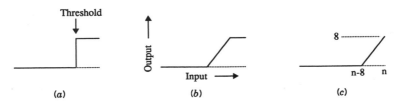

Figure 9.8 *Output functions: (a) hard limiting, (b) soft limiting, (c) an efficient soft limiting* function.

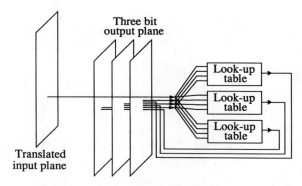

Figure 9.9   *Using truth tables for soft limiting.*

If no inputs satisfy the above two conditions so that the cell would normally accumulate to the maximum value, then that accumulator would not be decremented and remain at the maximum value. Thus the accumulator output is represented by the function in Figure 9.8c.

There are two advantages to counting an accumulator down, rather than the more natural scheme of counting up. First, only three bits of memory storage are needed, no matter how many connections there are. Second, the hardware truth tables can be used with good efficiency according to the method in Figure 9.9, which shows schematically that an input connection is translated and then applied to three truth tables that encode the decrement process. A 3-bit stationary accumulator is shown connected to three input lines of the truth table, and the neural input connection is connected to the forth input. The truth tables evaluate the accumulator output, and the result is written back into the accumulator. Three look-up table operations are needed for each connection, and for a 8×8 neighborhood, an average of four cycles are needed for an image translation, for a total of 19 cycles. For 512 processing elements, the system can compute 512 connections in 1.9 microseconds, or 270 million connections per second.

9.4   TRAINING HIDDEN LAYERS

Hard or soft limiting functions as defined above are not differentiable, and therefore back propagation cannot be used for training hidden layers [19]. Furthermore back propagation cannot be used because of the assumption that the weights are ± 1. In the training to be covered here the task is to find a number of connections with ± 1 weights that meet certain criteria of acceptability.

Hidden layers are very useful in complex classification applications such as character recognition. Rather than sending a raw image to the final layer, it is more efficient to reduce the image to a number of characteristic features that define all the patterns that occur in the image. The final layer will not have the burden of redundantly locating these features over the image for each character. Some useful features in character recognition are line segments at various angles and the locations of intersections of lines. In this section, a method of unsupervised competitive learning of features defined by matrix kernels is presented.

In Figure 9.3 there are a number of binary vector components input from a previous layer **S** to layer **Y**, which has a fixed number of neural cells at each pixel site. The problem is to choose connections for each of the **Y** component sublayers that meet three criteria: orthogonality, completeness, and meaningfulness. Orthogonality means that the features derived from each component sublayer of output **Y** are distinct from each other. Completeness here means that areas of activity in the input layer will result in activity in some cells in the output layer. If some potentially important activity is not covered by some Y_j output, then that information is lost. Meaningfulness simply refers to an attempt to prevent features in the input layer from being duplicated in the output layer by a trivial set of connections. The sets of connections will define matrix convolution kernels that represent the weights.

9.4.1 Choosing Candidate Features

A trial candidate refers to a trial set of connections corresponding to a single sublayer in the hidden layer under training. The current, or existing feature set refers to the connections corresponding to a layer (all sublayers). In training a hidden layer, meaningful trial candidate connections are randomly chosen, and then compared with a current feature set for orthogonality and completeness. If the trial connections do not improve the orthogonality of the current feature set, then the candidate is discarded. In the next section orthogonality and completeness will be discussed. In this section a method for choosing meaningful candidate connections will be presented.

The procedure for choosing candidate features is described as follows. First, a training image that has a representative sample of all the image patterns that are important, is input to the system. All layers are processed up to, but not including, the hidden layer that is to be trained. The layer that is input to the hidden layer is a vector space with several components, corresponding to the several sublayers. The connections that comprise a trial candidate are chosen, one at a time. There are two parameters for each candidate connection that must be chosen: the input sublayer index k and the spatial location of that input x and y, as illustrated in Figure 9.10a. The triple, $c_m = (k_m, x_m, y_m)$ characterizes a single connection indexed by m, and the set of connections $c = \{c_m\}$, $m = 1, \ldots, 4$, represents the trial candidate feature as illustrated in Figure 9.10b.

In a layer there are a number of connection sets that define the full set of features illustrated in Figure 9.10c. The weights $W_{ij}(\mathbf{v})$ are completely described by the connection sets $c_m = (k_m, x_m, y_m)$ according to the following relation. For sublayer j,

$$W_{ij}(\mathbf{v}) = 1 \quad \text{if for some } m, \ \mathbf{v} = (x_m, y_m) \ \text{ and } \ k_m = i$$

$$= 0 \quad \text{otherwise}$$

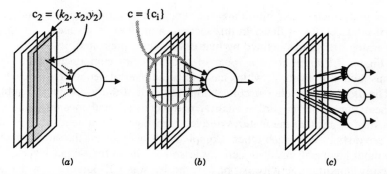

Figure 9.10 *Choosing candidate features: (a)* candidate connections, *(b)* candidate features, *(c)* full feature set for a layer.

The actual values of the weights are not necessarily 1, but are implicitly provided by the look-up table and are generally preset in an application. The number of all possible feature connections is too large for candidates to be chosen totally at random. The components of the input image vector are chosen at random, and the locations are chosen by a scheme that increases the probability of finding useful candidate connections.

The first and second components, k_1 and k_2, are randomly chosen. The coordinate position of the first component is chosen to be at the origin of the kernel element without loss of generality. Thus $c_1 = (k_1, 0, 0)$. A two-dimensional joint probability function is empirically computed for a few random sample points within a fixed neighborhood of $(0, 0)$ and gives the probability that the second feature is located at position (x, y) when it is given that the first feature is located at $(0, 0)$. A specific location, (x_2, y_2), is chosen where there is the largest probability in the random sample, so that the probability that a useful feature will be chosen is increased. Figure 9.11 is an example of the probability distribution for two input features: an east edge and a west edge. The training image is shown in Figure 9.11a. The two edges feature images are shown in Figure 9.11b. The probability distribution in Figure 9.11c illustrates the intuitively obvious result an east edge has a high probability of lying to the right of a west edge by an amount equal to the stroke width of the characters. For more complex images, the meaning of features may not be so obvious.

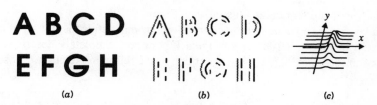

Figure 9.11 *Example of the probability distribution: (a)* training image, *(b)* two edge features, *(c)* probability of east edge given that a west edge is at $(0, 0)$.

Next, a third feature component k_3 is randomly chosen, and another joint probability function is computed for a few random points and is the probability that the third feature is located at position $(\mathbf{x}, \mathbf{y})$ when it is given that the first feature is $(k_1, 0, 0)$ and the second feature is (k_2, x_2, y_2). The third feature is chosen at a location (x_3, y_3) where the probability is the largest for the limited sample. The process is continued until all features and connection locations are chosen.

If two feature components are chosen from the same input layer $(k_m = k_n)$, the same connection location might be chosen twice. A second feature component will not be chosen at or near the same coordinate location when they are from the same input layer. The prevention of overlapping connections is enough to ensure that meaningful feature candidate are chosen because, even if all k_m are identical, the connection locations will all be different.

9.4.2 Evaluating Candidates

The above scheme supplies one feature candidate. If there are n neural cells in the layer under training, then n features chosen by the method given above will be generated, one for each hidden cell layer. The next task is to continue generating trial candidate features for potential replacement of the existing set of features. A new candidate is evaluated by testing for orthogonality and completeness with the existing set. If the new candidate is superior, one of the existing features is replaced.

Orthogonality.   There are a number of definitions of orthogonality depending on the mathematical discipline. In the field of vector analysis, two vectors $\mathbf{f}_i$ and $\mathbf{f}_j$ are defined to be orthogonal if their inner product is 0: $\mathbf{f}_i \cdot \mathbf{f}_j = 0$. An image can be represented by an expansion in terms of a set of orthogonal functions [20]

$$\varphi_{mn}: \iint \varphi_{mn}(x, y)\varphi_{pq}^*(x, y)\, dx\, dy = 0 \qquad \text{for} \quad m \neq p \quad \text{or} \quad n \neq q$$

Completeness means that an arbitrary image can be exactly reconstructed from the orthogonal expansion (e.g., from the coefficients of a Fourier transform). These definitions of orthogonality and completeness are used as a guide in training networks.

Neural cell responses will most likely never become exactly orthogonal or complete under any definition because the basic idea of a neural layer is to capture the most important properties of an image, such as shape, and remove unimportant properties, such as noise and illumination intensity. Orthogonal vectors have been defined by Stentiford [21] and used by others [22, 23] in order to generate features for recognizing characters using supervised learning. Orthogonality O is defined as

$$O = \sum_{j} \sum_{i \neq j} \frac{(\mathbf{f}_i \cdot \mathbf{f}_j)^2}{(\mathbf{f}_i \cdot \mathbf{f}_i)(\mathbf{f}_j \cdot \mathbf{f}_j)} \tag{9.5}$$

where $\mathbf{f}_i$ and $\mathbf{f}_j$ are the response vectors for characters i and j, and the inner product is used. During training, O must be minimized.

For iconic networks with unsupervised learning, the "vector" $\mathbf{f}_j$ in Eq. (9.5) will be defined as the output image from neural layer j during training. The image transformed by connections for layer j is $\mathbf{f}_j = Y_j = \Sigma \ W_{ij} * S_i$. The vectors have a length equal to the number of pixels in the image. Here the "inner product" between two images is defined as though the images were vectors with each pixel as a separate component. The inner product term $Y_j \cdot Y_j$ is the sum of the squares of the output pixels from cell i, and is equal to the area of image Y_j, since an output is either 0 or 1. The term $Y_i \cdot Y_j$ is equal to the number of output pixels that are 1 at the same location for both images Y_i and Y_j; thus $Y_i \cdot Y_j$ is the area of the logical intersection $Y_i \cap Y_j$. The objective to achieve orthogonality is realized by choosing a set of neural connections that have outputs Y_j that minimize O. Thus, a minimum orthogonality as defined by Eq. (9.5) will minimize the mutual overlap of all the images Y_j.

Completeness.   The definition of completeness for purposes of training features is quite different than that used in an orthogonal expansion. The idea of completeness is to try to ensure that features that uniquely describe all parts of a pattern are present, and no part of a pattern is left out because a critical descriptive feature is missing. The method to be discussed will not ensure completeness, but has been found experimentally to be useful. Completeness C is defined here as the area of the logical union of all the output images:

$$C = (\cup_i f_i) \cdot (\cup_i f_i). \tag{9.6}$$

The objective is to make the area of the union of images C large while making the mutual intersections O small. The orthogonality relation in Eq. (9.5) seems to favor completeness because larger areas given by $Y_i \cdot Y_i$ and $Y_j \cdot Y_j$ will diminish the value of O, as it should. It was found that orthogonality and many variations of the definition worked well for finding distinct features, but sometimes failed for completeness. Experiments showed that, for some features, the numerator of Eq. (9.5) would converge to 0 faster than the denominator could expand to a large value. Once the numerator is close to 0, the denominator becomes insignificant, and will generally become small. The result is that the output image features become sparse, and the completeness criterion is violated. Results are considerably improved if candidates are discarded that have areas $Y_c \cdot Y_c$ less than half of the average area. The instability where some feature areas approach 0 is aborted, and all features generally increase in area (completeness) while improving orthogonality.

Hamming Distance.   In choosing features it was found that the Hamming distance (HD) is also a good criterion to achieve both orthogonality and completeness:

$$\text{HD}_{ij} = (f_i \ \text{XOR} \ f_j) \cdot (f_i \ \text{XOR} \ f_j), \tag{9.7}$$

where XOR is the logical exclusive OR function. HD_{ij} is the area of the exclusive OR of two feature images. Orthogonality can be defined as the sum of the inverse of the squares of HD over the feature set:

$$O = \sum_{j} \sum_{i \neq j} \frac{1}{HD_{ij}^2}$$

The reciprocal of HD must be used so that good candidates will have a small 1/HD and poor candidates will have a large 1/HD. The mean squared criterion is then a more sensitive test for candidate quality because if a candidate is poor with respect to just one feature in the existing set, then the squaring will emphasize the poor quality. Completeness, defined in Eq. (9.6), is more strongly emphasized without degrading orthogonality if it is explicitly a part of the orthogonality definition.

$$O = \sum_{j} \sum_{i \neq j} \frac{1}{(HD_{ij} + C)^2} \tag{9.8}$$

Figure 9.12 shows a simple example of a two-component image along with the corresponding orthogonality, Hamming distance, and completeness. Equation (9.8) is used for training in the examples in this chapter.

In some applications [22, 23] involving the training of features using an orthogonality criteria, a list is kept of the orthogonality of each feature with respect to the set of existing features according to a partial sum of Eq. (9.5) defined as

$$O_j = \sum_{j} \frac{(f_i \cdot f_j)^2}{(f_i \cdot f_i)(f_j \cdot f_j)} \tag{9.9}$$

A new feature candidate is compared with the existing set, and has an orthogonality O_c according to Eq. (9.9). If O_c is less than the largest orthogonality O_L for an existing feature, then the new candidate feature will replace the existing feature. It is obvious that this scheme will diminish the orthogonality during training.

Experiments show that a better scheme is to try replacing every feature in the existing set with the trial candidate one by one, compute the orthogonality for every case, and then either choose the best feature to replace or discard the candidate if the orthogonality is made worse for all trial replacements. One reason for

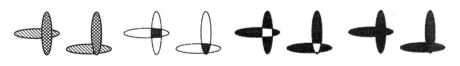

A two feature image   Orthogonality   Hamming distance   Completeness

Figure 9.12 *Example of an image showing definition of orthogonality, Hamming distance, and completeness.*

using this scheme is that the worst existing feature may represent a unique feature type (poorly). Eliminating it from the set will impede recovery of it later. A second more important reason is that a new trial feature may show a poor orthogonality with the existing feature set simply because it is very similar to just one of the existing features that has good orthogonality. Rather than discarding the trial feature, it would be more appropriate to perform a trial replacement with the similar existing feature because the candidate may prove to be superior.

9.4.3 Competitive Learning

With the orthogonality definitions (9.5), (9.7), or (9.8), and the candidate replacement strategy as described above, competitive learning takes place. Once a fairly strong feature (low orthogonality with the existing set) is in the set of existing features, it will most likely not be replaced by a different feature type, but will become stronger as better features of that type are found. For example, during training, a set of connections that detect vertical lines will not be replaced with other feature types, such as diagonal lines, but it will be replaced by connections that are better at detecting vertical lines. Other cells will not compete and be replaced with candidates that also attempt to detect vertical lines because they would have poor orthogonality with the existing vertical line detector.

A difficulty with any definition of orthogonality in a translation invariant network is that one output feature image Y_i may appear to be orthogonal to a feature image Y_j that is identical except for a translation. Achieving a large Hamming distance (good orthogonality) can result by simply translating away a large overlap of two competing features. Thus, the definition of orthogonality for feature candidate evaluation must refer to that translation of the candidate feature that gives the maximum value of orthogonality.

9.5 TRAINING THE FINAL LAYER

The final layers can be trained using supervised learning. There are two major issues that will be addressed in training the final layers. First, iconic networks have unique training properties. Second, the training of ± 1 weights is different than the usual incremental training rules in the literature.

9.5.1 Simulated Annealing

The supervised training of points that are members of a matrix of kernels can be provided using simulated annealing [24]. A relation between the network and a physical thermodynamic model is developed by explicitly defining temperature and energy in a manner such that the methods of thermodynamics can be applied. Details and examples of the use of simulated annealing in teaching network connections are covered in the references [13, 14].

Figure 9.13a is a graphic example of an IC chip, where the pattern to be rec-

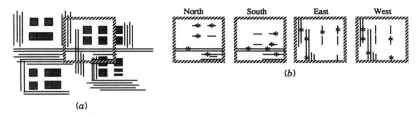

North   South   East   West

(b)

Figure 9.13 *IC chip (a)* image with training zone, *(b)* edges: quantum states (lines) and molecules (asterisks).

ognized is within the dotted box. Four edge direction components, shown in Figure 9.13*b*, are computed and act as inputs to the final layer. The image components that define the pattern of interest are called spatial *quantum states*. During training, a number *M* of candidate connections, called *molecules* are chosen from these quantum states to ensure that valid features are always used. The *M* molecular positions are the set of points that define the neural connections. The number of molecules will generally be much lower than the number of quantum states. Typical molecules are illustrated as asterisks in Figure 9.13*b*.

At the start of training, trial candidate connection points, or molecules, are randomly chosen. As training proceeds, molecules move around in a neighborhood about the position in the previous trial. The size of that neighborhood of movement, during each time cycle, from which new trial molecules are chosen, is called the *temperature* because the speed of random movement is analogous to the average kinetic energy of a physical system, which is related to the physical temperature. A very high temperature means that molecules are chosen almost at random from the quantum states, and corresponds to a global search over the energy space. At low temperatures there is only a slight difference from one connection configuration to the next and is a search about a local minimum.

The potential *energy* of the system is defined to be the largest matrix convolution value in the output image given by Eq. (9.3), with the exception of that value that refers to the pattern being trained. The large convolution values correspond to potential false recognitions. Figure 9.14 shows an example of a cross section of the convolution image. In this example there are 25 connections with weights of 1 in the kernels. The cross section includes a peak at the object being trained

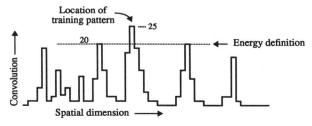

Location of training pattern

---- 25

20 ....

◀— Energy definition

Convolution

Spatial dimension ——▶

Figure 9.14 *Cross section of convolution output with potential false recognitions.*

at the maximum value of 25, along with two potential false recognitions that have the value 20. In this example the system energy has the value 20. For optimum convergence during annealing, the definition of energy must be modified according to a method covered in the references [13].

During annealing the temperature is lowered and the energy decreases. The usual definition of energy as a mean square of the convolution values does not eliminate false recognitions as effectively as the definition involving a maximum because a single image pattern very similar to the pattern under training will cause a very large narrow spike at the convolution output. The vast remainder of the rest of the output image can be small. Thus, as shown in Figure 9.14 the average output may be very small even though there are serious potentials for false recognitions. The definition of energy as a maximum value will be carried over to Hebbian learning.

9.5.2 Hebbian Learning

The delta rule for training weights has been given as [19]:

$$\Delta w_{ij} = \eta(t_j - o_j)s_i$$

where Δw_{ij} refers to the connection strength from input neuron i to output neuron j, η is a learning rate constant, t_j is a desired target for the training output; s_i are the input signals for a particular training input, and o_j are the outputs computed according to the current set of weights. During training, signals s_i are input to the network, the outputs o_j are computed using the existing weights, and then small adjustments Δw_{ij} are computed and added to the current weights w_{ij}:

$$w'_{ij} = w_{ij} + \Delta w_{ij}. \tag{9.10}$$

The training cycles are repeated until the error between the training set and output are low enough.

An Iconic Learning Model.   For iconic networks, the individual cells are indexed by spatial arguments, $\mathbf{u} = (x_u, y_u)$ and $\mathbf{p} = (x_p, y_p)$, which are vectors representing input and output image coordinates, respectively. The input, output, and training images, respectively, become $S(\mathbf{u})$, $Y(\mathbf{p})$, and $T(\mathbf{p})$ for consistency with the definition in Eq. (9.2). The delta rule becomes

$$\Delta W(\mathbf{p} - \mathbf{u}) = \eta(T(\mathbf{p}) - Y(\mathbf{p}))S(\mathbf{u})$$

Let $\mathbf{r} = \mathbf{p} - \mathbf{u}$, where the domain of $\mathbf{r}$ is limited to the size of the neighborhood of connections.

$$\Delta W(\mathbf{r}) = \eta(T(\mathbf{p}) - Y(\mathbf{p}))S(\mathbf{p} - \mathbf{r}) \tag{9.11}$$

Since each neuron (pixel) is associated with weights and connection patterns that are identical throughout the image space, each pixel can serve as a separate training site and still train the same set of weights. Thus, just one training image can furnish a large number of training sites. The delta rule in Eq. (9.11) is modified so that $\Delta W(\mathbf{r})$ is accumulated over all pixel coordinates $\mathbf{p}$ to get a large training sample before the weights are updated:

$$\Delta W(\mathbf{r}) = \eta \sum_{\mathbf{p}} \left[\frac{T(\mathbf{p})}{\Sigma T(\mathbf{p})} - \frac{Y(\mathbf{p})}{\Sigma Y(\mathbf{p})} \right] S(\mathbf{p} - r) \qquad (9.12)$$

where the normalization in the denominators is included because of the difference between the number of nonzero training locations $T(\mathbf{p})$ and output locations $Y(\mathbf{p})$. The weights are updated according to Eq. (9.10).

The Morphological Learning Rule.   If the weights are limited to $+1$, 0, and -1, they cannot be updated by Eq. (9.10) because $\Delta W(\mathbf{r})$ as computed by Eq. (9.12) can be outside these allowed values. In this case, only one weight is changed at a single position $\mathbf{r}'$, corresponding to the maximum value of $|\Delta W(\mathbf{r})|$ for all $\mathbf{r}$. If $\Delta W(\mathbf{r}')$ is positive, a new weight, $+1$, is added at position $\mathbf{r}'$, and corresponds to an excitation. If $\Delta W(\mathbf{r}')$ is negative, the new weight is -1, and corresponds to an inhibition. If $\Delta W(\mathbf{r})$ is maximum for more than one value of $\mathbf{r}$, then only one value of $\mathbf{r}$ is chosen at random, usually a value closest to $|\mathbf{r}| = 0$. Thus, the training rule for computing a new set of weights, as given by Eq. (9.10), is replaced by

$$W'(\mathbf{r}) = W(\mathbf{r}) + \delta(\mathbf{r} - \mathbf{r}') \left[\frac{\Delta W(\mathbf{r})}{|\Delta W(\mathbf{r})|} \right] \qquad (9.13)$$

where $\delta(0) = 1$ is the delta function, and $\mathbf{r}'$ is a location of the maximum $|\Delta W(\mathbf{r})|$. The output is defined by Eq. (9.2) as $Y = X_t(S * W)$, where X_t is shown in Figure 9.8(a) and t is the highest threshold that gives at least one false recognition output. Thus, threshold t has the same definition as that for the energy in simulated annealing. Equations (9.12) and (9.13) form what is called the Morphological Training Rule because of the relationship of binary signals and weights to mathematical morphology [15, 16]. Every time the training rule is applied, another connection is added to the layer being trained. The training rule is cycled a predetermined number of times to build up a specified number of connections. As more points located at various $\mathbf{r}'$ are added to $W(\mathbf{r})$, false recognitions will be eliminated, and threshold t will lower. However, the training cycles can be terminated if the false recognition energy t drops below a specified acceptable level.

The Morphological Training Rule starts out with all weights set to 0. Input image S has an area where a pattern is to be trained, centered at vector $\mathbf{t}$. The remainder of S generally contains confusing patterns where false detections are to be minimized. The training template T is an image where $T(\mathbf{t}) = 1$ at the point $\mathbf{t}$

where the constructed $W'(\mathbf{r})$ is to be referenced. $T(\mathbf{t}) = 0$ elsewhere. The domain of the vector $\mathbf{r}$ relative to t is such that it covers only the pattern to be trained. The image Y is computed according to the current $W'(\mathbf{r})$.

9.6 A NETWORK EXAMPLE

In this section an example is developed that illustrates the training of an iconic network with two hard limited hidden layers and a soft limited output layer. The advantages of hidden layers are that the output is more free of noise and that $\pm 10°$ of rotation can be accommodated. The network was found to work well at illumination intensities at half or twice the training intensity. The objective is to locate the specific area on a integrated circuit chip highlighted by a 60×30 pixel rectangle, as shown in Figure 9.15. Locating the chip at two different corners will allow the rotation and position of the chip to be determined so that a wire bonding machine can accurately proceed.

A four-layer network model for this application is shown in Figure 9.16. The neural cells for only one pixel are shown. Although Figure 9.16 only shows only connections within a single pixel site, most of the connections are not shown and are actually across pixel boundaries. The first layer performs an edge detection using the Difference Of Offset Gaussians (DOOG) [13], and a hard limited threshold. The output of the first layer is a four-component vector that indicates edges in the north, south, east, and west directions. The second two hidden layers (HL1 and HL2) consist of eight and four components, respectively, and are trained by the method given in Section 9.4 of this chapter. The final layer (FL) is a three-bit soft limited output layer with sixteen inputs, and is trained by the Morphological Training Rule.

In this application the DOOG has a Gaussian function with a sigma equal to 0. In this case there is no Gaussian filtering and the outputs are nothing but the differences in displaced images in the four compass directions. This is equivalent to

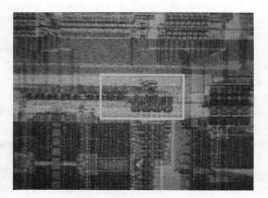

Figure 9.15 Chip with specific area to be located.

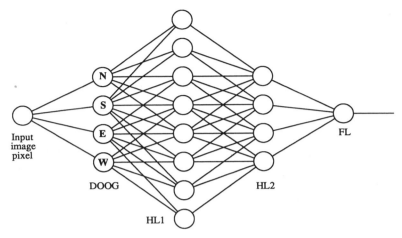

Figure 9.16 *Network model for locating a chip region.*

a discrete directional derivative and is characteristically noisy. The first hidden layer HL1 is trained by 100 to 200 iterations of the unsupervised learning method covered in Section 9.4. If the network adopts a new feature candidate, an orthogonality matrix is printed out, where each term in the sum of Eq. (9.8) is given as a separate element of the matrix. The sum of all the elements in a matrix is the orthogonality, as given by Eq. (9.8). Diagonal terms are set to 0. Figure 9.17*a* shows an example of the matrix early in the training and after training is completed. Layer HL2 is also trained in around 100 to 200 iterations. Examples of the HL2 orthogonality matrix are shown in Figure 9.17*b*.

The output of each hidden layer is dilated. That is, if a cell fires, then surrounding cells in a small neighborhood will also fire. Although the dilation can be conceived as a separate (but trivial) layer as in the Neocognitron [25], it is not trained and is not shown in the network diagram in Figure 9.16. The dilation allows a considerable relaxation in the exact location of features, so that the output of the final layer will still correctly respond if the location of an input strays by an amount equal to the sum of the dilations of the hidden layers. Figure 9.18 shows the result of dilations. A feature located in the first layer will be expanded by a radius r_1 at

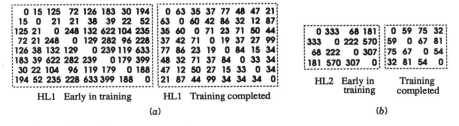

Figure 9.17 *Orthogonality matrix: (a)* first hidden layer, *(b)* second hidden layer.

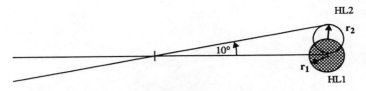

Figure 9.18   *Effect of dilations between layers.*

the output of layer HL1, and expanded again by r_2 at the output of HL2. In this application r_1 and r_2 are both set to roughly 1.5 pixels, so that the input can stray up to 3 pixels and still give a good output response, as seen in Figure 9.18. For a training window 60 pixels wide, a 3 pixel displacement is equivalent to around 5.7°.

Figure 9.19 shows the final layer soft limited output response of the trained pattern. The response is shown for networks with 0, 1, and 2 hidden layers as a function of rotation of the trained image of an IC chip. With no hidden layers, the final layer is connected directly to the four DOOG direction images. At 0° rotation the final layer output has one pixel with maximal response. An output of seven units indicates the maximum cell response at a pixel site. The extremely local response results in very little tolerance for image distortion or rotation, and is due to the fact that there is no Gaussian filtering.

The output of the network with one hidden layer is shown at 0° and 5°. At 0° there are 9 pixels that respond with an output of 6 or 7, and at 5°, there is still a significant response. The output of a network with two hidden layers is shown at 0° and 10°. At 0°, 16 pixels have maximum response. The response with two layers at 10° is much better than that for one layer at 5°.

Dilations will greatly increase the density of output features in an image. In order for dilations to work effectively, the density of features in an image must be small because if features are too dense, then there will be an increased probability of false recognitions. Each hidden layer cuts down the density of new output features compared with the density of features input to that layer as a result of a lack of completeness in training the layer.

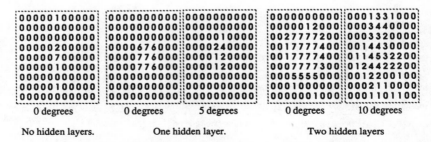

Figure 9.19   *Final layer output for different image rotations.*

9.7 CONCLUSIONS

The most important use of translation invariant (iconic) networks is in pattern recognition applications, where the object or pattern is very complex or embedded in a noisy background to the extent that the object cannot be separated from the background by a simple means. Thus the whole image must be searched using a complex but local neural model. The result is that there is a vast number of neurons and connections. The neurons must therefore be very simple in order to provide visual inspection in real-time.

Many neural hardware systems provide floating operations at rates of 10 to 100 million connections per second. Low cost SIMD systems such as the Applied Intelligent Systems, Inc. computers provide networks with up to 1000 million very simple connections per second. There are two extremes in system design: devote the hardware to fast floating point chips or to massive single bit parallelism. A basic unanswered question is this: What is the relative importance of systems that have weights with a wide dynamic range and high precision versus systems with low precision ± 1 weights and one or two orders of magnitude more connections? How is the potential for intelligence of a network distributed between weights and connections? These questions are difficult, and have not been explicitly addressed in this chapter, but it is shown that multilayer networks with a massive connectivity of ± 1 weights are very effective in real-time applications, and certainly have the robust performance expected of neural networks. These systems can be trained in less than a minute and run in industrial applications around 100 milliseconds.

A basic problem of neural network systems is conditioning the input signals in such a way that the information transmitted to the network is in a form that a network can effectively handle. Thus, there may be a need for high speed processing that lies outside the bounds of neural processing. An advantage of a general SIMD system is that there are many preexisting linear and nonlinear library functions that aid in filtering out background noise and irrelevant features, and prepare the image for the network stage of the processing.

The need for hidden layers in a network is well known. Two more advantages of hidden layers have been illustrated in this chapter. First, hidden layers can be very fast and simple, and consist of binary inputs from small neighborhoods and hard limited binary outputs. Some burden is taken off the final layers that use more complex soft limiting. It has been found that the number of output connections in the final layer can be reduced by 25% by including a simple local hidden layer. A second advantage of hidden layers is that a dilation, or spreading of the output signals from each hidden layer, allows a large degree of warping, rotation, and scale changes to be robustly handled. Feature outputs from successive hidden layers become increasingly more sparse so that false recognitions are not introduced by the dilations.

One basic problem with a network with ± 1 weights is that the training cannot be handled with delta rules or back propagation. This chapter has shown three methods for training this type of network. Hidden layers are trained by a type of unsupervised competitive learning, and the final layer can be trained by simulated annealing or the Morphological Training Rule. These training procedures take into account the ± 1 weights and the special properties of translation invariance.

REFERENCES

[1] H. Wechsler and G. L. Zimmerman, 2-D invariant object recognition using distributed associative memory, *IEEE Trans. Pattern Anal. Machine Intell.*, PAMI 10(6), 811–821 (1988).

[2] W. L. Reber and J. Lyman, An artificial neuron system design for rotation and scale invariant pattern recognition, *Proc. IEEE 1st Int. Conf. on Neural Network Systems*, Vol. IV, 277–283 (June 1987).

[3] B. Souček and M. Souček, *Neural and Massively Parallel Computers: The Sixth Generation*, Wiley-Interscience, New York, 1988.

[4] B. Souček, *Neural and Concurrent Real-time Systems: The Sixth Generation*, Wiley-Interscience, New York, 1989.

[5] S. C. J. Garth, A chipsset for high speed simulation of neural network systems, *Proc. IEEE 1st Internat. Conf. on Neural Network Systems*, Vol. III, 443–452 (June 1987).

[6] J. G. Cleary, A simple VLSI connectionist architecture, *Proc. IEEE 1st Int. Conf. on Neural Network Systems*, Vol. III, 419–426 (June 1987).

[7] H. P. Graf, W. Hubbard, L. D. Jackel, and P. G. N. deVegvar, A CMOS associative memory chip, *Proc. IEEE 1st Int. Conf. on Neural Network Systems*, Vol. III, 461–468 (June 1987).

[8] P. M. Flanders, D. J. Hunt, S. F. Reddaway, and D. Parkinson, "Efficient High speed Computing with the Distributed Array Processor," in D. J. Kuck, D. H. Lawrie, and A. H. Sameh, Eds., *High-Speed Computer and Algorithm Organization*, Academic Press, New York, 1979, pp. 113–127.

[9] S. S. Wilson, "One Dimensional SIMD Architectures—the AIS-5000," in S. Levialdi, Ed., *Multicomputer Vision*, Academic Press, London, 1988, pp. 131–149.

[10] S. S. Wilson, Massive parallelism in machine vision, *Vision '90, Soc. of Mnf. Eng. Conf. Proc.*, 7-43–7-54 (November 1990).

[11] T. J. Fountain, "A Review of SIMD Architectures," in M. J. B. Duff and J. K. Kittler, Eds., *Image Processing System Architectures*, Research Studies Press, Letchworth, England, November 1990, pp. 3–22.

[12] K. Preston, Jr., The Abingdon Cross benchmark survey, *IEEE Computer*, 22(7), 9–18 (July 1989).

[13] S. S. Wilson, "Teaching Network Connections for Real Time Object Recognition," to be published in B. Souček, and IRIS Group, *Neural and Intelligent Systems Integration*, Wiley, New York, 1991.

[14] S. S. Wilson, Teaching network connectivity using simulated annealing on a massively parallel processor, *Proc. IEEE*, 79(4), 559–566 (April 1991).

[15] S. S. Wilson, "Training Structuring Elements in Morphological Networks," to be published in Dougherty, E. R., Ed., *Mathematical Morphology in Image Processing*, Marcel Dekker, 1992.

[16] S. S. Wilson, Applications of matrix morphology, *Proc. SPIE*, 1350, 44–55 (1990).

[17] S. S. Wilson, Vector morphology and iconic neural networks, *IEEE Trans. on Systems, Man, and Cybernetics.*, SMC-19(6), 1636–1644 (Nov./Dec. 1989).

[18] S. S. Wilson, "Matrix Morphology-Mathematical Morphology on Matrices of Images," to be published in R. M. Haralick, Ed., *Mathematical Morphology: Theory and Applications*, 1992.

[19] D. E. Rumelhart, G. E. Hinton, and R. J. Williams, "Learning Internal Representations by Error Propagation," in D. E. Rumelhart and J. L. McClelland, Eds., *Parallel Distributed Processing:* Explorations in the Microstructures of Cognition, Vol. 1: *Foundations*, MIT Press, Cambridge, Mass., 1986, pp. 318–362.

[20] A. Rosenfeld and A. C. Kak, *Digital Picture Processing*, Academic Press, New York, 1976.

[21] F. W. M. Stentiford, Automatic feature design for optical character recognition using an evolutionary search procedure, *IEEE Trans. Pattern Anal. Machine Intell.*, PAMI 7(3), 349–355 (1985).

[22] M. Rizki, L. A. Tamburino, M. A. Zmuda, Adaptive search for morphological feature detectors, *Proc. SPIE*, 1350, 150–159 (July 10–12, 1990).

[23] A. M. Gillies, Automatic generation of morphological template features, *Proc. SPIE*, 1350, 44–55 (July 10–12, 1990).

[24] S. Kirkpatrick, C. D. Gelatt Jr., and M. P. Vecchi, Optimization by simulated annealing, *Science*, 220(4598), 671–680 (1983).

[25] K. Fukushima, Neocognitron: A hierarchical neural network capable of visual pattern recognition, *Neural Networks*, 1, 119–130 (1988).

CHAPTER 10 ————————————————

Higher Order Neural Networks in Position, Scale, and Rotation Invariant Object Recognition

LILLY SPIRKOVSKA
MAX B. REID

10.1 INTRODUCTION

An important aspect of the human visual system is the ability to recognize an object despite changes in the object's position in the input field, its size, or its angular orientation. A variety of models inspired by the architecture of biological neural systems have been designed with the goal of reproducing this characteristic in machine vision systems. One artificial neural system particularly well suited to this position, scale, and rotation invariant (PSRI) object recognition domain is based on higher order neural networks (HONNs).

We demonstrate higher order neural networks that can distinguish between classes of objects regardless of their position in the input field, their scale, or their angular orientation in a 127×127 pixel input field. These geometric distortions can be built into the network architecture of second and third order neural networks using information about the expected relationships between the input pixels. Because the invariances require no learning to produce, training is very quick, on the order of tens of passes. The networks are trained on just one view of each object and achieve 100% recognition accuracy on a test set of noisefree images characterized by the built-in distortions, provided pixelation does not induce errors.

HONNs are also robust with nonideal images, such as images characterized by white Gaussian noise or images containing occluding objects. With white noise added to images with a nearly ideal separation of background vs. foreground gray levels, we show that HONNs achieve 100% recognition accuracy for our test set for a standard deviation up to $\sim 10\%$ of the maximum gray value and continue to

Fast Learning and Invariant Object Recognition, By Branko Souček and the IRIS Group.
ISBN 0-471-57430-9 © 1992 John Wiley & Sons, Inc.

show good performance (defined as better than 75% accuracy) up to a standard deviation of ~14%. HONNs are also robust with respect to occlusion. For our test set for training images with very similar profiles, HONNs achieved 100% recognition accuracy for one occlusion of ~13% of the input field size and four occlusions of ~7% of the input field size. They showed good performance for one occlusion of ~23% of the input field size or four occlusions of ~15% of the input field size each. For training images with very different profiles, HONNs achieved 100% recognition accuracy for our test set for up to four occlusions of ~2% of the input field size and continued to show good performance for up to four occlusions of ~23% of the input field size each.

Finally, in the position, scale, and rotation invariant object recognition domain, our results show that HONNs are superior to other neural and symbolic learning techniques, in terms of recognition accuracy, training set size, and learning speed.

Neural networks have been applied to various domains including speech recognition, trend analysis and forecasting, process monitoring, robot control, and object recognition. We present work in the position, scale, and rotation invariant (PSRI) object recognition domain. The objective in this domain is to recognize an object despite changes in the object's position in the input field, size, or in-plane orientation, as shown in Figure 10.1.

Various techniques have previously been applied to achieve this objective in-

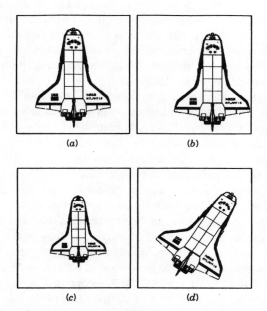

(a)   (b)

(c)   (d)

Figure 10.1   *PSRI object recognition. In the PSRI (position, scale, and rotation invariant) object recognition domain, all four of these objects would be classified as a single object. Three distortions of the prototype in (a) are shown. The object in (b) is a translated view, (c) is scaled, and (d) is rotated in-plane.*

cluding a number of neural network methods. Three of the more successful neural network methods are first order, backward-error propagation (backprop) trained networks [1], the neocognitron [2], and higher order networks [3–6]. We will focus on the higher order neural networks approach.

In a higher order neural network (HONN), known relationships are exploited and the desired invariances are built directly into the architecture of the network. Building such domain specific knowledge into the network's architecture results in a network that is pretrained and does not need to learn invariance to distortions. For each new set of training objects, a HONN only needs to learn to distinguish between the training objects; it does not need to generalize the concept behind the distortions. Therefore, training time is reduced significantly and HONNs need to be trained on just one view of each object, not on numerous distorted views. Moreover, 100% recognition accuracy is guaranteed for noisefree images characterized by the built-in distortions, providing pixelation does not induce errors.

In this paper, we explain how known relationships can be exploited and desired invariances built into the architecture of higher order neural networks, discuss some limitations of HONNs and how to overcome them, present simulation results demonstrating the usefulness of HONNs with practical object recognition problems, discuss the performance of HONNs with noisy test data, and, finally, compare them with other neural and nonneural techniques.

10.2 HIGHER ORDER NEURAL NETWORKS

10.2.1 Theory

The output of a node, denoted by y_i for node i, in a general higher order neural network is given by

$$y_i = \Theta(\Sigma_j w_{ij} + \Sigma_j \Sigma_k w_{ijk} x_j x_k + \Sigma_j \Sigma_k \Sigma_l w_{ijkl} x_j x_k x_l + \cdots) \qquad (10.1)$$

where $\Theta(f)$ is a nonlinear threshold function such as the hard limiting transfer function given by

$$y_i = 1, \quad \text{if } f > 0$$
$$y_i = 0, \quad \text{otherwise} \qquad (10.2)$$

The xs are the excitation values of the input nodes, and the interconnection matrix elements w determine the weight that each input is given in the summation. Using information about relationships expected between the input nodes under various distortions, the interconnection weights can be constrained such that invariance to given distortions is built directly into the network architecture [3, 4].

For instance, consider a second order network, as illustrated in Figure 10.2. In a second order network, the inputs are first combined in pairs and then the output is determined from a weighted sum of these products. The output for a strictly

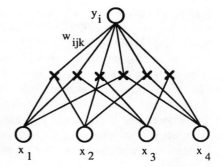

Figure 10.2 *Second order neural network. In a second order neural network, the inputs are first combined in pairs (at X) and the output is determined from a weighted sum of these products.*

second order network is given by the function:

$$y_i = \Theta(\Sigma_j \Sigma_k w_{ijk} x_j x_k) \tag{10.3}$$

The invariances achieved using this architecture depend on the constraints placed on the weights.

As an example, each pair of input pixels combined in a second order network define a line with a certain slope. As shown in Figure 10.3, when an object is moved or scaled, the two points in the same relative position within the object still form the endpoints of a line with the same slope. Thus, provided that all pairs of points that define the same slope are connected to the output node using the same weight, the network will be invariant to distortions in scale and translation. In particular, for two pairs of pixels (j, k) and (l, m), with coordinates (x_j, y_j), (x_k, y_k), (x_l, y_l), and (x_m, y_m), respectively, the weights are constrained according to

$$w_{ijk} = w_{ilm}, \quad \text{if } (y_k - y_j)/(x_k - x_j) = (y_m - y_l)/(x_m - x_l) \tag{10.4}$$

Alternatively, the pair of points combined in a second order network may define a distance. As shown in Figure 10.4, when an object is moved or rotated within a plane, the distance between a pair of points in the same relative position on the object does not change. Thus, as long as all pairs of points that are separated by

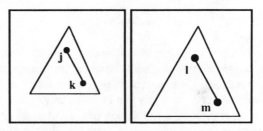

Figure 10.3 *Translation and scale invariance in a second order network. By constraining the network such that all pairs of points that define equal slopes use equal weights, translation and scale invariance are incorporated into a second order neural network.*

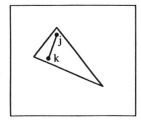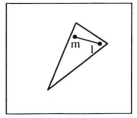

Figure 10.4 *Translation and rotation invariance in a second order network. By constraining the network such that all pairs of points that are equal distances away use equal weights, translation and rotation invariances are incorporated into a second order network.*

equal distances are connected to the output with the same weight, the network will be invariant to translation and in-plane rotation distortions. The weights for this set of invariances are constrained according to

$$w_{ijk} = w_{ilm}, \quad \text{if } \|\mathbf{d}_{jk}\| = \|\mathbf{d}_{lm}\| \tag{10.5}$$

That is, the magnitude of the vector defined by pixels j and k ($\mathbf{d}_{jk}$) is equal to the magnitude of the vector defined by pixels l and m ($\mathbf{d}_{lm}$).

To achieve invariance to translation, scale, and in-plane rotation simultaneously, a third order network can be used. The output for a strictly third order network, shown in Figure 10.5, is given by the function:

$$y_i = \Theta(\Sigma_j \Sigma_k \Sigma_l w_{ijkl} x_j x_k x_l) \tag{10.6}$$

All sets of input pixel triplets are used to form triangles with included angles (α, β, γ) as shown in Figure 10.6. When the object is translated, scaled, or rotated

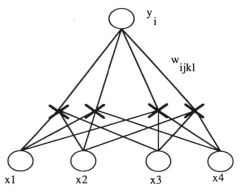

Figure 10.5 *Third order neural network. In a third order neural network, input nodes are first multiplied together in triplets (at **X**) and then the output is determined from a weighted sum of the products.*

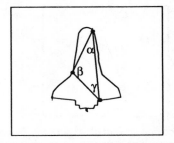 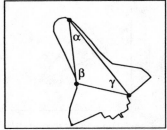

Figure 10.6 *PSRI in a third order network. As long as all similar triangles are connected to the output with the same weight, a third order network will be invariant to scale, in-plane rotation, and translation distortions.*

in-plane, the three points in the same relative positions on the object still form the included angles (α, β, γ). In order to achieve invariance to all three distortions, all sets of triplets forming similar triangles are connected to the output with the same weight. That is, the weight for the triplet of inputs (j, k, l) is constrained to be a function of the associated included angles (α, β, γ) such that all elements of the alternating group on three elements (group A3) are equal:

$$w_{ijkl} = w(i, \alpha, \beta, \gamma) = w(i, \beta, \gamma, \alpha) = w(i, \gamma, \alpha, \beta) \qquad (10.7)$$

Note that the order of the angles matters but not which angle is measured first.

Because HONNs are capable of providing nonlinear separation using only a single layer, once invariances are incorporated into the architecture, the network can be trained using a simple rule of the form:

$$\Delta w_{ijk} = (t_i - y_i)x_j x_k \qquad (10.8)$$

for a second order network, or

$$\Delta w_{ijkl} = (t_i - y_i)x_j x_k x_l \qquad (10.9)$$

for a third order network, where the expected training output t, the actual output y, and the inputs x, are all binary.

The main advantage of building invariance to geometric distortions directly into the architecture of the network is that the network is forced to treat all distorted views of an object as the same object. Distortion invariance is achieved before any input vectors are presented to the network. Thus, the network needs to learn to distinguish between just one view of each object, not numerous distorted views. The following section illustrates the rapid convergence attainable using this constraint.

10.2.2 Simulation Results: Fully Connected Networks

We simulated both second order and third order networks using a Sun 3/60 workstation [5]. The second order network had scale and translation invariances built into the architecture, whereas the third order network was designed for scale, translation, and in-plane rotation invariance.

The second order network was designed for a 16 × 16 pixel input field, with 256 input nodes (representing each of the input field pixels) and one output node. The weights were constrained to follow Eq. (10.4), the output was determined using a hard limiting transfer function given by Eq. (10.2) and the network was trained using Eq. (10.8).

The network was trained on just one view of two distinct objects. A sample set of objects is shown in Figure 10.7. Training took just 20 passes, and after training the network was able to distinguish between all translated and scaled (up to a factor of five) views of the two objects with 100% accuracy [5].

The third order network was designed for a 9 × 9 pixel input field, or 81 input nodes. Again, as for the second order simulations, the network had just one output node and one layer. To build in invariance to distortions in scale, translation, and in-plane rotation, the weights were constrained according to Eq. (10.7) and the network was trained using the rule in Eq. (10.9).

As for the second order network, the third order network was trained on just one view of each of the objects it was required to learn. In particular, we trained the network on the T/C recognition problem. As explained in Rumelhart [7], in the T/C problem, both objects are constructed of five squares, as illustrated in Figure 10.8, and the problem is to discriminate between them independent of translation or 90 degree rotations. In our work, the network was also required to distinguish between the objects invariant to distortions in scale.

The network learned to distinguish between all distorted views of a T and a C after just 10 passes through the training set, requiring less than 60 seconds on a Sun 3/60. The network was trained on just one view of a T and one view of a C, as shown in Figure 10.9. Nevertheless, because the invariances are built into the

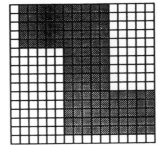

Figure 10.7 S/Z problem. Training set for distinguishing between an S and a Z invariant to distortions in scale or translation.

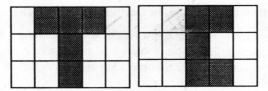

Figure 10.8 *T/C problem. In the T/C recognition problem, each pattern consists of five squares. Over all in-plane rotations and translations, the patterns can be discriminated only if combinations of triplets of pixels are examined.*

architecture of the network, it was able to distinguish between the two characters regardless of their position in the input field, 90 degree rotations, or changes in size over a factor of three. In principle, recognition is invariant for any rotation angle, given sufficient resolution to draw the objects accurately.

10.2.3   Implementation

This section presents the steps necessary for implementing a third order network. Second order networks require obvious modifications.

1. Constrain the network weights as specified by Eq. (10.7).
    (a) Calculate the included angles α, β, and γ (to some granularity) formed by each combination of three pixels for a given input field size. Since this computation is expensive and the combination of triplets for a given input field size does not depend on the objects to be distinguished, these angles can be precalculated and stored. This step would then be modified to read the included angles corresponding to each combination of three pixels from a file rather than calculating them.
    (b) Set up the correspondence between the angles α, β, and γ (same granularity) such that all triplets of the angles that are members of the alter-

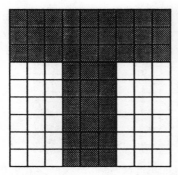
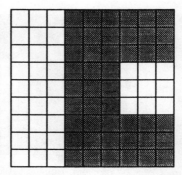

Figure 10.9 *Extended T/C problem. Training set for distinguishing between a T and a C invariant to distortions in scale, in-plane rotation, and translation.*

nating group (that is, the order of the angles matters, but not which one comes first) point to a single memory location. This assures that all similar triangles will manipulate the same weight value. Our implementation uses three matricies (*w*, *w_angle*, and *w_invar*) linked with pointers. Each location in *w* (indexed by the triple *i*, *j*, *k* representing the input pixels) points to a location in *w_angle* (indexed by the triple α, β, γ representing the angles formed by the triple *ijk*). Similarly, each location in *w_angle* points to a location in *w_invar*, also indexed by a triple of angles α, β, γ ordered such that the smallest angle is assigned to α. That is, *w_angle*[80][60][40] points to *w_invar* [40][80][60], as do the elements *w_angle*[60][40][80] and *w_angle*[40][80][60].

2. (a) Read in the training set data.
   (b) Assign the expected output value *t*, for each training object.
3. Train the network.
   (a) Compute the output *y*, as given by Eq. (10.6) and Eq. (10.2).
   (b) Modify the weight as specified by Eq. (10.9). To make learning more efficient, this step can be modified so that the weight is updated only once per training pass, not each time a similar triangle is encountered.
   (c) Repeat steps (a) and (b) until the network achieves 100% recognition of the training objects.

If the training set consists of just two objects, we can modify the above procedure to make learning more efficient. Between steps (2) and (3) above, determine which object contains more instances of each possible triangle and set a flag stating that ownership. During training, only weights belonging to each training object need to be updated. Weights for triangles that do not appear in either training object, or appear in equal numbers, need not be updated. Without this modification, if two training objects contain the same number of a particular triangle (denoted by *num*), the weight will first be increased by *num* and then decreased by *num*, resulting in a net change of zero.

10.3 LIMITATIONS

10.3.1 Scale Invariance

The advantages of HONNs stem from the fact that known relationships are incorporated directly into the architecture of the network. The network weights are constrained by this domain specific knowledge. Thus, fewer training passes and a smaller training set are necessary to learn to distinguish between the training objects.

The assumption behind incorporating specific knowledge into a network is that the weight values determined by the learning process result in the same output for one view of an object and a distorted view of the same object. Specifically, in our work, we assumed that the relationship expressed by Eq. (10.7), that all similar triangles have the same weight, constrained the network sufficiently so that an object and a distorted view of the same object would produce the same output. Using this relationship, we demonstrated that a third order network can achieve simultaneous invariance to translation, in-plane rotation, and scale on the T/C recognition problem in a 9 × 9 pixel input field. Unfortunately, Eq. (10.7) constrains the network adequately only in this limited domain but not when using a more general set of objects or a larger input field.

First, let us examine why using the same weight for similar triangles guarantees invariance to translation and (noisefree) in-plane rotation. As illustrated in Figure 10.10b, four triangles can be constructed in the object shown in Figure 10.10a. When the object is translated or rotated in-plane, as in Figure 10.10c, four triangles can still be constructed. Since the triangles formed in the distorted view are similar (in the strict geometric sense) to the ones in the original view, a network constrained by Eq. (10.7) would return the same output value for the object in Figure 10.10c as for the one in Figure 10.10a. Thus, since no new triangles are introduced, rotated and translated views of the training objects will be recognized with 100% accuracy.

In contrast, when the object in Figure 10.10a is scaled as shown in Figure 10.10d, not only are the triangles in Figure 10.10b present but also another 556 new triangles are introduced, two of which are shown in Figure 10.10d. Of these, only some are similar to the ones in Figure 10.10b. The introduction of nonsimilar triangles can lead to incorrect classification of scaled views of an object. As an example of a difficulty associated with the introduction of nonsimilar triangles, consider the two class case in which the weights that determine class 1 have pos-

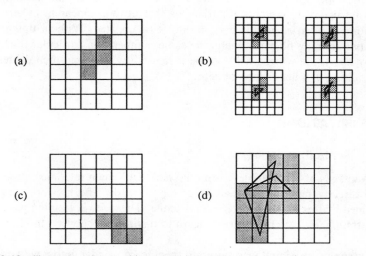

Figure 10.10   *Illustration of the problems associated with scale invariance. (a) A sample training object. (b) All the possible triangles that can be formed within the object in (a). (c) A rotated and translated view of the object in (a). (d) A scaled view of the object in (a). Two examples of the 556 new triangles introduced by scaling are shown.*

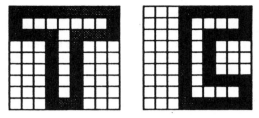

Figure 10.11 *Edge-only representation of a T and a C.*

itive values while the weights that determine class 2 have negative ones. If scaled versions of an object from class 1 contain many of the triangles that will be weighted by negative values, the final output value will be biased toward class 2. Thus, the network will incorrectly classify scaled views of the two objects.

In order to decrease the number of new triangles formed, edge-only images can be used, as shown in Figure 10.11. Since the interior pixels of an edge-only image are not turned on, scaling does not introduce as many new pixels with which triangles can be formed. However, even in this case, invariance to scale distortions cannot be guaranteed since scaling does introduce some triangles that were not used for training. This is not a problem unless the triangles introduced were used for recognizing the other images in the training set such that the extra triangles introduced could outweigh the original triangles and bias the answer toward the wrong training object.

Nevertheless, at least partial scale invariance can be achieved using Eq. (10.7) with edge only images. In particular, scale invariance is guaranteed when scaling an object does not introduce any new triangles. Instead, triangles are replaced with similar triangles, as in Figure 10.12. Moreover, invariance to a certain degree can be achieved if the number of similar triangles formed in a scaled version of a training object does not vary considerably from those which may be formed in the training object itself. This limitation is achieved by decreasing the resolution to which the included angles α, β, and γ are calculated. In simulations of the T/C problem, we have shown that for a 36 × 36 pixel input field, angles need to be rounded to the nearest 20° in order for the network to achieve scale down to 50%

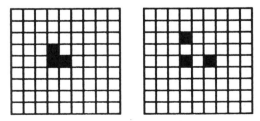

Figure 10.12 *A situation in which scale works correctly. As the image is scaled, triangles already present are replaced by similar triangles, but no new triangles are introduced.*

of the training image size. As the input field is increased to 80×80 pixels, the angle resolution can be increased to the nearest $10°$. Further increasing the input field resolution to 127×127 pixels allows the angle resolution to increase to $5°$. Thus, with larger input fields, both the image resolution and the resolution to which α, β, and γ are calculated can be increased.

10.3.2 Scaling the Network for Larger Input Scenes

As demonstrated in Section 10.2.1, higher order networks can be designed to quickly recognize objects invariant to geometric distortions such as scale, translation, and in-plane rotation. The networks need to be trained on just one view of each object, and since distortions are built into the architecture of the network, 100% recognition accuracy is achieved on all translated and rotated views for a large set of scaled views. However, the large number of interconnections possible in a third order network limits the input field size which can be fully connected. In this section, we examine the connectivity requirements of fully connected third order networks. Then, in the following section, we discuss a strategy of coarse coding useful for increasing the input field size to that required for practical object recognition problems.

A network with M inputs and one output using only rth order terms requires M-choose-r interconnections. For large M, this number, which is on the order of M^r, is clearly excessive. Building invariances into the architecture of the network partially solves this problem of the combinatoric explosion of interconnections by reducing the number of independent weights that must be learned. There is only one independent weight for each distinct set of included angles formed by triplets of input pixels. However, some storage must still be used to associate each triplet of pixels with a set of included angles. The most severe limitation of this method is that the number of possible triplet combinations increases as the size of the input field increases. In an $N \times N$ pixel input field, combinations of three pixels can be chosen in N^2-choose-3 ways. Thus, for a 9×9 pixel input field, the number of possible triplet combinations is 81-choose-3 or 85,320. Increasing the resolution to 128×128 pixels increases the number of possible interconnections to 128^2-choose-3, or 7.3×10^{11}, a number too great to store on most machines. On our Sun 3/60 with 30 MB of swap space, we can store a maximum of 5.6 million (integer) interconnections, limiting the input field size for fully connected third order networks to 18×18 pixels. Furthermore, this number of interconnections ($\sim 10^{12}$) is far too large to allow a parallel implementation in any hardware technology that will be commonly available in the foreseeable future.

To circumvent this limitation, in previous research we evaluated various strategies of connecting only a subset of input pixel triplets to the output node [8]. In particular, we evaluated regional connectivity in which triplets of pixels are connected to the output node only if the distances between all of the pixels composing the triplet fell within a set of preselected regions. Using this strategy, the input field size was increased to 64×64 while still retaining many of the advantages shown previously, such as a small number of training passes, training on only one view of each object, and successful recognition invariant to in-plane rotation and translation. However, using regional connectivity, we were unable to recognize images invariant to changes in scale. Also, as the input field size increased, the amount of time for each pass on a sequential machine increased dramatically. The 64×64 pixel input field network required on the order of days on a Sun 3/60 to learn to distinguish between two objects. This is despite the fact that the number of interconnections was greatly reduced from the fully connected version. The number of logical comparisons required to determine whether the distances between pixels fall within the preselected regions was still huge.

In the following section, we describe a coarse coding algorithm [9] which allows a third order network to be used with an input field size practical for object recognition problems while still retaining its ability to recognize images that have been scaled, translated, or rotated in-plane in an input field of at least 4096×4096 pixels. Training takes just a few passes and training time is on the order of minutes, instead of days, for regionally connected networks.

Coarse Coding. The coarse coding representation presented is a variation of a distributed representation described by Hinton [10]. A distributed representation is a memory scheme in which each feature is represented by a pattern of activity over many units [11]. By using units that are very coarsely tuned, a network requires few units to encode many features accurately. The maximum number of features is determined by the density and degree of overlap of the units' receptive fields [12].

The coarse coding algorithm involves overlaying fields of coarser pixels in order to represent an input field composed of smaller pixels [13], as shown in Figure 10.13. Figure 10.13*a* shows an input field of size 10×10 pixels. In Figure 10.13*b*,

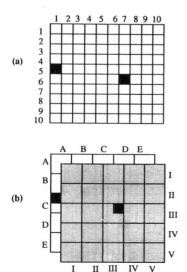

Figure 10.13 An example of a coarse coded input field. (a) A 10×10 pixel input field. (b) Two fields of 5×5 coarse pixels.

we show two offset but overlapping fields, each of size 5×5 coarse pixels. In this case, each coarse field is composed of pixels that are twice as large (in both dimensions) as in Figure 10.13a. To reference an input pixel using the two coarse fields requires two sets of coordinates. For instance, pixel ($x = 7$, $y = 6$) on the original image would be referenced as the set of coarse pixels (($x = $ D, $y = $ C) & ($x = $ III, $y = $ III)), assuming a coordinate system of (A, B, C, D, E) for coarse field 1 and (I, II, III, IV, V) for coarse field 2. This is a one-to-one transformation. That is, each pixel on the original image can be represented by a unique set of coarse pixels.

The above transformation of an image to a set of smaller images can be used to greatly increase the resolution possible in a higher order neural network. For example, a fully connected third order network for a 10×10 pixel input field requires 10^2-choose-3, or 161,700, interconnections. Using 2 fields of 5×5 coarse pixels requires just 5^2-choose-3, or 2300, interconnections, accessed once for each field. The number of required interconnections is reduced by a factor of ~ 70. For a larger input field, the savings are even greater. For instance, for a 100×100 pixel input field, a fully connected third order network requires 1.6×10^{11} interconnections. If we represent this field as 10 fields of 10×10 coarse pixels, only 161,700 interconnections are necessary. The number of interconnections is decreased by a factor of $\sim 100,000$.

One aspect of coarse coding that needs to be addressed is how the part of the image that is not intersected by all coarse fields is handled. That is, how is pixel (1, 5) in the original image shown in Figure 10.13a represented using the two fields in Figure 10.13b. There are at least two ways to implement coarse coding: (1) with wraparound, or (2) by using only the intersection of the fields. If coarse coding is implemented using wraparound, pixel (1, 5) could be represented as the set of coarse pixels ((A, C) & (V,II)). On the other hand, of coarse coding is implemented as the intersection of the coarser fields, the two fields shown in Figure 10.13b would be able to uniquely describe an input field of 9×9 pixels, not 10×10.

Using wraparound, the relationship between the number of coarse fields (n), input field size (IFS), and coarse field size (CFS) in each dimension is given by

$$\text{IFS} = (\text{CFS} * n) \qquad (10.10)$$

On the other hand, using the intersection of fields implementation, the relationship between number of coarse fields, input field size, and coarse field size in each dimension is given by

$$\text{IFS} = (\text{CFS} * n) - (n - 1) \qquad (10.11)$$

The effective input field size IFS is not significantly different with either implementation for small n.

Coarse Coding and HONNs.   As discussed in the previous section, coding an image as a set of coarser images greatly increases the size of the input field possible in a higher order neural network. As an example of how coarse coding can be applied to HONNs, refer to Figure 10.14. In order to train the network to distinguish between a T and a C in an 8 × 8-pixel input field, we could either train the network on the two images shown in Figure 10.14*a* directly or apply coarse coding. Simulations presented in Section 10.2.2 demonstrated the first option. With coarse coding implemented with wraparound, as explained previously, there are two possible combinations which will provide an effective input field of 8 × 8 pixels: two fields of 4 × 4 coarse pixels or four fields of 2 × 2 pixels. Both possibilities are shown in Figure 10.14*b*.

Applying coarse coding by using two fields of 4 × 4 coarse pixels, the two images shown in Figure 10.14*a* are transformed into the four images shown in Figure 10.14*c*. Training of the network then proceeds in the usual way with one modification: the transfer function thresholds the value obtained from summing the weighted triangles over *all* coarse images associated with each training object. That is,

$$y = 1, \quad \text{if } \{\Sigma_n (\Sigma_j \Sigma_k \Sigma_l w_{jkl} x_j x_k x_l)\} > 0$$

$$y = 0, \quad \text{otherwise}$$

(10.12)

where j, k, and l range from one to the coarse pixel size squared, n ranges from one to the number of coarse fields, the xs represent coarse pixel values, and w_{jkl} represents the weight associated with the triplet of inputs (j, k, l).

During testing, an input image is again transformed into a set of coarse images. Each of these coarser vectors are then presented to the network and an output value determined using Eq. (10.12).

Simulation Results: Coarse-Coded Networks. We evaluated the coarse coding technique using the expanded version of the T/C problem. Implementing coarse coding using the intersection of fields, we increased the input image resolution for

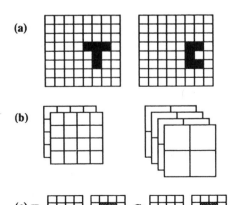

(a)

(b)

(c) T: C:

Figure 10.14 Using coarse coded fields with higher order neural networks. (a) Two training images in an 8 × 8 pixel input field. (b) Two possible configurations of coarse pixels to represent the input field in (a). (c) Coarse coded representation of the training images in (a) using two layers of 4 × 4 coarse pixels.

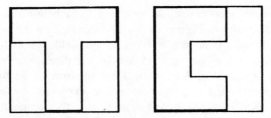

Figure 10.15 *A binary edge-only representation of a T and a C, drawn in a 127 × 127 pixel window.*

the T/C problem to 127 × 127 pixels using nine fields of 15 × 15 coarse pixels. The network was trained on just two images: the largest T and C possible within the input field, as shown in Figure 10.15. Training took just five passes.

A complete test set of translated, scaled, and one degree rotated views of the two objects in a 127 × 127-pixel input field consists of ~135 million images. Assuming a test rate of 200 images per hour, it would take about 940-computer-months to test all possible views. Accordingly, we limited the testing to a representative subset consisting of four sets:

1. All translated views, but with the same orientation and scale as the training images.
2. All views rotated in-plane at 1° intervals, centered at the same position as the training images, but only 60% of the size of the training images.
3. All scaled views of the objects, in the same orientation and centered at the same position as the training images.
4. A representative subset of approximately 100 simultaneously translated, rotated, and scaled views of the two objects.

The network achieved 100% accuracy on all test images in sets (1) and (2). Furthermore, the network recognized, with 100% accuracy, all scaled views, from test set (3), down to 38% of the original size. Objects smaller than 38% were all classified as C's. Finally, for test set (4), the network correctly recognized all images larger than 38% of the original size, regardless of the orientation or position of the test image.

A third order network also learned to distinguish between practical images such as a space shuttle orbiter versus an F-18 aircraft (Fig. 10.16) in up to a 127 × 127-pixel input field. In this case, training took just six passes through the training set, which consisted of just one (binary, edge-only) view of each aircraft. As for the T/C problem, the network achieved 100% recognition accuracy of translated and in-plane rotated views of the two images. Additionally, the network recognized images scaled to almost half the size of the training images, regardless of their position or orientation.

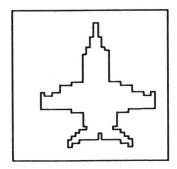 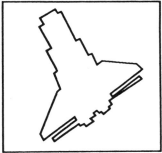

Figure 10.16 *A binary edge-only representation of an F-18 aircraft and a space shuttle orbiter.*

Coarse Coding and Scale Invariance.   As the above examples illustrate, the amount of scale invariance a network achieves is not constant. As discussed in Section 10.3.1, invariance to scale is affected by the resolution to which the included angles α, β, and γ are calculated. Briefly, as the resolution of the input field is increased, the resolution to which α, β, and γ are calculated can also be increased, generally increasing scale invariance. Angle resolutions of either 5, 10, or 20° were used in all the simulations presented below.

In addition, scale invariance varies with the coarse field size (CFS) as well as the number of coarse fields (n) used. In this section, we discuss these two relationships in more detail.

In order to determine how CFS and n affect scale invariance, we simulated three scenarios using a third order network trained on the T/C problem:

1. For a given CFS, we varied n.
2. For a given n, we varied CFS.
3. For a given input field size (IFS), we varied both CFS and n.

Table 10.1 shows the values for n, CFS, and IFS used for scenario one along with the scale invariance attained. The metric given for invariance is the ratio of the size of the training images, which were the largest scale T and C that could be drawn in the given IFS, to the size of the smallest test images correctly identified. Using a coarse field size of 10×10 pixels, we increased the number of fields, thereby increasing the effective input field size up to 127×127 pixels. As Figure 10.17 illustrates, the amount of scale invariance attained did not vary considerably relative to the number of coarse fields used.*

Similarly, Table 10.2 shows the values for n, CFS, IFS, and scale invariance

---

*For $n = 1$ and CFS $= 10 \times 10$, test images smaller than the training images could not be drawn, and the network was limited to scale invariance of 1. For $n = 2$ and CFS $= 10 \times 10$, three scales of T and C could be drawn giving three possibilities for scale invariance: 1, 1.5, or 2.1.

TABLE 10.1 Values Used for Determining the Relationship between the Number of Coarse Fields (*n*) and Scale Invariance, Assuming the Coarse Field Size (CFS) Remains Constant

CFSxCFS	n	IFSxIFS	Scale invariance
10x10	1	10x10	1.00
	2	19x19	1.49
	3	28x28	1.79
	4	37x37	1.72
	5	46x46	1.67
	6	55x55	1.64
	7	64x64	1.75
	8	73x73	1.72
	9	82x82	1.70
	10	91x91	1.75
	11	100x100	1.72
	12	109x109	1.79
	13	118x118	1.79
	14	127x127	1.75

Note: Scale invariance is the ratio of the size of the training images (which were the largest views of the two objects that could be drawn in the given IFS) to the size of the smallest test images correctly identified. Also shown is the effective input field size (IFS).

attained for scenario two. Using five coarse fields, we increased the coarse field size up to the maximum possible (18 × 18 pixels, as previously shown). As illustrated in Figure 10.18, as the coarse field size is increased, the amount of scale invariance attained generally increases.

Finally, for scenario three, we designed a third order network to solve the T/C

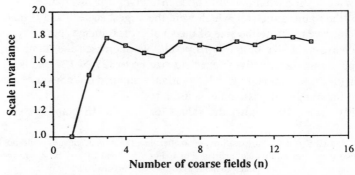

Figure 10.17 *Relationship between scale invariance and the number of coarse fields used in coarse coding an image. The coarse field size is constant.*

**TABLE 10.2 Values Used for
Determining the Relationship
between the Coarse Field Size
(CFS) and Scale Invariance,
Assuming the Number of Coarse
Fields (*n*) Remains Constant**

n	CFSxCFS	IFSxIFS	Scale invariance
5	4x4	16x16	1.00
	5x5	21x21	1.16
	6x6	26x26	1.14
	7x7	31x31	1.43
	8x8	36x36	1.20
	9x9	41x41	2.63
	10x10	46x46	1.67
	11x11	51x51	1.70
	12x12	56x56	1.49
	13x13	61x61	1.67
	14x14	66x66	1.81
	15x15	71x71	1.92
	16x16	76x76	1.67
	17x17	81x81	2.27
	18x18	86x86	2.33

Note: Also shown is the effective input
field size (IFS).

problem in an input field as close to 127×127 pixels as possible using the intersection of fields implementation. Table 10.3 shows the values for *n*, CFS, and IFS
used in simulations, as well as the scale invariance attained. As illustrated in Figure 10.19, the amount of scale invariance attained generally increases as the coarse
field size increases. Alternatively, scale invariance increases as the number of fields
decreases.

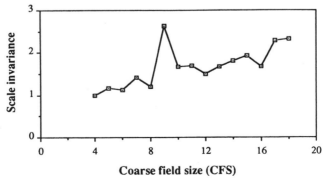

Figure 10.18 *Relationship between scale invariance and the number of coarse fields used
in coarse coding an image. The coarse field size is constant.*

**TABLE 10.3 Values Used for
Determining the Relationship
between the Coarse Field Size
(CFS), the Number of Fields (*n*), and
Scale Invariance Attained**

CFSxCFS	n	IFSxIFS	Scale invariance
3x3	63	127x127	1.00
4x4	42	127x127	1.20
5x5	31	125x125	1.18
6x6	25	126x126	1.14
7x7	21	127x127	1.14
8x8	18	127x127	1.27
9x9	16	129x129	1.35
10x10	14	127x127	1.75
11x11	13	131x131	1.43
12x12	12	133x133	2.00
13x13	11	133x133	2.56
14x14	10	131x131	2.38
15x15	9	127x127	2.63
16x16	9	136x136	1.72
17x17	8	129x129	2.70
18x18	8	137x137	3.45

Note: Also shown is the effective input field
size (IFS).

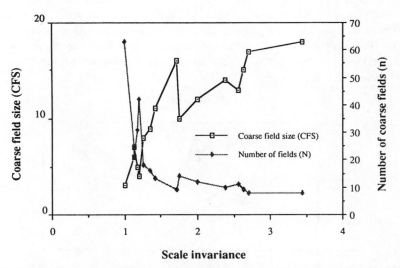

Figure 10.19 *Relationship between scale invariance and the coarse field size and number
of coarse fields. Both coarse field size and number of coarse fields are allowed to vary while
the input image size is held approximately constant.*

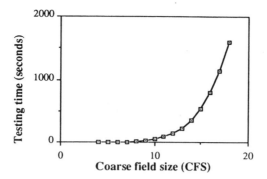

Figure 10.20 *Relationship between learning time and coarse field size. The input field size was held approximately constant at 127 pixels and the number of passes required to learn to distinguish between the training objects did not vary significantly relative to the coarse field size (CFS).*

In general, a larger coarse field size yields greater scale invariance. However, the testing time also increases as the coarse field size increases, as illustrated in Figure 10.20. Thus, if less scale invariance can be tolerated, a desired input field size can be represented with a smaller coarse field size and greater number of coarse fields. Even if the speed is not critical, scale invariance can be increased but is still limited by the coarse field size. In the next section, we examine this limit as well as some of the other limits of coarse coding.

Limits of Coarse Coding.   This section discusses some of the limitations of the coarse coding technique including the minimum and maximum coarse field size, the minimum and maximum number of fields that can be used and still achieve position, scale, and rotation invariant recognition, and the maximum input field resolution possible.

The minimum possible coarse field size is determined by the training images. The network is unable to distinguish between the training images when the size of each coarse pixel is increased to the point where the training images no longer produce unique coarse coded representations. As an example, for the T/C problem, the minimum course field size that still produces unique representations is 3×3 pixels.

In contrast, the maximum limit is determined by the HONN architecture and the memory available for its implementation, and not by the coarse coding technique itself. As discussed previously, the number of possible triplet combinations in a third order network is N^2-choose-3 for an $N \times N$-pixel input field and given the memory constraints of our Sun 3/60, the maximum possible coarse field size is 18×18 pixels.

Regarding the number of coarse fields which can be used and still achieve PSRI object recognition, the minimum is one field, whereas the maximum has not yet been reached. A minimum of one coarse field represents the noncoarse coded HONN case discussed in Section 10.2.2. In order to determine the limit for the maximum number of fields possible, we ran simulations on the T/C problem coded with a variable number of 3 × 3 coarse pixels. A third order network was able to learn to distinguish between the two characters in less than ten passes in an input field size of up to 4095 × 4095 pixels using 2047 fields.* Increasing the number of fields beyond this was not attempted because 4096 × 4096 is the maximum resolution available on most image processing hardware that would be used in a complete HONN based vision system. Also, each object in such a large field requires 16 MB of storage space. It takes only a few such objects to fill up a disk.†

Finally, as with the maximum number of coarse fields, the maximum input field resolution possible with coarse coded HONNs has not been delimited. As discussed above, we trained a third order network on the T/C problem in up to a 4096 × 4096 pixel input field. We expect a resolution of 4096 × 4096 is sufficient for most object recognition tasks. Notwithstanding, we also expect a greater resolution is possible.

10.4   TOLERANCE TO NOISE

All of the above simulations demonstrate the performance of HONNs in a noisefree environment. In this section, we explore the recognition accuracy of HONNs with nonideal test images. We consider white Gaussian noise and occlusion.

We evaluated the performance of HONNs with noisy images on two object recognition problems: an SR-71/U-2 discrimination problem and an SR-71/space shuttle discrimination problem. All simulations used a coarse coded, third order network designed for a 127 × 127 pixel input field. For ease of implementation, we used the intersection of fields approach to coarse coding. Also, because we wanted scale invariance over the range between 70 and 100% of the original size, we used large coarse pixels and a small resolution for the angles α, β, and γ in Eq. (10.2), as explained in [3, 6]. Specifically, we used nine fields of 15 × 15 coarse pixels and an angle resolution of 10°. Each instantiation of the network was trained on just one binary, edge-only view of each object, as shown in Figure 10.21, and training required less than ten passes through the training set.

The training sets were generated from actual models of the aircraft. The 8-bit gray level images of the aircraft are shown in Figure 10.22. The images were thresholded to produce binary images, and then edge detected using a digital Laplacian convolution filter with a positive derivative to produce the silhouettes shown in Figure 10.21. For rotated and scaled views of the objects, the original gray level images were first scaled, then rotated, and then thresholded and edge-detected. Because the position of the object is irrelevant in Eq. (10.2), ensuring translation

*An input field resolution of 4096 × 4096 was also achieved by using 273 fields of 16 × 16 coarse pixels.
†Note that this is not a limitation of the coarse coding scheme itself. If a 4096 × 4096 pixel image could be stored on disk, using the intersection of fields approach to coarse coding, we could represent it as 228 fields of 18 × 18 coarse pixels, requiring only 5.6 MB memory.

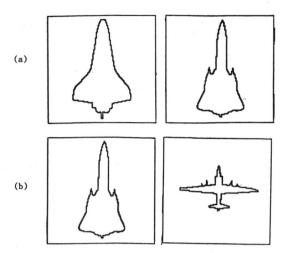

(a)

(b)

Figure 10.21 *Training images. One binary edge-only view each for (a) space shuttle orbiter vs. SR-71 and (b) SR-71 vs. U-2.*

invariance, the test images were positioned arbitrarily. Notice that the profiles of the SR-71 and space shuttle are somewhat similar whereas those of the SR-71 and U-2 are very different.

10.4.1 White Gaussian Noise

To test the tolerance of higher order neural networks to white noise, each instantiation of the network (one for the SR-71/U-2 problem and one for the shuttle/SR-71 problem) was tested on 1200 images generated by modifying the 8-bit gray level values of the original images using a Gaussian distribution of random numbers with a mean of 0 and a standard deviation of between 1 and 50. The test set consisted of fifty images (with increasing standard deviation from 1 to 50)* for each of four scales ranging from 70 to 100% in 10% increments, and each rotation of 0, 30, and 45°. For 90° angles, our rotation routine produces an image in which all combinations of three-input pixels produce the same included angles as those produced by the unrotated image. Thus, the three angles used represent a much wider variety of distorted images than is initially apparent. The noisy images were then binarized and edge-detected. Typical test images, along with their values for standard deviation (σ), scale, and rotation, are shown in Figure 10.23.

To have an affect on the processed binary image, the modified gray level value must cross the threshold value. Hence, the amount of noise tolerated will depend on the distribution of gray level values in the original images such that for a

---

*For values falling outside [0, 255], the modified gray scale value was rounded to the nearest in-range value.

Figure 10.22 *8-bit gray level images from which the training images are generated: (a) space shuttle, (b) SR-71, and (c) U-2.*

given σ, images with low contrast foreground/background values appear noisier than images with high contrast foreground/background values. In our case, the lighting conditions present when the images in Figure 10.22 were taken produced dark areas with gray level values of approximately 20 and light areas with gray level values of approximately 220, with decreasing light area values near the edges

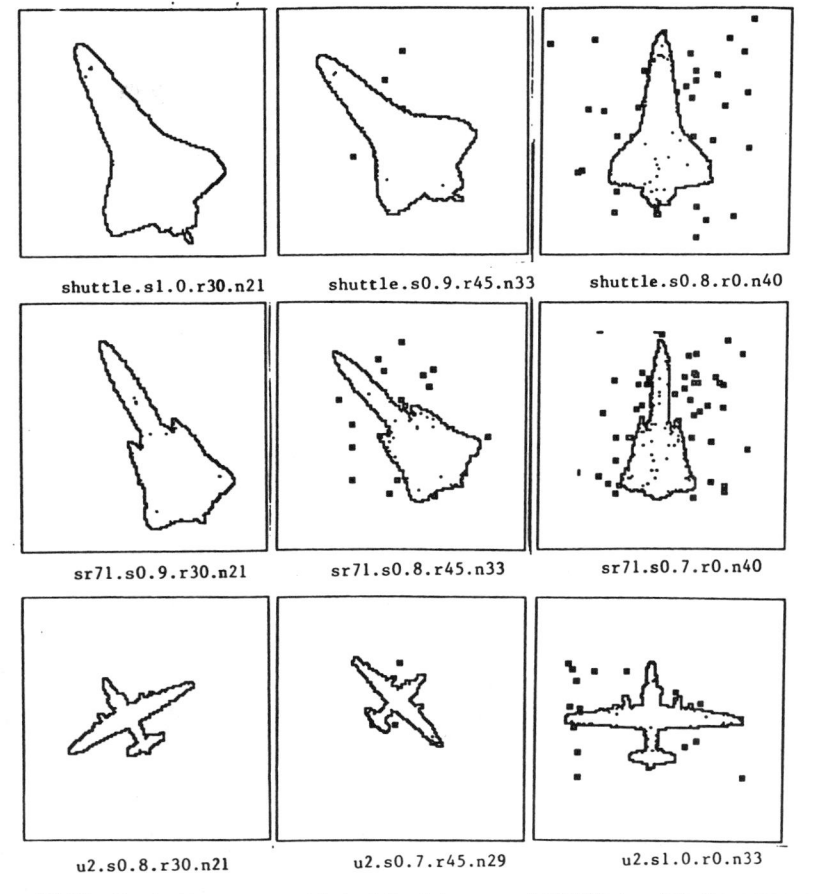

shuttle.s1.0.r30.n21 shuttle.s0.9.r45.n33 shuttle.s0.8.r0.n40

sr71.s0.9.r30.n21 sr71.s0.8.r45.n33 sr71.s0.7.r0.n40

u2.s0.8.r30.n21 u2.s0.7.r45.n29 u2.s1.0.r0.n33

Figure 10.23 *Typical images used to test the tolerance of HONNs to white Gaussian noise. Test images were generated automatically by adding a normally distributed random gray value (with a mean of 0 and a standard deviation from 1 to 50) to the original gray level value and then binarizing and edge-detecting the resulting image. Values for scale, rotation, and standard deviation are shown under each image. For example, "s0.7.r30.n20" is an image of scale 70%, rotation 30°, and standard deviation of 20. For each object, we show a noise level recognized with an accuracy of 100, 75, and 50%.*

and where the original model had decals or other anomalies, such as windows. Our threshold value was 128. Thus, our results show the performance of HONNs with white noise in almost ideal conditions.

The results are summarized in Figure 10.24. The network performed with 100% accuracy for our test set for a standard deviation of up to 23 on the SR-71/U-2 problem and 26 on the shuttle/SR-71 problem. For the similar images of the shuttle and SR-71, the recognition accuracy quickly decreased to 75% at a σ of 30 and to 50% (which corresponds to no better than random guessing) for σ greater than 33. The SR-71/U-2 remained above 75% accuracy up to a σ of 35 (or ~14% of the

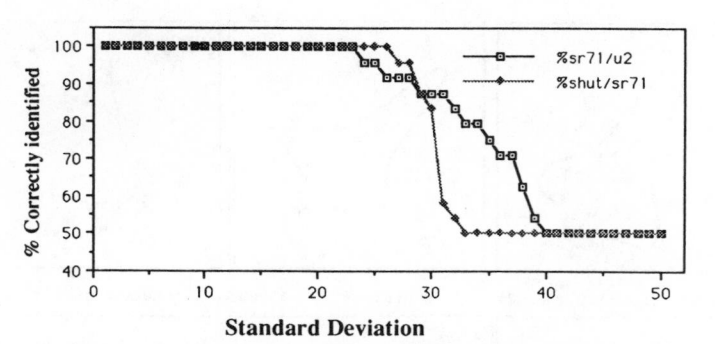

Figure 10.24   *Tolerance of HONNs to white Gaussian noise introduced as in Figure 10.23. Each instantiation of a third order network designed to be invariant to distortions in scale, translation, and in-plane rotation (one for the SR-71/U-2 problem and one for the shuttle/ SR-71 problem) was tested on 1200 images generated by modifying the 8-bit gray level values of the original images using a Gaussian distribution of random numbers with a mean of 0 and a standard deviation between 1 and 50. The test set consisted of fifty images (with increasing standard deviation from 1 to 50) for the four scales ranging from 70 to 100% in 10% increments, and each rotation of 0, 30, and 45°. For 90° angles, our rotation routine produces an image in which all combinations of three-input pixels produce the same included angles as those produced by the unrotated image. Thus, the three angles used represent a much wider variety of distorted images than is initially apparent. The noisy images were then binarized and edge-detected.*

gray level range) and gradually decreased to 50% at a σ of 40 (or ~16% of the gray level range). If we define "good performance" as greater than 75% accuracy, HONNs have good performance for σ up to 35 (or ~14% of the gray level range) for images with very distinct profiles and σ up to 30 (or ~12% of the gray level range) for images with similar profiles. It should be noted that these results apply only to images with an ideal separation of background/foreground gray levels. For images with a lower contrast, the performance may be quite different.

10.4.2   Occlusion

To test the tolerance of HONNs to occlusion, the two instantiations (one for the shuttle/SR-71 problem and one for the SR-71/U-2 problem) of the third order network built to be invariant to scale, in-plane rotation, and translation as described above were tested on occluded versions of the image pairs for each of four scales ranging from 70 to 100% in 10% increments, and each rotation of 0, 30, and 45°. Again, as for white noise, these three angles represent a much wider variety of distorted images than is initially apparent. We started with binary, edge-only images and added automatically-generated occlusions based on four variable parameters: the size of the occlusion, the number of occlusions, the type of occlusion, and the position of the occlusion. Objects used for occlusion were squares with a linear dimension between one and twenty-nine pixels. The number of occlusion objects per image varied from one to four, and the randomly chosen type of occlusion determined whether the occlusion objects were added to or subtracted from

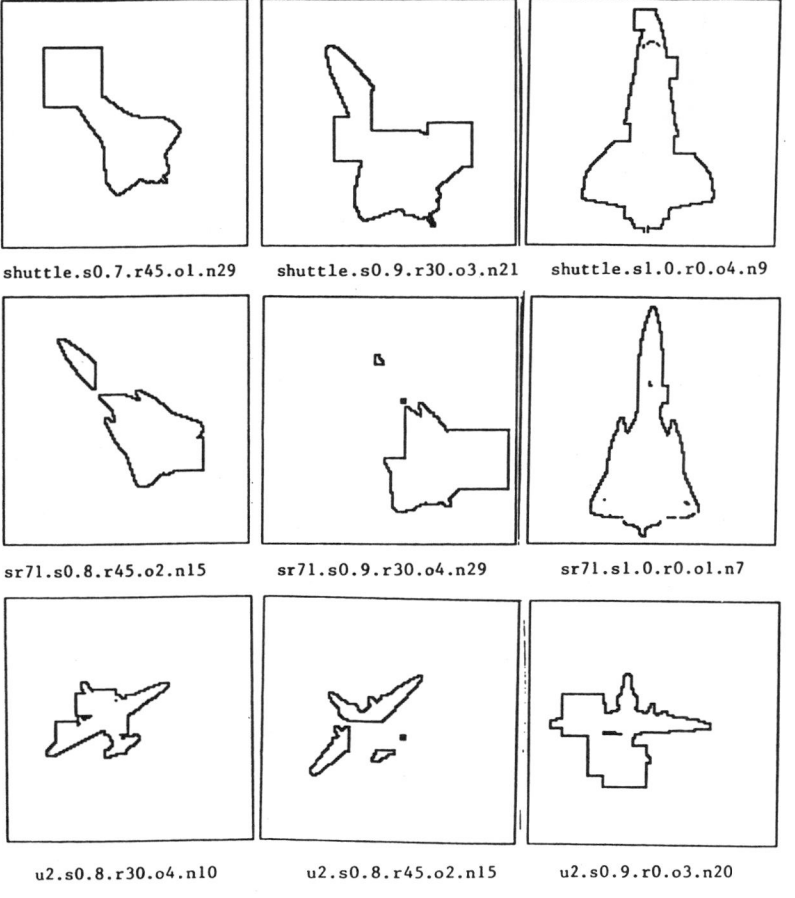

shuttle.s0.7.r45.o1.n29   shuttle.s0.9.r30.o3.n21   shuttle.s1.0.r0.o4.n9

sr71.s0.8.r45.o2.n15   sr71.s0.9.r30.o4.n29   sr71.s1.0.r0.o1.n7

u2.s0.8.r30.o4.n10   u2.s0.8.r45.o2.n15   u2.s0.9.r0.o3.n20

Figure 10.25 *Typical images used to test the tolerance of HONNs with respect to occlusion. Values for number of occlusions and occlusion size range are shown under each typical test image. For example, "s1.0.r30.o3.n20" is an image of scale 100%, rotation 30°, and three 20 pixel occlusions.*

the original image. Finally, the occlusions were randomly (uniform distribution) placed on the profile of the training images. The test set consisted of 10 samples for each combination of scale, rotation angle, occlusion size, and number of occlusions for a total of 13,920 test images per training image or 27,840 test images per recognition problem. Typical test images are shown in Figure 10.25.

As shown in Figure 10.26, the performance of HONNs with occluded test images depends mostly on the number and size of occluding objects and to a lesser degree on the similarity of the training images. In the case of the shuttle/SR-71 recognition problem, the network performed with 100% accuracy for our test set for one 16-pixel occlusion and up to four 10-pixel occlusions. It performed with better than 75% accuracy ("good performance") for up to four 19-pixel occlu-

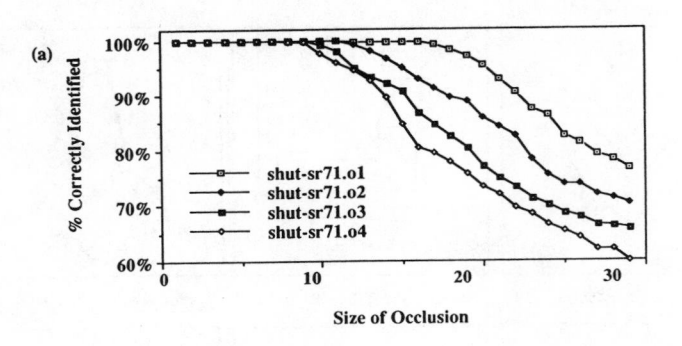

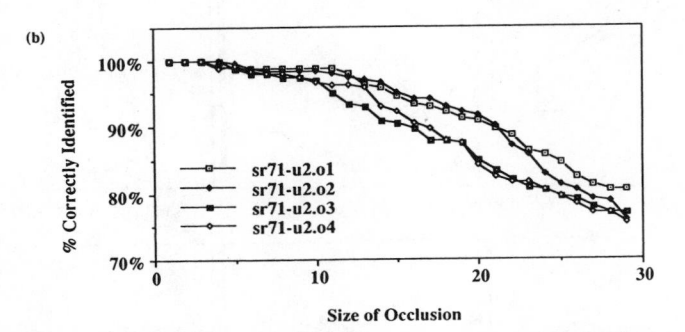

Figure 10.26 *Tolerance of HONNs with respect to occlusion: (a) shuttle/SR-71 discrimination problem and (b) SR-71/U-2 discrimination problem. Each graph shows the recognition accuracy for images generated as stated in the text.*

sions, three 21-pixel occlusions, two 24-pixel occlusions, and one 29-pixel occlusion.

For the SR-71/U-2 problem, the network exhibited good performance for the entire test set but achieved 100% accuracy only for one 4-pixel occlusion and up to four 3-pixel occlusions.

10.5 COMPARISON TO OTHER APPROACHES

In the position, scale, and rotation invariant object recognition domain, higher order neural networks offer numerous advantages over both neural and nonneural approaches. This section will discuss some of the limitations of the other methods. We consider back-propagation-trained first order networks, the neocognitron, and a symbolic classification method, ID3.

Back-prop-trained first order networks [1], illustrated in Figure 10.27, are the most popular method used in neural network based object recognition. The training process consists of applying input vectors sequentially and adjusting the network weights using a gradient descent learning rule until the input vectors produce the

Output nodes

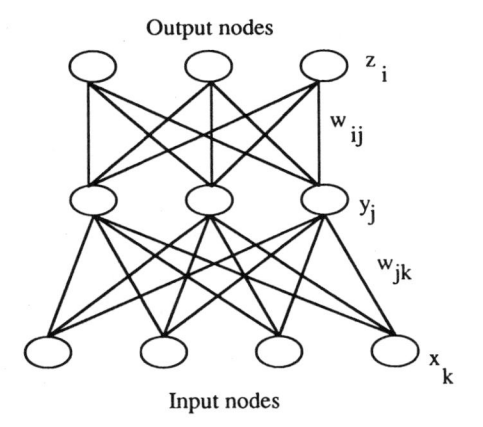

z_i

w_{ij}

y_j

w_{jk}

x_k

Input nodes

Figure 10.27   *First order neural network. In a first order neural network, input nodes are connected directly to output or hidden layer nodes. No advantage is taken of any known relationships between the input nodes.*

desired output vectors within some predetermined error. For a first order network to learn to distinguish between a set of objects independent of their position, scale, or in-plane orientation, the network must be trained on a large subset of distorted views. The desired effect of including distorted views into the training set is that the hidden layers will extract the necessary invariant features and the network will generalize the input vectors so that it can also recognize distorted views that are not part of the training set. Such generalization has been demonstrated in numerous simulations, including Rumelhart's T/C problem [7]. Typically, because first order networks do not take advantage of predefined relationships between the input nodes, they require a large number of training passes to generalize the concepts behind the distortions. Also, even after extensive training with a large training set, they usually achieve only 80–90% recognition accuracy on novel examples [1, 14].

A different approach to neural based object recognition is the neocognitron. The human visual system is believed to be organized in a hierarchical structure in which first simple features are extracted and then combined into more complicated features. Moreover, a neuron in a higher stage of the hierarchy generally receives signals from a wide area of the preceding stage, thus correcting for small positional errors in the input. The neocognitron is based on this model of the human visual system.

Like the visual system, the neocognitron is arranged as a hierarchy of layers. The first stage is the input layer—a two-dimensional array of receptor cells. Each successive stage consists of two layers: "S-cells" followed by "C-cells." S-cells are feature extracting cells. The S-cells in the lower stages of the hierarchy extract local features such as lines in a particular orientation, whereas S-cells in higher stages extract global features such as substructures of the training pattern. Within each stage, a C-cell receives signals from a group of S-cells that extract the same feature, but from a slightly different position. Thus, the C-cells desensitize the model to the exact position of the input. For a mathematical analysis of the training process, see Fukushima [2].

Following training, the neocognitron can recognize a pattern independent of its position in the input field, a slight change in size, or a slight deformation. Though deformations can include small rotations (up to a few degrees), the neocognitron has not been demonstrated for rotation invariance over a wider range [2].

The neocognitron has at least two limitations. First, the number of cells in the model increases almost linearly with the number of objects it is required to learn to distinguish. This makes the training process very slow. Also, the weights are pattern specific and thus the network must be completely retrained for each new set of patterns.

We also compared HONNs to a symbolic learning algorithm, ID3 [15]. ID3 was chosen as a representative of the symbolic learning approach primarily for consistency with previous comparisons [16–18], in which it was studied because of its simplicity and popularity. It is the ancestor of several commercial rule induction systems and has been extensively tested on large data sets. Further, in experimental comparisons, ID3 generally performs as well or better than other symbolic learning algorithms [15].

The ID3 approach to pattern recognition and classification consists of a procedure for building an efficient decision tree from a set of training objects represented by attributes or feature values. At each node of the tree, the training objects are partitioned based on the value of the feature which provides the most information. The training set is recursively decomposed in this manner until the tree can correctly classify all the objects in the training set. A detailed description of the algorithm used to build a decision tree is presented in Quinlan [15].

Like back-prop-trained first order networks, ID3 requires a large, if not exhaustive, training set of distorted images. Thus, if training data is difficult to obtain, HONNs have an advantage over ID3. Also, if the input pixels are used as features, ID3 cannot always build a decision tree by decomposing the training set based on the value of just one feature at a time [19].

10.6 CONCLUSIONS

The most important advantage of the HONN architecture is that distortion invariance can be incorporated into the network and does not need to be learned. Compared with other neural network methods, such as back-prop-trained first order neural networks and the neocognitron, or symbolic learning algorithms, such as Quinlan's ID3, HONNs have demonstrated clear advantages in terms of training time, training set size, and recognition accuracy.

In simulations, we showed that third order neural networks can be trained to distinguish between two objects regardless of their position, angular orientation, or scale and achieve 100% accuracy on test images characterized by the built-in distortions. Only one view of each object was required for learning, and the network successfully learned to distinguish between all distorted views of the two objects in tens of passes, requiring only minutes on a Sun 3/60 workstation. In contrast, other neural network approaches require thousands of passes through a training set consisting of a much larger number of training images.

The major limitations of HONNs is that the size of the input field is limited because of the memory required for the large number of interconnections in a fully connected network. In an $N \times N$-pixel input field, combinations of three pixels can be chosen in N^2-choose-3 ways. Thus, for a 128 $\times$ 128-pixel input field, the number of possible triplet combinations is $\sim 7.3 \times 10^{11}$, a number too great to store on most machines. To circumvent this limitation, we demonstrate a coarse coding algorithm which allows a third order network to be used with a practical input field size of at least 4096 $\times$ 4096 pixels while retaining its ability to recognize images that have been scaled, translated, or rotated in-plane. As for non-coarse coded networks, training takes just a few passes and training time is on the order of minutes on a Sun 3/60 workstation.

Finally, we explored the tolerance of higher order neural networks (HONNs) to white Gaussian noise and to occlusion. We demonstrated that for images with an ideal separation of background/foreground gray levels, it takes a great amount of white noise in the gray level images to affect the binary, edge-only images used for training and testing the system to a sufficient degree that the performance of HONNs was seriously degraded. Specifically, we demonstrated that the gray level values must be changed by a standard deviation of at least 10% before the recognition accuracy of HONNs drops below 100%. HONNs continue to show good performance (greater than 75% recognition accuracy) on white noise for a standard deviation up to $\sim 14\%$. For images with a lower contrast, the performance may be quite different.

HONNs are also robust with respect to occlusion. We trained a third order network on two sets of images (shuttle vs. SR-71 and SR-71 vs. U-2) and tested it using numerous occluded images generated automatically by varying the size of the occlusions, the number of occlusions, the type of occlusions, and the location of the occlusions. The amount of occlusion tolerated depends mostly on the size of the occlusion and the number of occlusions, and slightly on the similarity of the training images. On the test set for training images with very similar profiles, HONNs achieved 100% recognition accuracy for one occlusion of $\sim 13\%$ of the input field size and four occlusions of $\sim 7\%$ of the input field size. They showed good performance for one occlusion of $\sim 23\%$ of the input field size or four occlusions of $\sim 15\%$ of the input field size each. On the test set for training images with very different profiles, HONNs achieved 100% recognition accuracy for up to four occlusions of $\sim 2\%$ of the input field size and continued to show good performance for up to four occlusions of $\sim 23\%$ of the input field size each. For tolerance of occlusions, unlike for white Gaussian noise, the initial gray levels do not have as great an affect on the performance and thus can be generalized more readily.

REFERENCES

[1] D. E. Rumelhart, G. E. Hinton, and R. J. Williams, "Learning Internal Representations by Error Propagation," in D. E. Rumelhart and J. L. McClelland, Eds., *Parallel Distributed Processing: Explorations in the Microstructures of Cognition*, Vol. 1: *Foundations*, MIT Press, Cambridge, Mass., 1986, pp. 318–362.

[2] K. Fukushima, Analysis of the process of visual pattern recognition by the neocognitron, *Neural Networks*, 2, 413–420, (1989).

[3] G. L. Giles and T. Maxwell, Learning, invariances, and generalization in high-order neural networks, *Applied Optics*, 26, 4972–4978, (1987).

[4] G. L. Giles, R. D. Griffin, and T. Maxwell, Encoding geometric invariances in higher-order neural networks, *Neural Information Processing Systems, American Institute of Physics Conference Proc.*, 301–309, (1988).

[5] M. B. Reid, L. Spirkovska, and E. Ochoa, Simultaneous position, scale, and rotation invariant pattern classification using third-order neural networks, *Internat. J. of Neural Networks*, 1, 154–159 (1989).

[6] M. B. Reid, L. Spirkovska, and E. Ochoa, Rapid training of higher-order neural networks for invariant pattern recognition, *Proc. Joint Internat. Conf. on Neural Networks*, Vol. 1, 689–692 (1989).

[7] D. E. Rumelhart, G. E. Hinton, and R. J. Williams, "Learning Internal Representations by Error Propagation," in D. E. Rumelhart and J. L. McClelland, Eds., *Parallel Distributed Processing: Explorations in the Microstructures of Cognition*, Vol. 1: *Foundations*, MIT Press, Cambridge, Mass., 1986, pp. 348–352.

[8] L. Spirkovska and M. B. Reid, Connectivity strategies for higher-order neural networks applied to pattern recognition, *Proc. Joint Internat. Conf. on Neural Networks*, 121–126, (1990).

[9] L. Spirkovska and M. B. Reid, Coarse-coded higher-order neural networks for PSRI object recognition, *IEEE Trans. on Neural Networks* (to be pub.).

[10] G. E. Hinton, J. L. McClelland, and D. E. Rumelhart, "Distributed Representations," in D. E. Rumelhart and J. L. McClelland, Eds., *Parallel Distributed Processing: Explorations in the Microstructures of Cognition*, Vol. 1: *Foundations*, MIT Press, Cambridge, Mass., 1986, pp. 77–109.

[11] R. Rosenfeld and D. S. Touretzky, A survey of coarse-coded symbol memories, *Proc. 1988 Connectionist Models Summer School*, Carnegie Mellon University, Pittsburgh, 256–264 (1988).

[12] J. Sullins, "Value Cell Encoding Strategies," Tech. Rep. TR-165, Computer Science Department, University of Rochester, Rochester, N.Y. (1985).

[13] D. P. W. Graham, pers. comm.

[14] S. E. Troxel, S. K. Rogers, and M. Kabrisky, The use of neural networks in PSRI recognition, *Proc. Joint Internat. Conf. on Neural Networks*, 593–600 (1988).

[15] J. R. Quinlan, Induction of decision trees, *Machine Learning*, 1, 81–106 (1986).

[16] R. Mooney, J. Shavlik, G. Towell, and A. Gove, An experimental comparison of symbolic and connectionist learning algorithms, *Proc. 11th Internat. Joint Conf. on Artificial Intelligence*, 775–780 (1989).

[17] D. H. Fisher and K. B. McKusick, An empirical comparison of ID3 and back-propagation, *Proc. 11th Internat. Joint Conf. on Artificial Intelligence*, 788–793 (1989).

[18] S. M. Weiss and I. Kapouleas, An empirical comparison of pattern recognition, neural nets, and machine learning classification methods, *Proc. 11th Internat. Joint Conf. on Artificial Intelligence*, 781–787 (1989).

[19] L. Spirkovska and M. B. Reid, "An empirical comparison of ID3 and HONNs for distortion invariant object recognition," *Proc. 2nd Internat. Conf. on Tools for Artificial Intelligence* (1990), pp. 577–582.

CHAPTER 11 ⸺⸺⸺⸺⸺⸺⸺⸺

Visual Tracking with Object Classification: Neural Network Approach

A. DOBNIKAR
A. LIKAR, B. JURČIČ-ZLOBEC
D. PODBREGAR

11.1 INTRODUCTION

The tracking of moving objects and their classification belong among the classic tasks in the image processing problem domain. Because they are far from being trivial ones, every new approach is evaluated according to the best previously obtained solutions for the same problems. The neural network approach is one unconventional way of attacking the above problems, as it differs considerably from current computer technology.

In this chapter we introduce two specialized neural networks, one for tracking and another for classification functions. Their structures follow directly from the analysis of the corresponding functions. We show that this approach gives equally good results in tracking tasks as the optimal Kalman filtering procedure and that it even overcomes classification results obtained with Fourier transformations of an object's contours. With parallel processing real-time applications seem feasible.

It has been commonly accepted by the neural network society that all kinds of communications and basic processings regarding human environments can effectively be solved by the neural network approach. Some of the most well known problems in this area are certainly image and speech processing, pattern recognition and classification, and knowledge base processing. They are all closely related to the perception of environments, its analysis, and fundamental processing. Visual perception of the environment and its processing, with the goal of dynamic extraction from moving objects for tracking purposes and its additional classifi-

Fast Learning and Invariant Object Recognition, By Branko Souček and the IRIS Group.
ISBN 0-471-57430-9 © 1992 John Wiley & Sons, Inc.

cation, are typical but not at all trivial problems of this kind. As these are also problems of real time, as much as possible, parallelism in the processing should be involved, which makes hardware realization of the neural network approach even more promising.

The aim of this paper is to show that it is possible to solve the above problems successfully with the help of neural networks. We propose two neural networks, one for the visual tracking of moving objects and another one for their classification. The input images are taken sequentially from digitized TV pictures showing the 3-D object's movement along its trajectories. The following steps are necessary to solve the above problem: detection of objects in movement, attention to one of the moving objects, tracking, and classification of the observed object. Only the last two functions were realized with neural networks. The other two were less important for us, although they might be easily accomplished with neural networks as well.

In the following pages, we concentrate on the functions of the neural networks. Therefore, only a brief explanation of the preprocessor functions is given here. To perform detection of moving objects some time filtering should be realized over the sequence of input images. Scanning the obtained binary image enables us to make a window that encloses the moving objects within the limited area of interest. After attention to the particular window has been performed, the tracking procedure, realized by the first neural network TNN (Tracking Neural Network), is activated.

There are three steps that complete the tracking cycle. Each step is realized within one neural network layer, as is outlined in detail in the next section. The first is responsible for the topologically correct mapping of the input window into the neural network. The second performs the dynamic filtering function of the first order over the first layer. The dynamic model is a general one supposing noisy acceleration with zero average. The third layer finally detects the center of mass of the object within the observed window. It therefore defines the difference between the center of the object's mass and the center of the layers, which actually corresponds to the velocity of the object in the window. According to this difference, the movement of the camera is performed. Such prompt adjustment of the input window relative to the observed object ensures smooth tracking, provided that the object dynamics are within the expected ones.

When the tracking achieves sufficient quality, the classification function, performed by CNN (Classification Neural Network) is activated. Again the input information for the second neural network comes from the window under observation. The object in this window is centered because of the tracking procedure. As the number of projections from a 3-D object is very large, the classification procedure performed by the neural network must be invariant to all rotations around body axes and changes in size. The problem can be significantly reduced if the speed vector and range to the object are known. A reference system suitable for classification purposes can be chosen with an axis along the known projection of the speed vector to the image plane. The transformation of the detected shape to this system considerably reduces the number of possible attractors. Furthermore, measured range to the object makes the scale correction easy. The neural network must, therefore, be taught the rotations invariantly around the two axes of the image plane only. We extracted the learning patterns from the five 3-D TETRIS objects. Two layers of the classification neural network are proposed. The first one is the well known MAXNET layer or neural network that performs the so called "winner take all" function, while the second one simply associates the nearest attractor object to the input one with a corresponding output classification vector.

A lot of research work has already been done in the area of visual tracking and classification. Among the most important are the contributions of Malsburg and Willshaw [1, 2, 3], Amari [4], Kohonen [5, 6, 7], Fukushima [8], Carpenter and Grossberg [9], Hopfield [10], and, most recently, Seibert and Waxman [11], Coolen and Kuijk [12], Udpa and Udpa [13], Austin [14], Pao [15], and Hecht-Nielsen [16]. We were particularly influenced by Kohonen's self-organizing neural network for topologically correct mapping, the adaptive resonance theory of Grossberg and Carpenter, the multilayered Neocognitron invented by Fukushima, and recurrent neural networks introduced by Hopfield. Our basic idea was to design neural networks that follow directly the analysis of the tracking and classification functions. Therefore, we developed some special neural networks. From Kalman filter equations we derived a neural network layer that performs suboptimal filtering of dynamic and measurement noises. In constructing neural network topology for classification functions we followed the well known principle of matching the unknown object with attractors or references. Here we found that logical equivalence in the matching layer greatly improves the classificational results. The aim of this paper is to detail our approach and to compare it with the classic procedures.

11.2 TRACKING NEURAL NETWORK

Living organisms perform optical processing by perception of light through specialized sensors (eyes), recording it into a receptor (retina), and distributing to different areas of the neural system (cortex), where processing is actually realized. We somehow followed this basic concept by introducing Input Array (IA), where the camera's signals are stored, and the Multilayered Artificial Neural Network (MANN) for different kinds of processing. Figure 11.1 shows the organization of the system for visual tracking, based on this concept.

MANN accepts input information from IA, records it topologically correctly into the first layer, performs filtering in the second, and finds the center of mass in the third layer. Each succeeding layer of MANN performs specialized operations that represent higher or a more abstract degree of processing. Its operation is synchronized in such a way that all elements on the same layer act simultaneously, while succeeding layers are sequentially enabled.

11.2.1 The First Layer of MANN

The neurons in the first layer follow the well known equations in order to make a weighted record of input image from IA:

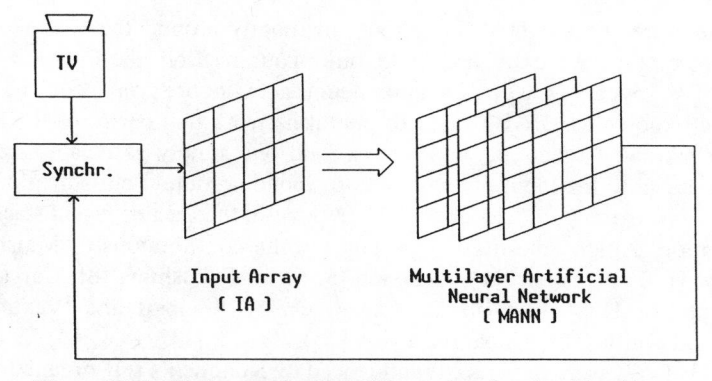

Figure 11.1   *Basic organization of the system for visual tracking.*

$$\eta_i = \left[\sum_{j=1}^{N} \omega_{ij} \xi_j \right], \quad i = 1, \cdots, N \tag{11.1}$$

Here and in all expressions that follow, if not specified otherwise, we used vector notation for input array and all layers of MANN. Therefore $\xi = (\xi_1, \xi_2, \ldots, \xi_N)$ is the binary vector that defines IA, $\eta = (\eta_1, \eta_2, \ldots, \eta_N)$ defines the first layer of MANN, while ω_{ij} denotes the weight from ξ_j to η_i. The weights from IA to the first layer are defined through the learning procedure, which uses an algorithm similar to the one described in Kohonen [5]. Considering the convergence of the learning procedure (Fig. 11.2), applied to the visual tracking case, the dis-

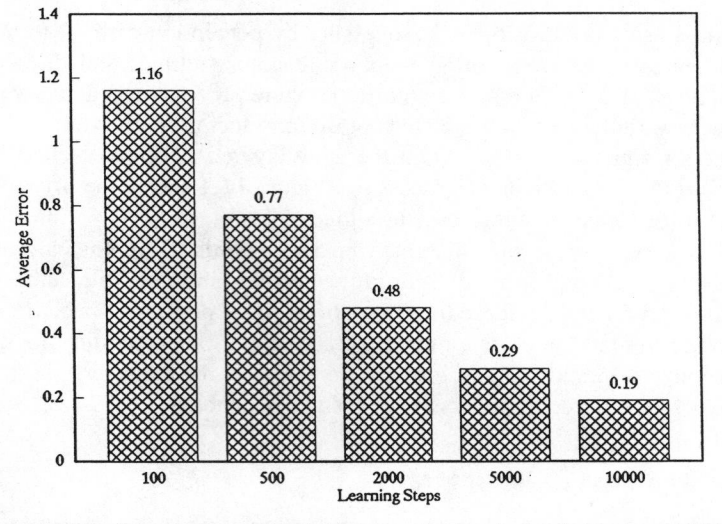

Figure 11.2   *Convergence of the learning procedure in the first layer of MANN.*

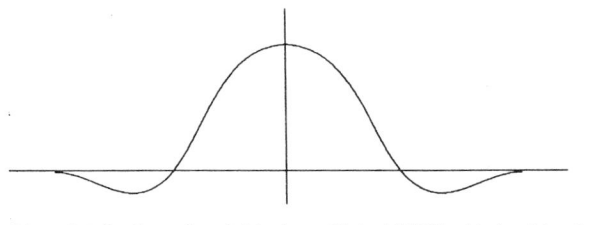

Figure 11.3 *Limiting distribution of weights from IA to MANN obtained by the learning procedure that follows the algorithm similar to Kohonen's [5].*

tribution of weights approaches the shape whose radial form is shown in Figure 11.3. This is a well known function, called the Lateral Inhibition Function (LIF), which is used in the learning algorithm for quantification of weight modifications. Simulations have shown that the width and the height of the limiting distribution closely correlate with the size of testing objects and the LIF function in the learning algorithm. In order to avoid on-line learning we tested LIF distribution of weights. We found out that for large objects these weights cause mapping of convex intensity distribution to concave distribution. This prevents accurate detection of the center of mass by searching the maximum of intensity distribution. We have therefore modified the original proposal of Kohonen [5] by changing the LIF to the Gaussian shape. In this case, the distribution of weights is Gaussian also, and the convexity of object intensity is preserved. Figure 11.4 proves the superiority of

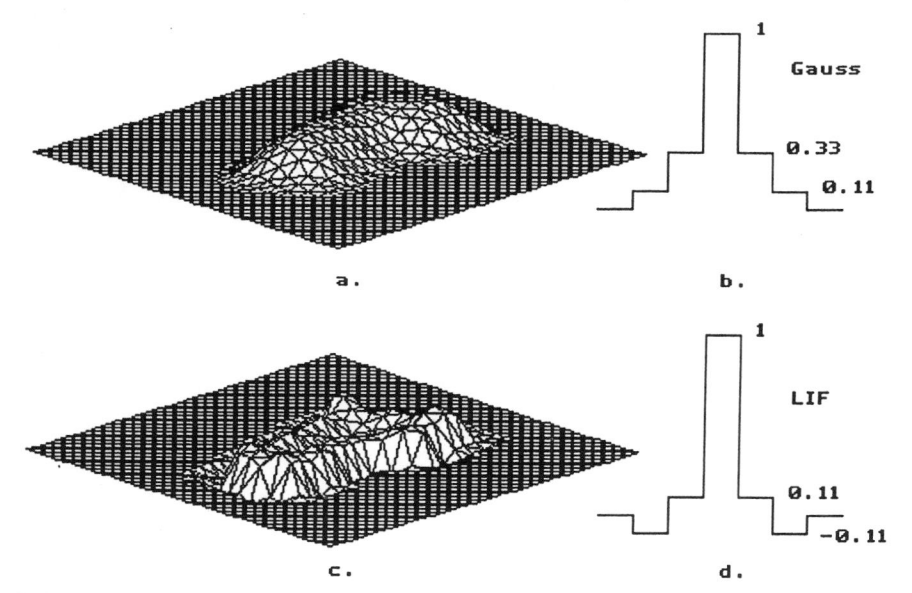

Figure 11.4 *Influence of weights distribution on input mapping of the first layer in MANN: (a) Image in first layer, Gaussian distribution; (b) G distribution used; (c) Image in first layer, LIF; (d) LIF distribution used.*

Gaussian distribution over LIF in cases when the distribution width is comparable to the object's. One might say instead that the first layer diminishes the influence of finite resolution of the neural network by performing the convolution filtering. Without this layer, tracking performances decrease significantly.

11.2.2 The Second Layer of MANN

The second layer performs the filtering operation to remove noise and other deviations from expected features in IA. It follows the equations:

$$\mu_i(t + T) = \mu_i(t) + k(t)(\eta_i(t) - \mu_i(t)), \quad i = 1, \cdots, N \qquad (11.2)$$

where T is the time between subsequent exposures of MANN from the camera and k is the gain factor of the dynamic filter of the second order whose values can be approximated by equation:

$$k(t + T) = (k(t) + q)/(k(t) + q + 1) \qquad (11.3)$$

The parameter q represents the ratio between covariances of dynamic and measurement noises. In a case without measurement noise $q \to \infty$, so $k = 1$, which means that filtering is suppressed. Properly chosen, q defines limiting value of $k(\infty)$ by requirement $k(t + T) = k(t)$.

The tracking procedure performed by MANN is based on optimal filtering with modified model equations in a global coordinate system:

$$\dot{x} = v + K_x(z - x)$$
$$\dot{v} = K_v(z - x) \qquad (11.4)$$

where x is the component of the vector to one of the object's points and v its velocity. The original model equations of actual variables x_a, v_a in this system are

$$\dot{x}_a = v_a$$
$$\dot{v}_a = w \qquad (11.5)$$

where w is the dynamic noise due to unpredictable acceleration. In the optimal case the gain factors K_x and K_v are time dependent. The innovation $(z - x)$ is obtained from the noisy measurement of the actual component x_a:

$$z = x_a + r \qquad (11.6)$$

where r and w are assumed to be stationary white noises with covariances:

$$\langle r(t)r(t + \tau) \rangle = R\delta(\tau)$$
$$\langle w(t)w(t + \tau) \rangle = Q\delta(\tau) \qquad (11.7)$$

Here, $\langle \ \rangle$ denotes the expected values and δ is the Dirac impulse function.

The camera follows the object using the filtered velocity v. As the neural network cannot accept continuous information from the camera, one must expose the MANN repeatedly to fresh information at regular time intervals T.

In the ideal case the filtered image should be displaced from the center of the MANN by vT as a consequence of neural network computation. Dividing the displacement by time interval T, we obtain the filtered velocity to steer the camera properly. In order to deduce the connection between the optimal filtering and corresponding neural network computation, we first discretize Eqs. (11.4) as follows:

$$x_{i+1} = x_i + v_i T + k_x(z_i - x_i) \tag{11.8a}$$

$$v_{i+1} = v_i + k_v(z_i - x_i) \tag{11.8b}$$

with the time step T. The time dependence of modified gains k_x and k_v due to discretization is $1/i$ for small i. Eq. (11.8b) requires the innovation $(z_i - x_i)$, which is not known to the MANN. However, this innovation is equivalent to $(z_i'' - v_i^T + (Tk_v - k_x)(z_{i-1} - x_{i-1}))$, where z_i'' can be considered as noisy measurement of the actual velocity v_a because of this relation:

$$z_i'' = z_i - x_{i-1} = v_a T + r' \tag{11.9}$$

The white noise r' has a slightly larger covariance than r because of noise in the filtered value x_{i-1}.

Equation (11.8b) can now be rewritten as

$$Tv_{i+1} = Tv_i + Tk_v(z_i'' - Tv_i) \tag{11.10}$$

where $(Tk_v - k_x)(z_{i-1} - x_{i-1})$ was neglected since $|Tk_v - k_x|$ is small compared to 1. This equation is equivalent to Eq. (11.2) if we identify

$$k = Tk_v$$

$$CM(\eta(t)) = z_i''$$

$$CM(\mu(t + T)) = Tv_{i+1} \tag{11.11}$$

$$CM(\mu(t)) = Tv_i$$

Here the operator $CM(\eta)$ extracts the coordinates of the center of mass from a particular vector η:

$$CM(\eta) = 1/N \left(\sum_{i=1}^{N} \rho_i \eta_i \right) \tag{11.12}$$

where ρ_i stands for the radius-vector from the center of MANN to the pixel i. The processing in MANN follows within approximations the Eqs. (11.8) with $k_x = 0$. The stability of the approach could be demonstrated from original Eqs. (11.4), where in the simplest case we put $K_x = 0$ (no filtering of x coordinate) and $(z - x) = z''/T - v$,

$$\dot{x} = v$$
$$\dot{v} = K_v(z''/T - v)$$

(11.13)

or equivalently,

$$\ddot{x} = K_v(z''/T - \dot{x})$$

(11.14)

Equation (11.14) describes forced movement of a particle in a dissipative medium. Equation (11.2), therefore, represents the stable suboptimal filtering of the velocity of the object.

In the above approach the velocity of the object and its filtered shape are both encoded within the MANN. For classification purposes it is more interesting to keep the filtered image close to the center of MANN by properly steering the camera motion. In the system of MANN that moves together with the camera with velocity v_i we may rewrite Eq. (11.8a) as

$$x'_{i+1} = x'_i + v'_i T + k_x(z'_i - x'_i)$$

(11.15)

Variables x'_i, v'_i and z'_i refer now to the system of MANN:

$$z'_i = z_i - v_i T$$
$$x'_i = x_i - v_i T$$
$$v'_i = 0$$

(11.16)

Equation (11.15) is equivalent to Eq. (11.2) if we identify

$$k = k_x$$
$$\text{CM}(\eta(t)) = z'_i$$
$$CM(\mu(t + T)) = x'_{i+1}$$
$$\text{CM}(\mu(t)) = x'_i$$

(11.17)

The camera is moved by using modified Eq. (11.8b):

$$v_{i+1} = v_i + k_v(z'_i - x'_i) + \alpha x'_i$$

(11.18)

where $\alpha x'_i$ is term which reinforce the camera towards the center of the object, $\alpha > 0$. k_x and k_v are expected to be stationary solutions of the corresponding Ricatti matrix equation [19].

To prove the stability of the method we conclude that the processing in the MANN for constant gains k_x, k_v is equivalent to the discretized form of Eqs. (11.4),

$$\ddot{x} = K_v(z - x) + K_x(\dot{z} - \dot{x}) + \alpha x \tag{11.19}$$

which is the equation of the forced movement of the damped harmonic oscillator. The filtered image in the second layer of the MANN is in this case adequate for processing in CNN.

11.2.3 The Third Layer of MANN

The third layer is intended to enhance the convexity of image intensity. The procedure performed by this layer must be adaptive, according to the size of the object, and local because of its cellular realization. The main purpose of this procedure is to enable the detection of the center of the object's mass. For this purpose we could also use any local shrinking algorithm [17]. However, we shall describe here the procedure that we found convenient for our particular application. For that purpose we shall use matrix notations for positions of neurons. The algorithm is a parallel version of standard operator CM, described in Eq. (11.12). It works in two steps according to row and column calculations:

$$\begin{aligned}
\mathrm{CM}(x) &= \sum_i \chi_i(x) \Big/ \sum_i \sum_j \mu_{ij} \\
\mathrm{CM}(y) &= \sum_j \chi_j(y) \Big/ \sum_i \sum_j \mu_{ij}
\end{aligned} \tag{11.20}$$

where

$$\chi_i(x) = \sum_j j\mu_{ij}$$

$$\chi_j(x) = \sum_i i\mu_{ij} \tag{11.21}$$

We demonstrate the processing of all layers in MANN by showing the values of all three layers. Figure 11.5 gives the results of the two simulation runs, one for each of the two distributions (LIF and G), where in both cases random noise is added.

11.3 CLASSIFICATION NEURAL NETWORK

As we mentioned above, the classification procedure follows the tracking operation, which means that the observed object should first be followed smoothly. At that moment both neural networks, TNN and CNN, are activated so that the tracking and classification functions run simultaneously.

The overall organization of the classification procedure is outlined in Figure 11.6. It is shown that the information from the observed window in IA is first transformed according to velocity and range vectors and then loaded into the input

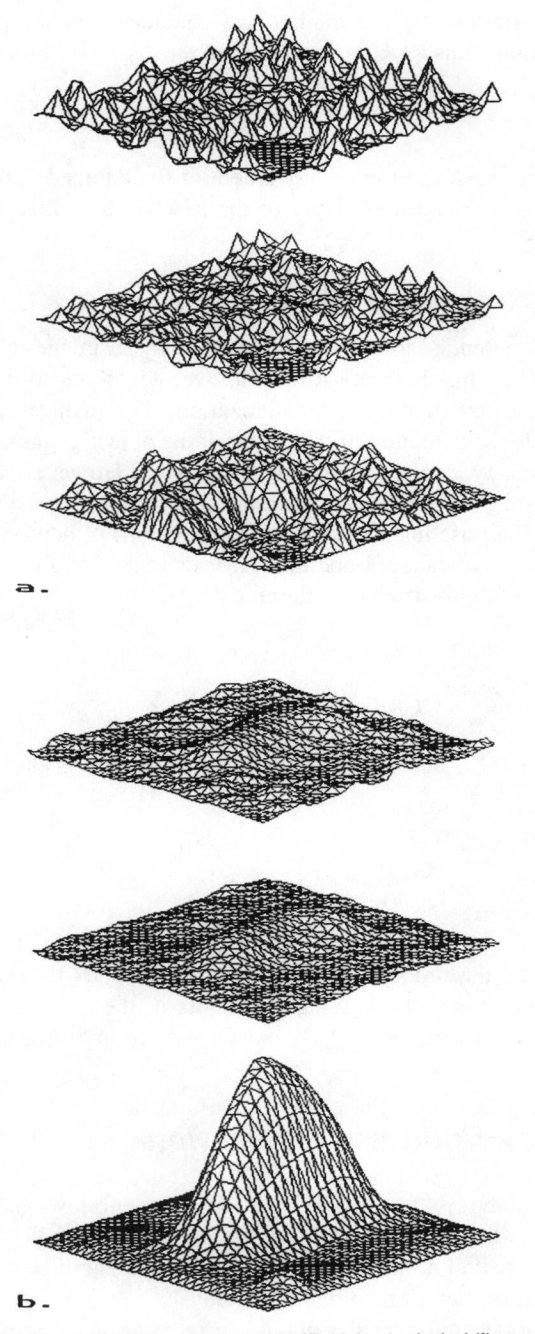

Figure 11.5   *Illustration of MANN processing: (a) LIF, Noise included (first, second, third layer); (b) G, the same as above.*

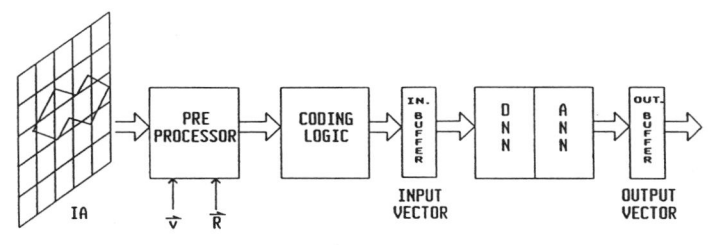

Figure 11.6   *Basic organization of the classification neural network*

vector by a coding logic, which reduces the information through the sensors that are placed on the joint points of the radii-vectors and circles illustrated in Figure 11.7. As the window has resolution 32 × 32 in our case, the input buffer receives 32 × 16 = 512 binary components.

In the following we first explain how the two layer *NN* structure performs the classification function. It is supposed that the first layer (Dynamic Neural Network) is taught to perform mapping that corresponds to the best matching of the input object to some attractor object. In order to do this, weights from the input buffer to the neurons are chosen to be equal to the binary components of the corresponding attractors. One should note here that these weights are binary. Moreover, there are still other weights that connect each neuron with itself and all others in the same layer. This enables the so called MAXNET or "winner take all" function. After calculation of the weighted sum of the inputs, these values are iteratively compared to find the neuron with the largest value. It represents the attractor to which the input object matches most. In our experiments we chose 100 attractors for each TETRIS object according to rotations between 0 and 90° around two perpendicular axes lying in the projection plane.

The so-called fired neuron in the DNN layer then enables its weights to enter the second or Associative Neural Network (ANN) layer. This means that the input vector to ANN is replaced by the weights of the best matched reference object in the DNN layer. In that case, the disturbance in the input vector is filtered out before the final classification mapping is performed by the ANN layer. The asso-

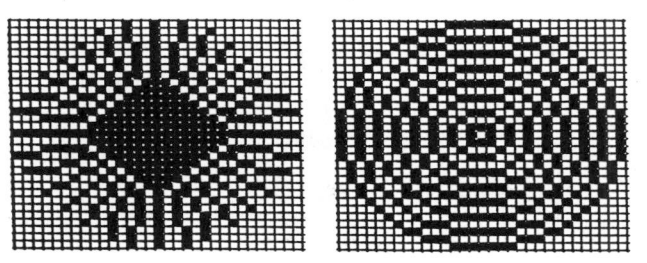

Figure 11.7   *Positions of sensors for image extraction defined by joint points of radii-vectors and circles.*

ciative layer is supposed to be taught to classify or group attractor neurons into an output vector that defines which object is shown in the input.

11.3.1   Learning Procedures in CNN

As we explained above, there is no need for a learning procedure in the DNN layer, as all the weights are predetermined. In the case of ANN, the input pattern represents the weights of the winning neuron in the DNN layer, while the output vector actually defines the classification pattern that is supervised according to the input object in the input image. Therefore, the learning or modifications of the weights in ANN are given by

$$dω_{ij} = α \left(\left(z_i' - \sum_j ω_{ij} y_j \right) \cdot y_j \right) \qquad (11.22)$$

where z_i' means the desired output of ith neuron in the ANN layer, y_j is the input to ANN, and $α$ is the learning parameter. $ω_{ij}$ represents the weight between the jth input component and ith cell of ANN. As noted above, there are 500 input components in our particular case, which correspond to the number of all reference objects and five neurons in the ANN layer, one for each 3-D TETRIS object.

11.3.2   Processing in CNN

The DNN layer performs its function in two steps. First, each neuron calculates the weighted sum according to the equation:

$$k_i = \sum_j w_{ij} \cdot ξ_j \qquad (11.23)$$

where w_{ij} is the weight between input component $ξ_j$ and neuron k_i, and "." means logical conjunction. The result of this calculation corresponds to the number of matchings between active input variables and neuron weights. We see in the next section that the results can be greatly improved if we take the logical equivalence instead of the logical product. In the second step, the neuron with the maximum number is searched iteratively, as is explained by the following equations:

$$k_i(t + 1) = g \left(k_i(t) - ε \sum_j k_j(t) \right), \quad i, j = 1, 2, \cdots, N \qquad (11.24)$$

$$g(o) \; α \; o \quad \text{for } o > 0$$

$$g(o) = 0 \quad \text{for } o < 0$$

where k_i denotes the ith neuron in DNN and the weights t_{ij} between neurons have the following values:

$$t_{ij} = \begin{cases} 1 & \text{for } i = j \\ -\epsilon & \text{for } i \langle \rangle j, \epsilon < 1/N, \quad i, j = 1, 2, \cdots, N \end{cases} \tag{11.25}$$

After the iterative process is completed, only the neuron with the greatest weighted sum is set to one and all others to zero.

When the neuron in DNN with the maximum value is found, its weights are selected and used as the input in the ANN layer. There, the output values of the corresponding neurons are calculated according to this equation,

$$z_i = \sigma \left(\sum_j \omega_{ij} \cdot y_j - \tau_i \right) \tag{11.26}$$

where y_j is the jth input to the ANN layer, σ is a nonlinear function, and τ_i the threshold of the ith neuron in ANN. The CNN structure is shown in Figure 11.8.

11.4 RESULTS OF TRACKING AND CLASSIFICATION PERFORMANCES

We made several simulation runs of the entire MANN using the first variant of tracking (see Section 11.3) to find out the convergence of tracking with or without the presence of noise. The experiments show that the neural network approach gave the same quality of tracking in comparison with the optimal Kalman filtering procedure. To outline the simulation results, two runs are shown in Figure 11.9.

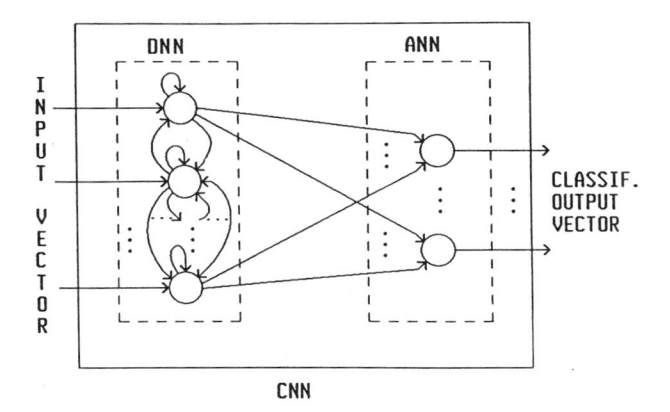

Figure 11.8 *Structure of the classification neural network*

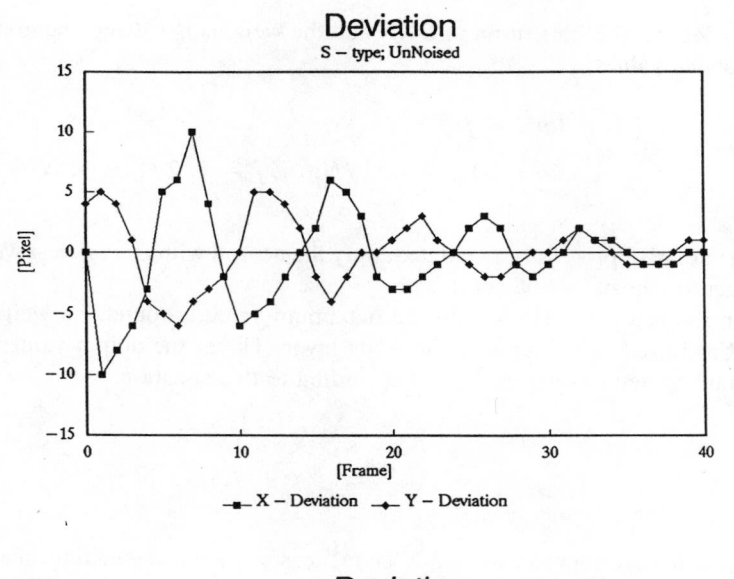

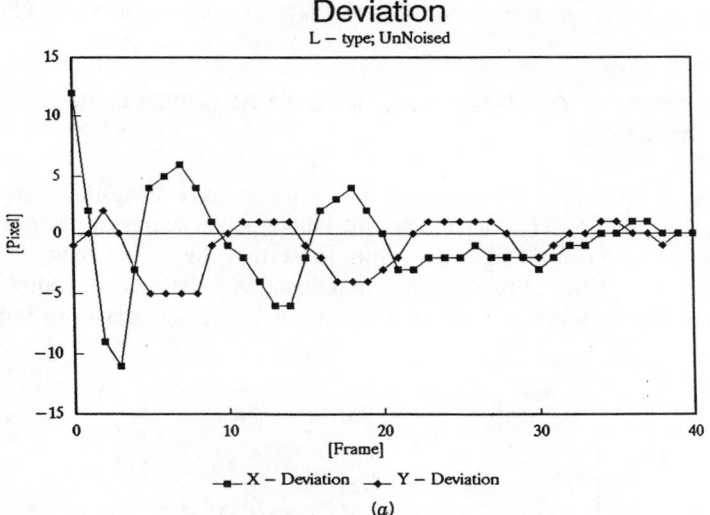

(a)

Figure 11.9 *Tracking performance of TNN: deviations in x and y axis (a) without noise (S and L type); (b) with dynamic and measurement noise (S and L type).*

In the first simulation run we chose L and S type 3-D TETRIS objects (one symmetric and one asymetric object) and their movement along the linear 3-D trajectory without any dynamic or measurement noise. In the second run we again took both representative objects, this time with a chosen linear 3-D trajectory, and added random dynamic noise between 0 and 1% of radian in all three angles, and random measurement noise of the "pepper and salt" type from between 0 and 40% of

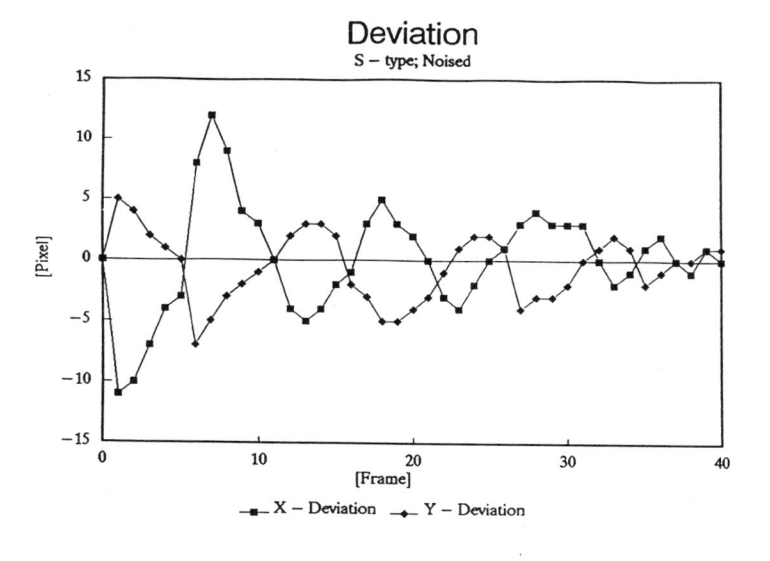

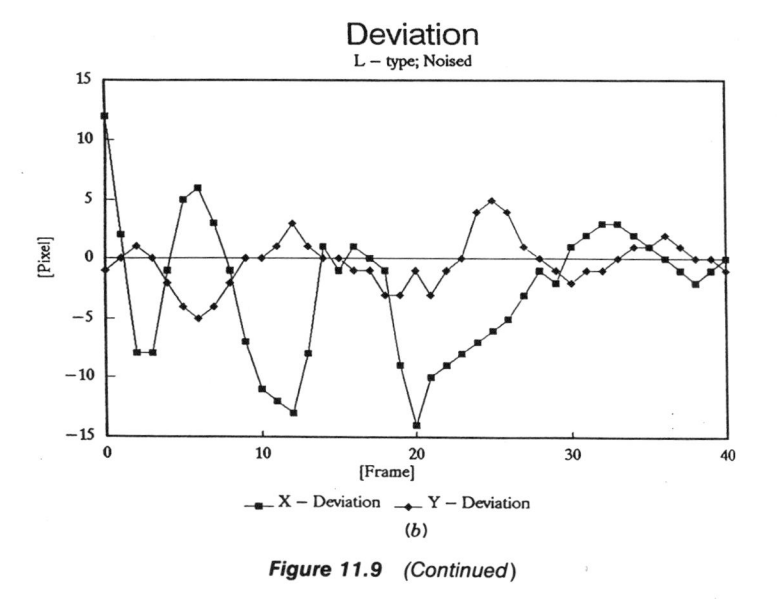

(b)

Figure 11.9 *(Continued)*

pixels within IA. The results indicate that TNN performs tracking comparable with the standard method regardless of the presence of noise. Its potential advantage lies in the parallel processing feature in the case where specific hardware realization is provided. Real-time applications then become feasible.

We explained above the close connection between the tracking and classification procedures. The quality of tracking has a strong impact on the classification results. We proposed that the classification procedure is enabled after the tracking procedure smoothly follows the observed object, which is expected to be in the center of the MANN. As the object moves along the 3-D trajectory, its projection seen by MANN is not invariant, so the classification is degraded because of the limited number of reference objects. The classification procedure is therefore repeated during the movement of the object, which gives the system a greater chance of recognizing and classifying it correctly. Figure 11.10 outlines the resulting dis-

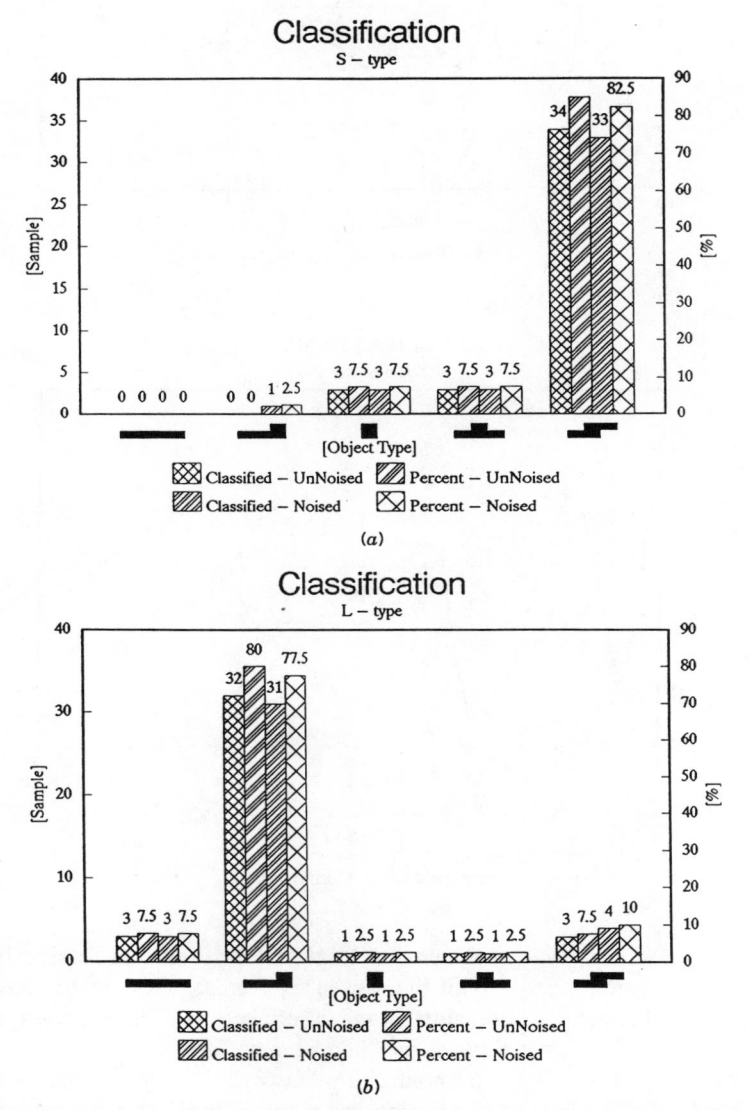

Figure 11.10 *Classification results from experiments shown in Figure 11.9: (a) S type, with and without noise; (b) L type, as above.*

tributions that follow from the examples in Figure 11.9, together with the percentage of the correct classification. In these simulations we used the window from IA instead of the filtered image. The results can be improved by taking the window from the filtered image of the second layer of MANN. To further illustrate the above experiments, Figure 11.11 shows some characteristic pictures of the exposed object under observation.

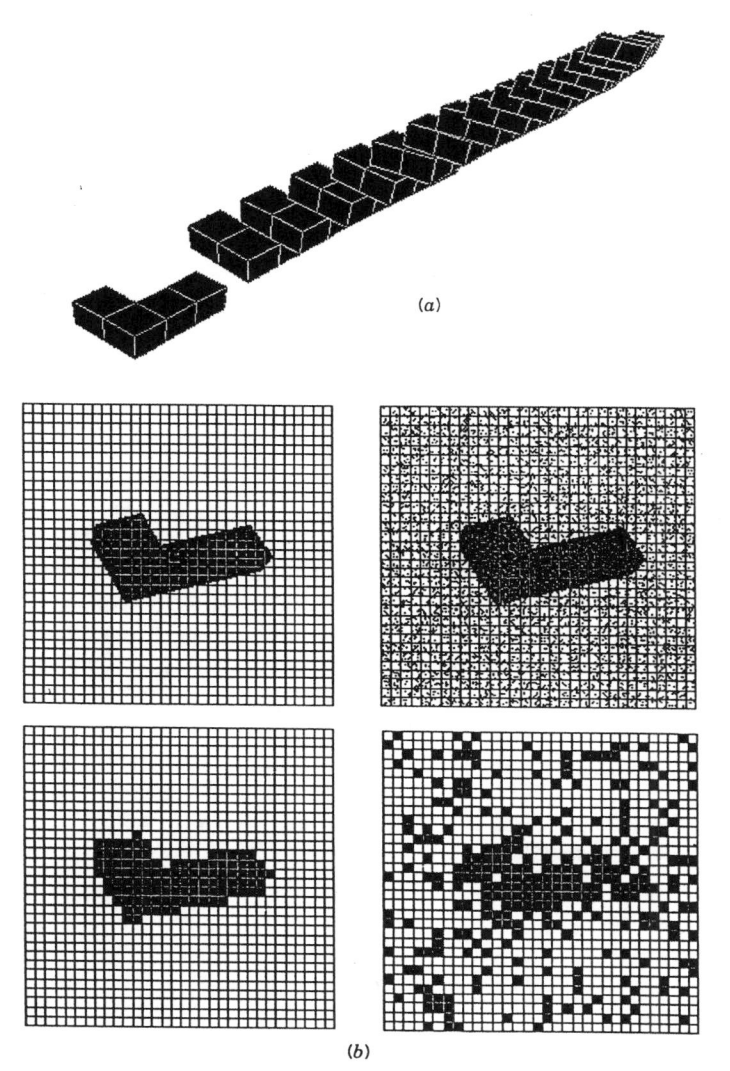

(a)

(b)

Figure 11.11 *Illustration of experiments, described in Figures 11.9 and 11.10: (a) L type of object, exposed to MANN while moving along noised 3-D trajectory; (b) L type of object, with and without noise and corresponding bit images; (c) detection of center of mass for L type of object along its trajectory.*

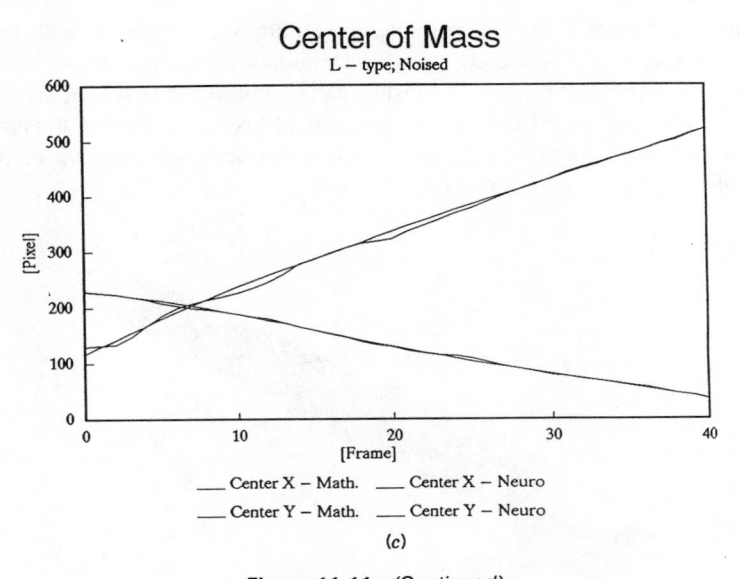

Figure 11.11 (Continued)

In order to evaluate the classification results obtained by CNN with the standard methods based on Fourier transformations, we simplified our experiments. Namely, we suggested the 2-D TETRIS objects that vary in size and angle of rotation. The classification is performed statically, with and without noise. The corresponding experiments showed the superiority of the neural network approach over the standard method, where we used the amplitude spectrum of the object's contour as the criterion for similarity with the referenced amplitude spectrums. Without going further into details, which can be found in Dobnikar [18], we only illustrate the results with Tables 11.1 and 11.2. In these experiments CNN was taught to be invariant on size and rotation in image plane.

TABLE 11.1 Testing Results of Classifying Seven 2-D TETRIS Objects of Different Size and Angle of Rotation

No. of Tests	Noise (%)	Correct Classif. FT − (%)	Correct Classif. NN(AND) − (%)
10 × 100	0	83	87
"	2	67	69
"	4	56	72
"	6	43	59
"	10	31	50
1000	0–10	55	63

Note: FT versus NN approach (with logic AND operation).

TABLE 11.2   Testing Results with NN, when AND Operation Is Replaced with Logic Equivalence (EQ)

No. of Tests	Noise (%)	Correct Classif. NN(EQ) − (%)
10 × 100	0	100
"	2	100
"	4	100
"	6	99
"	10	99
1000	0–10	99.8

11.5 CONCLUSION

The neural network approach is introduced for visual tracking and classification problems. We show that with the proposed tracking neural network the same quality of tracking can be achieved as with the Kalman filtering method. The classification of moving objects performed by the classification neural network also gives results that indicate the superiority over the method based on the Fourier transformation. The real benefit of the neural network approach, however, is expected when the proposed NN is actually realized in hardware and therefore the processing in real time according to potential parallelism becomes feasible.

REFERENCES

[1] Ch. von der Malsburg, Self-organization of orientation sensitive cells in the striate cortex, *Kybernetic*, 14, 85–100 (1973).

[2] D. J. Willshaw and von der Malsburg, Ch. How patterned neural connections can be set up by self-organization, *Proc. Roy. Soc. (London)*, B194, 431–445 (1976).

[3] D. J. Willshaw and Ch. von der Malsburg, A marker induction mechanism for the establishment of ordered neural mappings; its application to the retino-tectal problem, *Philos. Trans. Roy. Soc. (London)*, B287, 203–243 (1979).

[4] S. I. Amari, Topographic organization of nerve fields, *Bull. Math. Biol.*, 42, 339–364 (1980).

[5] T. Kohonen, Self-organized formation of topologically correct feature maps, *Biol. Cybern.*, 43, 59–69 (1982).

[6] T. Kohonen, Clustering, taxonomy and topological maps of patterns, *Proc. 6th Internat. Conf. on Pattern Recognition* (October 1982), pp. 114–128.

[7] T. Kohonen et al., Phonotopic maps insightful representation of phonological features for speech recognition, *Seventh Internat. Conf. on Pattern Recognition* (August 1984), pp. 182–185.

[8] K. Fukushima, Analysis of the process of visual pattern recognition by neocognitron, *Neural Networks*, 2(6), 413–420 (1989).

[9] G. A. Carpenter and S. Grossberg, ART 2: Self-organization of stable category recognition codes for analog input patterns, *Applied Optics*, 26(23), 4919–4930 (1987).

[10] J. J. Hopfield, Neural networks and physical systems with emergent collective computational abilities, *Proc. National Acad. Sci. USA*, 79, 2554–2558 (1982).

[11] M. Seibert, and A. M. Waxman, Spreading activation layers, visual cascades and invariant representations for neural pattern recognition systems, *Neural Networks*, vol. 2(1), pp. 9–27 (1989).

[12] A. C. C. Coolen and F. W. Kuijk, A learning mechanism for invariant pattern recognition in neural networks, *Neural Networks*, 2(6), 495–506 (1989).

[13] L. Udpa and S. S. Udpa, Application of neural networks to nondestructive evaluation, *1st Internat. Conf. on Artificial Neural Networks*, London (1989), pp 143–147.

[14] J. Austin, ADAM: An associative neural architecture for invariant pattern classification, *Proc. 1st Internat. Conf. on Artificial Neural Networks*, (1989), pp. 196–200.

[15] Y. H. Pao, *Adaptive Pattern Recognition and Neural Networks*, Addison Wesley, Reading, Mass., 1989.

[16] R. Hecht-Nielsen, Counterpropagation networks, *Proc. 1st IEEE Conf. on Neural Networks*, Vol. 2, 19–32 (1987), pp. 19–32.

[17] M. Onoe et al., *Real-Time/Parallel Computing: Image Analysis*, Plenum Press, New York, 1981.

[18] A. Dobnikar, "Invariant Pattern Classification—Neural Network versus FT Approach," International Summer School and Workshop on Neurocomputing, ECPD, Dubrovnik, 1990.

[19] A. Dobnikar, A. Likar, B. Jurčič-Zlobec, and D. Podbregar, Tracking and classifying 3D objects from TV pictures, *IJCNN '91*, Singapore, 1, 313–325 (1991).

CHAPTER 12 _____

A Neural Network Approach to Landmark Based Shape Recognition

NIRWAN ANSARI
KUOWEI LI

12.1 INTRODUCTION

In this chapter, a new method is introduced to achieve partial shape recognition by means of a modified Hopfield neural network. To recognize partially visible object, each object is represented by a set of *landmarks*. The landmarks of an object are points of interest relative to the object that have important shape attributes. Given a scene consisting of partially occluded objects, a model object in the scene is hypothesized by matching the landmarks of the model with those in the scene. A measure of similarity between two landmarks, one from a model and the other from the scene, is needed to perform this matching. A local shape measure, known as the sphericity of a triangular transformation, is used. The hypothesis of a model object in a scene is completed by matching the model landmarks with the scene landmarks. The landmark matching task is performed by a modified Hopfield neural network. The location of the model in the scene is estimated with a least squares fit among the matched landmarks. A heuristic measure is then computed to decide if the model is in the scene.

The problem of recognizing partially occluded objects is of considerable interest in the field of industrial automation, especially in robotic applications where multiple objects, touching objects, or overlapping objects cause many problems in identifying and locating the objects in the workcell of a robot. This problem has intrigued many researchers in the areas of computer vision. Recent works on 2-D partial shape recognition have exhibited an increasing interest in developing methods capable of recognizing objects when global information about the objects is

Fast Learning and Invariant Object Recognition, By Branko Souček and the IRIS Group.
ISBN 0-471-57430-9 © 1992 John Wiley & Sons, Inc.

not available. The recognition task can be modeled as searching for a match between model and scene features. Commonly used features are holes and points [1–5], line segments [6–10], curve segments [11–15], or a combination of these features [16, 17]. The features are obtained by a preprocessing step such as edge detection, polygonal approximation, and corner extraction. A similar view is taken in this chapter by posing the recognition task as a landmark matching problem [5]. Detailed literature reviews can be found in many of the above mentioned publications and in reference [18]. Among the voluminous literature on this subject, five recently proposed methods [4, 5, 7, 8, 10] will be briefly discussed. The problem of 3-D object recognition such as recognizing polyhedral objects [19] is not considered in this chapter. A rather detailed survey of 3-D object recognition can be found in reference [20].

Bhanu and Faugeras [7] cast the shape matching problem as a segment matching problem. An object contour is first approximated by a polygon from which feature values such as the length of a segment, the slope of a segment, the angle between two adjacent segments, and the intervertice distance are computed. The sum of the weighted absolute differences of the feature values between a model and a scene segment is the shape measure between the two segments. This measure indicates the goodness of match between the two segments. A stochastic labeling scheme is then used to label each model segment either as one of the scene segments or NIL (no match).

Since this method uses relaxation labeling, it is computationally intensive. A good estimate of the initial assignment of the labels is important relative to the convergence of the algorithm and the validity of the result.

In Price's approach [8], the shape features of an object are the line segments of the approximated polygon of the object. Each model segment is then compared with every scene segment in terms of their lengths and the included angles between successive segments. If the lengths and angles are within certain thresholds, the model segment is said to be compatible with the scene segment, and their orientation difference is stored in an array known as a disparity array. Since segments of an object are arranged sequentially along the object contour, segments between the model and the scene are likely to be matched in a sequence. The longest consecutive sequence of matched segments between the model and the scene corresponds to the longest compatible consecutive diagonal entries of the disparity array that have similar orientation differences. A transformation that aligns the model segments with the matched scene segments is evaluated. Applying this transformation to the model segments, disparity values based on the segment position and orientations are updated and stored in the disparity array. The final matches between the model and scene segments are determined by finding the longest compatible consecutive diagonal entries of the new disparity array.

Price's procedure is simple but not computationally efficient, since every entry of the disparity array has to be tested for the starting location of the longest sequence. Furthermore, the technique is sensitive to scale variation because the feature value, such as the length of a line segment, used in this technique is inherently scale dependent.

Bhanu and Ming [10] improve Price's approach by using the same disparity array but with a different matching process. The matching process first applies the K-*mean* clustering algorithm iteratively on the disparity array until the optimal number of clusters is found. It then checks for the elements of each cluster that are in sequential order, and finds the sequences. The process then clusters the sequence averages using the same clustering algorithm described above. The cluster that contains the largest number of sequences determines the final matches between the model and the scene segments. A confidence value, which is the ratio of the cumulative length of the segments in the final match to the total length of all segments of the model, is evaluated to verify the final match. Although it is computationally more efficient than Price's approach, it remains computationally expensive because of the iterative nature of the algorithm.

Wei and Nasrabadi [4] propose a neural network approach to solve the partial shape recognition problem. They use the Hopfield neural network, which provides a parallel processing mechanism for feature matching. The shape features of an object are the corners (nodes) of the approximated polygon of the object. Each object characterized by its set of nodes constitutes an object graph. The local feature property of the node is represented by the corresponding angle of the vertices and their lengths between the nodes. First, node assignments between every two pairs of matching nodes have to be formed. If the difference between the feature values of a node in the model graph and a node in the input scene is within certain threshold, the node of the model object is said to be compatible with the node of the input scene. The Hopfield binary network is implemented to perform a graph isomorphism to obtain the optimal compatible match. This algorithm provides good results for a scene consisting of a single object scene or lightly occluded objects, but the algorithm may fail in the case of heavily occluded objects. If the numbers of the false matches are larger than the numbers of the feature points, the algorithm will generate incorrect hypotheses. Besides, this technique is sensitive to scale variation. The main reason of scale variation is that the relational constraints, such as the length of two nodes, are inherently scale dependent.

The shape recognition approach reported in reference [5] uses landmarks as the shape features. The feature matching algorithm is based on a procedure known as hopping dynamic programming. This technique provides good results even for a scene with heavily occluded objects, and it is not sensitive to scale variation.

The approach proposed in this chapter inherits the benefits of the above two approaches [4, 5]. That is, it inherits the parallelism of the Hopfield neural network [4] and the merit of scale invariance [5]. Figure 12.1 shows the landmark based shape recognition system. Similar to Ansari and Delp's approach [5], landmarks are used as the shape features. In order to characterize the similarity between two features, a function known as sphericity [5] is used to discriminate the dissimilarity between two landmarks. The matching technique is based on Hopfield neural network [21, 22, 23]. The *sphericity*, a local shape measure, is used as one of the relational constraints. The extraction of landmarks and the sphericity is discussed in Section 12.2. In contrast to Wei and Nasrabodi's approach [4], the new approach is not sensitive to scale variation. The new approach to partial shape rec-

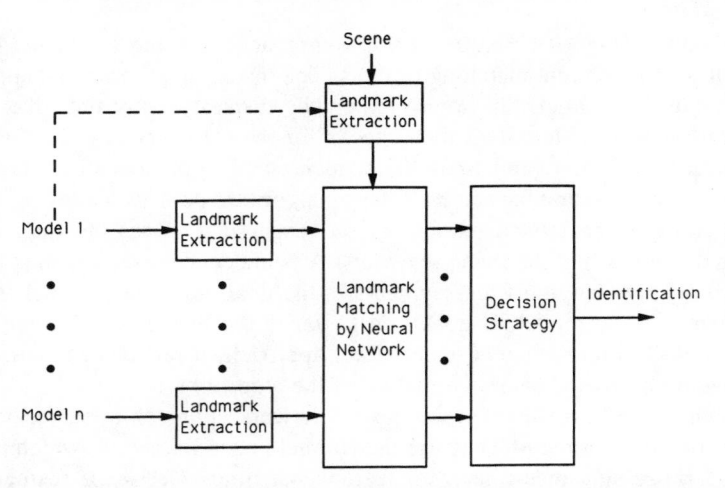

Figure 12.1   *Landmark based shape recognition system using Hopfield Neural Network.*

ognition by means of a modified Hopfield method is discussed in details in Section 12.3. Finally, experimental results are presented in Section 12.4, along with a discussion on the merits of the new approach as compared to references [4] and [5].

12.2   LANDMARK EXTRACTION AND SPHERICITY

When objects are occluded, many shape recognition methods that use global information will fail. To recognize partially occluded objects, we represent each object by a set of *landmarks*. In this section, the landmark extraction task [24] and the properties of sphericity [25], a local shape measure used in the new algorithm, are briefly discussed.

12.2.1   Landmark Extraction

For the purpose of shape recognition, much of the visual data perceived by a human being is highly redundant. It has been suggested from the viewpoint of the human visual system [26] that some dominant points along an object contour are rich in information content and are sufficient to characterize the shape of the object. These dominant points of an object are called the landmarks of the object. The landmarks of an object are defined as points of interest relative to the object that have important shape attributes. Examples of landmarks are corners, holes, protrusions, and high curvature points.

It is important to note that the entire contour of an object is not needed to use landmarks to achieve recognition. The approach only requires knowledge of the positions of the landmarks of the object in the image. It is necessary to impose a consistent ordering of the landmarks.

Among the extreme points, points with high curvature along the object contour are features that are most attractive. The contour, as in the case of a model, usually represents one object. However, in a general scene, when occlusion is allowed, the contour could represent merged boundaries of several objects. In this chapter, only points of high curvature along an object contour are considered as landmarks. Other problem specific types of landmarks will not be considered. Note that erroneous landmarks of objects in a scene may occur due to occlusion or noise in the scene.

As a result of the discrete boundary representation and quantization error, false local concavities and convexities along a boundary are introduced. Smoothing is thus necessary to reduce false concavities and convexities. A Gaussian filter, which has been shown to be an ideal smoothing filter for numerical differentiation [27], is used. The extreme (positive maximum and negative minimum) curvature points of a boundary that has been smoothed by a Gaussian filter with a large width w are stable with respect to orientation and scaling; that is, their corresponding locations along the unsmoothed boundary remain relatively unchanged when the boundary is rotated or scaled within a reasonable range. These stable local extreme curvature points are referred to as the *cardinal curvature points* [24].

The cardinal curvature points along an object boundary are obtained by successively smoothing the boundary with a Gaussian filter with various widths w, until the extreme curvature points do not change (their number remains the same and their locations deviate little) for a range of w. Points along the original unsmoothed boundary that correspond to the cardinal curvature points are considered as the landmarks of the object. Landmarks obtained for a library of objects by this approach are shown in Figure 12.2.

12.2.2 Sphericity

After extracting the shape features from a model and a scene, some sort of similarity or dissimilarity measure must be used to quantify the difference between the shape features. In this chapter, the sphericity [25] is used as the similarity or dissimilarity measure.

The sphericity of a triangular transformation that maps a triangle to another triangle is a measure of similarity between the two triangles. Under the triangular transformation, the inscribed circle of one triangle is mapped onto an inscribed ellipse of the other triangle. As shown in Figure 12.3, the sphericity is defined as the ratio of the geometric mean to the arithmetic mean of the lengths of the principal axes of the inscribed ellipse; that is,

$$\text{sphericity} = (2\sqrt{d_1 d_2})/(d_1 + d_2)$$

If the two triangles are similar, the sphericity is one. The less similar the two triangles are, the smaller is the value of the sphericity. If the vertices of one tri-

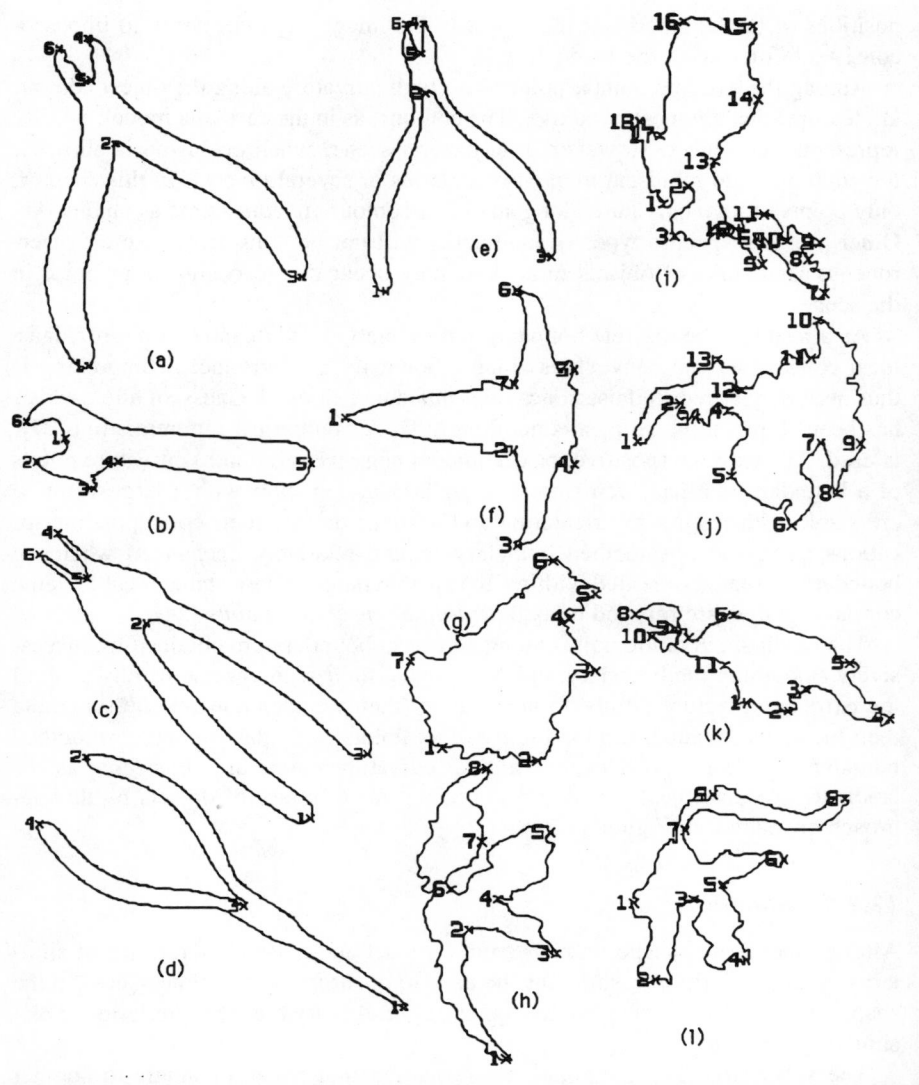

Figure 12.2 The landmarks of a library of objects obtained based on the cardinal curvature points: (a) wire stripper, (b) wrench, (c) specialty plier, (d) needle-nose plier, (e) wire cutter, (f) spacecraft, (g) Island of Borneo, (h) Island of Halmahera, (i) Island of Luzon, (j) Island of Mindanão, (k) Island of New Guinea, (l) Island of Sulawesi.

angle are considered as the coordinates of three consecutive landmarks belonging to a model, and the vertices of the other triangle as those belonging to a scene, the sphericity is thus a measure of the similarity between the set of three model landmarks and the set of three scene landmarks. The triangular transformation is uniquely defined by an affine transform [28].

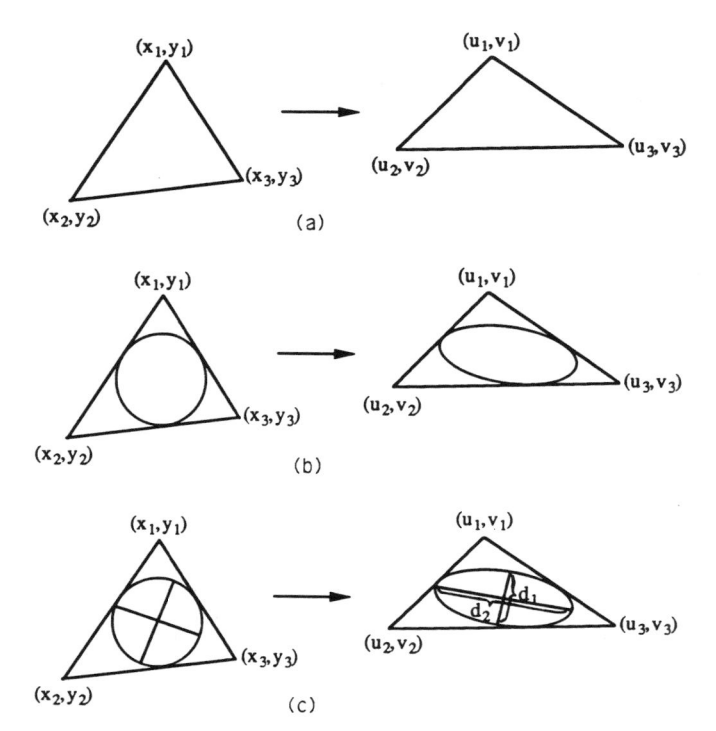

Figure 12.3 *Representation of a mapping from a triangle to another: (a) original triangles, (b) mapping from the inscribed circle to an inscribed ellipse, (c) mapping of the principal axes.*

Definition: An affine transform is the mapping of **x** to **u**, where **x, u** belong to $\mathbf{R}^2$ defined by

$$\mathbf{u} = \mathbf{A}x + \mathbf{t} \tag{12.1}$$

where

$$\mathbf{x} = \begin{bmatrix} x \\ y \end{bmatrix}, \quad \mathbf{u} = \begin{bmatrix} u \\ v \end{bmatrix}, \quad \mathbf{t} = \begin{bmatrix} e \\ f \end{bmatrix}, \quad \mathbf{A} = \begin{bmatrix} a & b \\ c & d \end{bmatrix}$$

and $\det (A) \neq 0$.

Coefficients of the affine transform that maps one triangle into another, as shown in Figure 12.3, are computed using the following equation:

$$\begin{bmatrix} a \\ b \\ e \end{bmatrix} = B^{-1} \begin{bmatrix} u_1 \\ u_2 \\ u_3 \end{bmatrix} \quad \text{and} \quad \begin{bmatrix} c \\ d \\ f \end{bmatrix} = B^{-1} \begin{bmatrix} v_1 \\ v_2 \\ v_3 \end{bmatrix} \tag{12.2}$$

where

$$B = \begin{bmatrix} x_1 & y_1 & 1 \\ x_2 & y_2 & 1 \\ x_3 & y_3 & 1 \end{bmatrix}$$

(u_i, v_i) are the image points of the points (x_i, y_i), $i = 1, 2,$ and 3, under the transform described by Eq. (12.1). Since vertices of a triangle are noncollinear, det $(B) \neq 0$ and B^{-1} exists. The sphericity of an affine transformation defined by Eq. (12.1), for $|A| \geq 0$, can be computed by the following [25]:

$$S = \frac{t_1^2 + t_3^2 - (t_2^2 + t_4^2)}{t_1^2 + t_2^2 + t_3^2 + t_4^2} \tag{12.3}$$

where

$$t_1 = a + d, \qquad t_2 = a - d$$
$$t_3 = b - c, \qquad \text{and} \qquad t_4 = b + c$$

The above expression provides a simple equation to compute the sphericity of a triangular transformation. It can be shown [25] that the sphericity of an affine transform is invariant when the affine transform undergoes a similarity transformation.

12.3 THE NEURAL NETWORK APPROACH TO LANDMARK BASED SHAPE RECOGNITION

The hypothesis of a model object in a scene is completed by matching the model landmarks with the scene landmarks. The landmark matching task is performed by the modified Hopfield neural network. The location of the object in the scene is then estimated by a least squares fit among the matched landmarks. A heuristic measure based on the least squared error of the fit is finally used to verify the hypothesis.

12.3.1 The Partial Shape Recognition Problem

As mentioned in Section 12.2, each object is represented by a set of "landmarks" because the landmarks are the dominant points that have important shape attributes. For partial shape recognition, only knowledge of the positions of the landmarks of the object in the image is required. It is important to impose a consistent ordering of the landmarks and arrange landmarks in a predefined order reflecting the shape and geometry of the object. Example of landmarks of object are shown in Figure 12.2. Given a scene consisting of M landmarks, and a model consisting of N landmarks, the hypothesis of this model object in the scene is determined by how well the model landmarks are matched to the scene landmarks. The landmark matching task is thus to find the correspondence between the model landmarks and the scene landmarks. Each correspondence between a model landmark and a scene landmark constitutes a ''landmark correspondence pair.'' To map the landmark matching task into the framework of the Hopfield neural network, each ''landmark correspondence pair'' is represented by the value of a neuron; that is, the correspondence pair is established if the neuron has a value of 1. Since there are N model landmarks and M scene landmarks, a network with $N \times M$ neurons is needed to achieve the landmark matching task. The network is represented by a matrix in which each matrix entry, denoted by V_{Xi}, represents a neuron. Each neuron takes on binary values 1 or 0. The first and second subscript of V_{Xi} denote the row index and the column index, respectively. Consider a scene with two overlapping object (wire stripper and wrench) as shown in Figure 12.4. The scene consists of 12 landmarks. To match landmarks of the wire stripper (Fig. 12.2a) which consists of six landmarks to the scene, a network with 6×12 neurons, as shown in Figure 12.5, is needed. The row index corresponds to a model landmark while the column index corresponds to a scene landmark. In this example, as shown in Figure 12.5c, neurons $V_{2,11}$, $V_{3,12}$, $V_{4,1}$, $V_{5,2}$, and $V_{6,3}$ are turned on ''1's,'' indicating that model landmarks 2, 3, 4, 5, and 6 match scene landmark 11, 12, 1, 2, and 3, respectively. Note that, as shown in Figure 12.5c, which shows the final (steady) state of the network, each row or column only have at most one neuron turned on. This is due to the physical constraint that one model landmark can match to only one scene landmark, and vice versa.

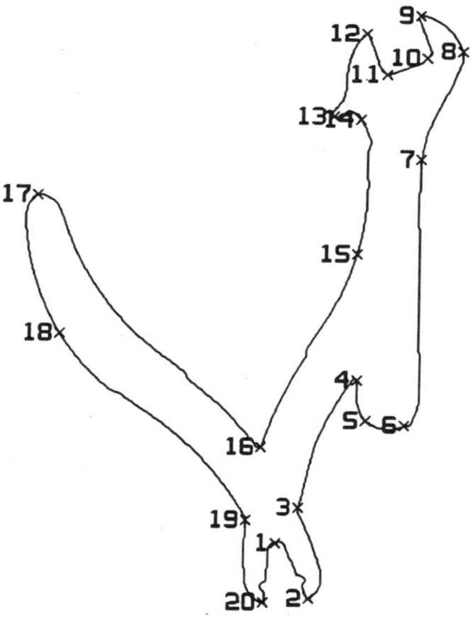

Figure 12.4 *A scene that consists of a wire stripper and a wrench overlapping each other. Each landmark is labeled and indicated by an "×."*

	1	2	3	4	5	6	7	8	9	10	11	12
1	0	0	0	0	0	0	0	0	0	0	0	1
2	0	0	0	0	0	0	1	0	0	0	1	0
3	0	0	0	0	0	0	0	0	0	0	0	1
4	1	0	1	0	0	0	0	0	0	0	0	0
5	0	1	0	1	0	0	0	0	0	0	0	0
6	1	0	1	0	1	0	0	0	0	0	0	0

(a)

	1	2	3	4	5	6	7	8	9	10	11	12
1	0	0	0	0	0	0	0	0	0	0	0	0
2	0	0	0	0	0	0	0	0	0	0	1	0
3	0	0	0	0	0	0	0	0	0	0	0	1
4	1	0	1	0	0	0	0	0	0	0	0	0
5	0	1	0	1	0	0	0	0	0	0	0	0
6	0	0	1	0	1	0	0	0	0	0	0	0

(b)

	1	2	3	4	5	6	7	8	9	10	11	12
1	0	0	0	0	0	0	0	0	0	0	0	0
2	0	0	0	0	0	0	0	0	0	0	1	0
3	0	0	0	0	0	0	0	0	0	0	0	1
4	1	0	0	0	0	0	0	0	0	0	0	0
5	0	1	0	0	0	0	0	0	0	0	0	0
6	0	0	1	0	0	0	0	0	0	0	0	0

(c)

Figure 12.5 *Network status during the landmark matching process: (a) initial state, (b) the state after the preprocessing step, (c) the final state.*

12.3.2 The Neural Network Architecture

To enable the $N \times M$ neural network to perform the landmark matching task, the network is described by an energy function in which the lowest energy state corresponds to the "best" set of landmark correspondence pairs. The network must satisfy the following constraints and assumptions:

1. each model landmark can match no more than one scene landmark,
2. each scene landmark can match no more than one model landmark, and
3. the lowest energy should favor the best set of correspondence pairs.

The modified Hopfield energy function is given as follows:

$$
E = \sum_{X=1}^{N} \sum_{i=1}^{M} \sum_{j \neq 1}^{M} V_{Xi} V_{Xj} + \sum_{i=1}^{M} \sum_{X=1}^{N} \sum_{Y \neq X}^{N} V_{Xi} V_{Yi}
$$

$$
+ \left\{ \sum_{X=1}^{N} \left(1 - \sum_{i=1}^{M} V_{Xi} \right)^2 + \left(\sum_{i=1}^{M} \left(1 - \sum_{X=1}^{N} V_{Xi} \right)^2 \right) \right\}
$$

$$
- \sum_{X,i,Y,j} \left(W_1 F_1(V_{X,i}) + W_2 F_2(S_{YX(X+1),ji(i+1)}) \right) \qquad (12.4)
$$

where the first term achieves the minimum, 0, if each row contains no more than one "1," that is, each model landmark matches with no more than one scene landmark. Likewise, the second term achieves minimum if each scene landmark matches with no more than one model landmark. However, the first two terms would yield 0 when there is no match between the model and the scene landmark at all. Thus, the third term is used to enforce that one model landmark can only match to one scene landmark, and vice versa. Therefore, for each row or column, at most one neuron can be active. These three terms thus enforce the first two constraints. The fourth term which is used to impose the third condition represents the strength of the interconnection among the neurons. This term is repeated and explained as follows:

$$- \sum_{X,Y,i,j} (W_1 F_1(V_{X,i}) + W_2 F_2(S_{YX(X+1),ji(i+1)})) \tag{12.5}$$

where $W_1 + W_2 = 1$,

$$F_1(V_{X,i}) = \begin{cases} 1 & \text{if } V_{X,i} = 1 \\ -1 & \text{if } V_{X,i} = 0 \end{cases} \tag{12.6}$$

$$F_2(S_{YX(X+1),ji(i+1)}) = \begin{cases} 1 & \text{if } S_{YX(X+1),ji(i+1)\,+1} \geq \theta \\ -1 & \text{else} \end{cases} \tag{12.7}$$

$V_{X,i}$ is the neuron value at the current state. $V_{X,i} = 1$ at the current state implies that at the current state the network hypothesizes that model landmark X likely matches scene landmark i. Thus, $F_1(1) = 1$ favors a lower energy as opposed to $F_1(0) = -1$. $S_{YX(X+1),ji(i+1)}$ is the sphericity value derived from the triangular transformation mapping model landmarks Y, X, $X + 1$ to scene landmarks j, i, $i + 1$, respectively. This sphericity value indicates how the neighboring landmarks of the model and the scene "support" the hypothesis that model landmark X matches scene landmark i. It is like a tally system, all neighboring model and scene landmarks can "vote" for the match between model landmark X and scene landmark i. If the sphericity value is greater than θ, there is a supporting evidence that model landmark X matches scene landmark i. Hence, the function F_2 yields a value of 1 favoring a lower energy. The terms described by Eq. (12.5) thus impose the third condition. Note that the first set of subscripts in the terms $V_{X,i}$ and $S_{YX(X+1),ji(i+1)}$ indicates the row indices of the network, while the second set indicates the column indices of the network.

The original energy function of the Hopfield neural network [22] is given as follows:

$$E = -1/2 \sum_{i,j} T_{ij} V_i V_j - \sum_i V_i I_i \tag{12.8}$$

where V_i indicates the output of neuron i, T_{ij} indicates interconnection strength from neuron j to i, and I_i is the external input to neuron i.

Note that Eq. (12.4) can be rewritten into an equation similar to the energy function of the original Hopfield neural network. Using double subscripts to index neurons, Eq. (12.8) can be rewritten as

$$E = -1/2 \sum_{X,Y,i,j} T_{Xi,Yj} V_{Xi} V_{Yj} - \sum_{X,i} V_{Xi} I_{Xi} \qquad (12.9)$$

Now, Eq. (12.4) can be written into a form similar to Eq. (12.9). Let the connection matrix that indicates the interconnection among neurons in the network be

$$T_{Xi,Yj} = -\delta_{XY}$$
$$-\delta_{ij}$$
$$+ \{W_1 F_1(V_{X,i}) + W_2 F_2(S_{YX(X+1),ji(i+1)})\}$$

where δ_{XY} and δ_{ij} are Kronecker delta functions; that is, $\delta_{XY} = 1$, if $X = Y$, and 0, otherwise. Similarly, $\delta_{ij} = 1$, if $i = j$, and 0, otherwise. Thus Eq. (12.4), the energy function, can be rewritten as

$$E = -\sum_{X,Y,i,j} T_{Xi,Yj} V_{Xi} V_{Yj} + \sum_{X}\left(1 - \sum_{i} V_{Xi}\right)^2 + \sum_{i}\left(1 - \sum_{X} V_{Xi}\right)^2 \qquad (12.10)$$

To minimize the energy function defined by Eq. (12.10) is equivalent to minimizing

$$-\sum_{X,Y,i,j} T_{Xi,Yj} V_{Xi} V_{Yj} - 4 \sum_{X,i} V_{Xi} \qquad (12.11)$$

which has a similar form of Eq. (12.9). The network will be shown to converge to the steady state (minimum) energy.

The proof of the convergence of the new network is similar to that of the original Hopfield network except that each neuron in the new network is indexed by double subscripts, and the interconnection matrix is not symmetric ($T_{Xi,Yj} \neq T_{Yj,Xi}$). Note that the change of energy ΔE due to a change of the state of neuron (X, i) by ΔV_{Xi} is

$$\Delta E = \left\{ -\sum_{Y \neq X} \sum_{j \neq i} (T_{Xi,Yj} + T_{Yj,Xi}) V_{Yj} - 4 \right\} \Delta V_{Xi} \qquad (12.12)$$

Denote U_{Xi} as the input to the neuron (X, i) at an iteration, and let U_{Xi} be

$$U_{Xi} = \sum_{Y \neq X} \sum_{j \neq i} (T_{Xi, Yj} + T_{Yj, Xi}) V_{Yj} + 4 \qquad (12.13)$$

where $T_{Xi, Yj} = -\delta_{XY} - \delta_{ij} + W_1 F_1(V_{Xi}) + W_2 F_2(S_{YX(X+1), ji(i+1)})$

Note that $T_{Xi, Yj} \neq T_{Yj, Xi}$. If the following updating rule to the next iteration is adopted:

$$V_{Xi} = \begin{cases} 1 & U_{Xi} > 0 \\ 0 & U_{Xi} < 0 \\ \text{unchanged} & U_{Xi} = 0 \end{cases} \qquad (12.14)$$

the energy of the network will be decreasing monotonically because ΔE is non-positive. This can be seen from the fact that

$$\Delta E = -(U_{Xi}) \Delta V_{Xi}$$

If $U_{Xi} > 0$, $\Delta V_{Xi} \geq 0$ since V_{Xi} will be activated for the next iteration regardless of the current state of the neuron. Likewise, $\Delta V_{Xi} \leq 0$ if $U_{Xi} < 0$. Since the energy is bounded, the network will converge to a stable state with the above updating rule.

In vision, many problems can be modeled as optimization problems. The new shape recognition procedure can be described below:

1. The initial states of neurons are set to 1 or 0, depending on the following two conditions:

(a) sphericity value $S_{(X-1)X(X+1), (i-1)i(i+1)}$ which indicates the local compatibility between the Xth model landmark and the ith scene landmark.

(b) curvature matching function $C_{X,i}$. The curvature matching function $C_{X,i}$ is defined by

$$C_{X,i} = \left| \frac{C_X - C_i}{|C_X| + |C_i|} \right| \qquad (12.15)$$

where C_X, C_i is the curvature of model landmark X and the curvature of scene landmark i, respectively.

$$V_{X,i} = \begin{cases} 1 & \text{if } C_{X,i} \leq \theta_1 \text{ or } S_{(X+1)X(X+1), (i-1)i(i+1)} \geq \theta_2 \\ 0 & \text{else} \end{cases} \qquad (12.16)$$

where θ_1 and θ_2 are two thresholds.

In the experiments, $\theta_1 = 0.09$ and $\theta_2 = 0.85$ are used. Both sphericity value $S_{(X+1)X(X-1), (i-1)i(i+1)}$ and curvature matching function $C_{X,i}$ are used to determine the initial states of the network, thus alleviating the disadvantage of either sphericity or curvature matching function. Even a scene landmark and a model landmark are compatible; the sphericity derived from the model landmark and its two adjacent landmarks to the respective three scene landmarks may not be close to 1, owing to occlusion. Likewise, the distortion of the object will create a wrong curvature value. Therefore, the two local measures $S_{(X-1)X(X+1),(i-1)i(i+1)}$ and $C_{X,i}$, which indicate the compatibility between model and scene landmarks, are used to set the initial state of the network. For example, the initial state of the network is shown in Figure 12.5a.

Owing to occlusion, noise, and other distortions, some landmarks of the object may be missing in the scene and some extraneous landmarks may be introduced in the scene. In addition, the landmark locations may be corrupted with noise. As shown in Figure 12.5a, there are six mismatched neurons being activated. If the scene consists of heavily occluded objects, it may take many iterations for the network to converge to a stable state, and the converged state may not be correct because too many neurons are initially falsely activated. To alleviate the above-mentioned problems, a preprocessing step is introduced: that is, all activated neurons that are isolated are set to be inactive. Thus, an active neuron is said to be isolated if none of its diagonally ($-45°$) adjacent neurons are activated. For example, in the initial network shown in Figure 12.5a, the activated neurons $(2, 7)(1, 12)(6, 1)$ are said to be isolated. After this preprocessing step the network for the above example is shown in Figure 12.5b.

2. Compute the input value to each neuron according to Eq. (12.13). W_1 is usually small because the previous hypothesis (previous iteration) may not be correct. W_2 is usually larger than W_1 because F_2 indicates the support from the neighboring landmarks.

3. Update each neuron according to Eq. (12.14). As shown earlier, such updating rule will guarantee the network to converge.

$$V_{Xi} \Rightarrow 1 \quad \text{if } U_{Xi} > 0$$
$$V_{Xi} \Rightarrow 0 \quad \text{if } U_{Xi} < 0 \tag{12.17}$$
$$V_{Xi} \Rightarrow \text{unchanged} \quad \text{if } U_{Xi} = 0$$

4. Repeat Steps (2) and (3) until convergence. The final state of the network indicates the "landmark correspondence pairs." Final state of the network for the earlier example is shown in Figure 12.5c.

5. After having determined the landmarks of a model that match well with those in the scene using the proposed modified Hopfield neural network, the location of the model object in the scene is estimated by a procedure that is discussed in the next section.

6. A match error that is discussed in the next section is finally computed to validate the match.

12.3.3 Location Estimation and Matching Verification

After having determined the landmarks of a model that match well with those in the scene using the modified Hopfield neural network, the location of the model object in the scene is estimated. Location of the object in the scene is estimated by finding a coordinate transformation consisting of translation, rotation, and scaling that maps the matched landmarks of the model to the corresponding scene landmarks in a least squares sense. A score based on the least squared error of the mapping is used to quantify the overall goodness of the match between the model and the scene.

Continuing from the earlier example, the least squares coordinate transformation is derived from the matched pairs of landmarks between the model and the scene. Note that if a priori knowledge of the scale of the object in the scene is available, the scale factor derived from the least squares coordinate transformation can be used as an additional parameter for verifying the match.

The least squares error only quantifies how well a portion of the model landmarks match with the corresponding scene landmarks. A small error indicates that only portion of the model landmarks match well with the corresponding scene landmarks. It does not, however, account for the overall goodness of match. Denote ϵ as the least squares error derived from the matched pairs of landmarks between the model and the scene; the following heuristic measure [5], which penalizes incomplete matching of the landmarks of the model, is used:

$$
\epsilon' = \begin{cases} \left(1.0 + \left(\dfrac{n-2}{k-2}\right)\log_2\left(\dfrac{n-2}{k-2}\right)\right)\bar{\epsilon} & \text{for } k \geq 3 \\ \infty & \text{for } k = 0, 1, 2 \end{cases}
\tag{12.18}
$$

where n is the total number of landmarks of the model, k is the number of model landmarks that match the scene landmarks, and $\bar{\epsilon} = \epsilon/(k(\text{scale factor}))$, that is, $\bar{\epsilon}$ is the normalized least squares error

The scale factor is derived from the coordinate transformation. The heuristic measure, ϵ', which can be regarded as the error measure for the overall goodness of match between the model and the scene, is referred to as the match error. If only one or two model landmarks match those in the scene, the least squares error is always zero because there always exists a coordinate transformation that perfectly maps a set of one or two points to another set. Such cases where two or less model landmarks match with those in the scene are considered as undetermined cases; that is, these cases have insufficient evidence of match between the model and the scene. Note that when $k = n$, $\epsilon' = \bar{\epsilon}$, that is, no penalty is added to the normalized least squares error when all model landmarks match those in the scene. The penalty is larger if k is smaller. In the earlier example, since five out of six of the model landmarks match with those in the scene, the match error value is 0.81 as shown in Table 12.1(a). The hypothesis of the model in the scene is finally determined by the value of the match error—with a small error, the hypothesis is

TABLE 12.1   Summary of the Results of Matching the Library Objects with the Scene Shown (a) in Figure 12.4, (b) in Figure 12.7, and (c) in Figure 12.9

(a)

Model	Model Figure Numbers	Total Number of Model Landmarks	Number of Matched Model Landmarks	Match Error
wrench*	2b	6	4	1.1
needle-nose plier	2d	4	0	∞
wire cutter	2e	6	2	∞
specialty plier	2c	6	0	∞
wire stripper*	2a	6	5	0.81
Borneo	2g	7	0	∞
Halmahera	2h	8	2	∞
Luzon	2i	18	0	∞
Mindanão	2j	13	0	∞
New Guinea	2k	11	0	∞
Sulawesi	2l	9	0	∞
spacecraft	2f	7	0	∞

(b)

Model	Model Figure Numbers	Total Number of Model Landmarks	Number of Matched Model Landmarks	Match Error
wrench	2b	6	1	∞
needle-nose plier	2d	4	0	∞
wire cutter	2e	6	2	∞
specialty plier	2c	6	0	∞
wire stripper*	2a	6	5	0.83
Borneo	2g	7	0	∞
Halmahera	2h	8	2	∞
Luzon	2i	18	4	206
Mindanão	2j	13	2	∞
New Guinea*	2k	11	6	5.4
Sulawesi*	2l	9	7	0.5
spacecraft*	2f	7	5	0.63

(c)

Model	Model Figure Numbers	Total Number of Model Landmarks	Number of Matched Model Landmarks	Match Error
wrench*	2b	6	4	0.74
needle-nose plier	2d	4	0	∞
wire cutter	2e	6	0	∞
specialty plier*	2c	6	0	∞

TABLE 12.1   (*Continued*)

(c) continued

Model	Model Figure Numbers	Total Number of Model Landmarks	Number of Matched Model Landmarks	Match Error
wire stripper	2a	6	0	∞
Borneo*	2g	7	3	8.4
Halmahera*	2h	8	5	0.92
Luzon*	2i	18	11	1.16
Mindanão	2j	13	2	∞
New Guinea	2k	11	1	∞
Sulawesi	2l	9	3	195
spacecraft*	2f	7	3	3.03

Note: Objects that are in the scene are indicated by *.

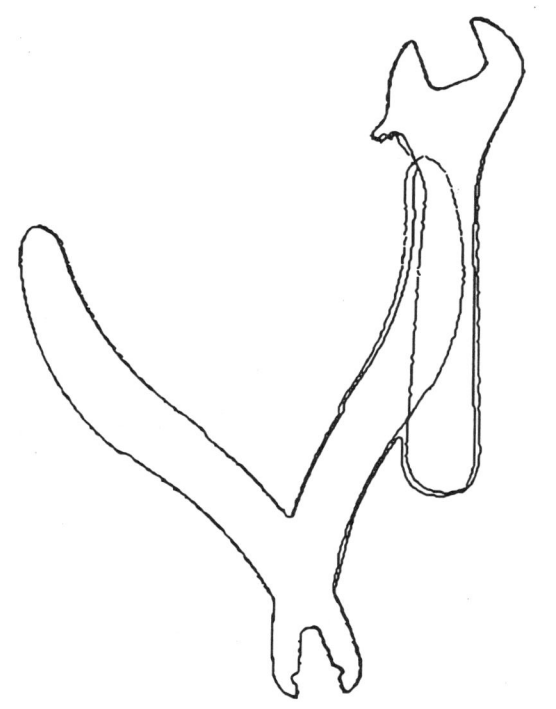

Figure 12.6   *The result of mapping the wire stripper and wrench into the scene shown in Figure 12.4 by the least squares coordinate transformation.*

accepted. The results of mapping the wire stripper and wrench into the scene are shown in Figure 12.6.

12.4 EXPERIMENTAL RESULTS

In the following examples, landmarks in the scene are similarly extracted based on the cardinal curvature points. Now consider the scene shown in Figure 12.7, which consists of four overlapping objects. Compared to their respective models, the spacecraft has been rotated by 45° and scaled by 1.4, the wire stripper has been scaled by an area factor of 1.5, the Island of Sulawesi has been scaled by 1.3, and the Island of New Guinea has been scaled by an area factor of 1.4. Compared to their respective model landmarks, one out of six of the landmarks of the spacecraft, one of seven of the landmarks of wire stripper, one out of nine of the landmarks of Sulawesi, and five out of the landmarks of New Guinea are missing. With respect to each model, those landmarks in the scene not belonging to the model are eventually made inactive by the new algorithm. The results of matching each model object of the library with the scene are summarized in Table 12.1(*b*). The model that correctly match with the scene has the smallest match errors. Figure 12.8 shows the result of mapping the spacecraft, wire stripper, Sulawesi, and Luzon into the scene shown in the Figure 12.7.

Figure 12.9 shows a more complicated scene, which consists of six overlapping objects. Compared to their respective models, the specialty plier has been rotated by 20° and scaled by an area factor of 0.5. The wrench and Halmahera have been rotated by 90°; the spacecraft has been rotated by 180°. Luzon has been scaled

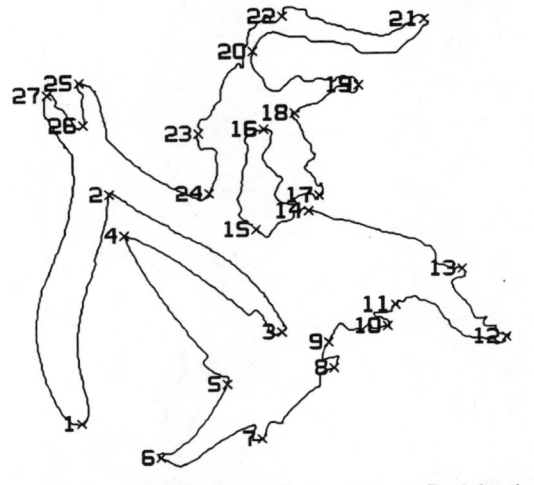

Figure 12.7 *A scene that consists of four overlapping objects. Each landmark is labeled and indicated by an "×."*

Figure 12.8   *The result of mapping the spacecraft, wirestripper, Sulawesi, and Luzon into the scene shown in Figure 12.7 by the least squares coordinate transformation.*

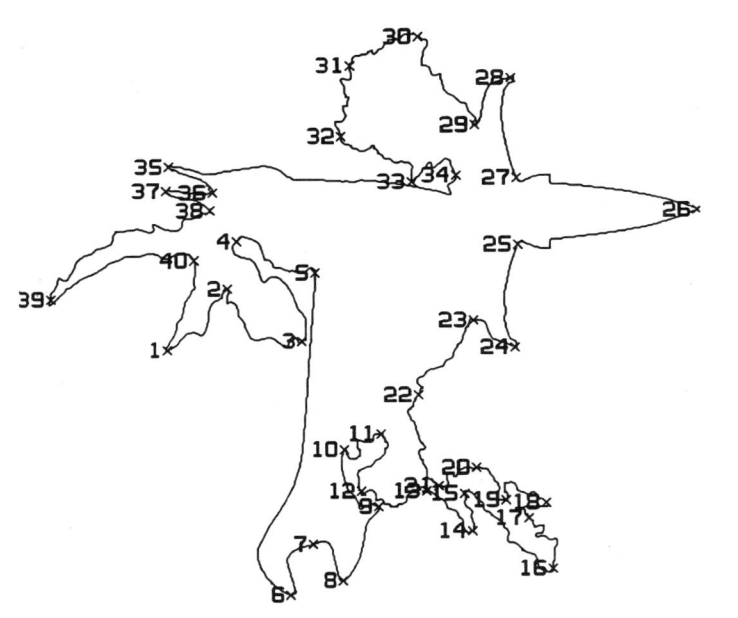

Figure 12.9   *A scene consisting of six overlapping objects. Each landmark is labeled and indicated by an "×."*

Figure 12.10 *The result of mapping Luzon, Borneo, Halmahera, the spacecraft, and New Guinea into the scene shown in Figure 12.9 by the least squares coordinate transformation.*

by an area factor of 1.4, and Borneo has been rotated by 90° and scaled by an area factor of 0.6. Compared to their respective model landmarks, three out of six of the landmarks of the specialty plier, one out of six of the landmarks of wrench, two out of seven of the landmarks of the spacecraft, two out of eight of the landmarks of Halmahera, five out of the eighteen of the landmarks of Luzon, and three out of seven of the landmarks of Borneo are missing. With respect to each model, those landmarks in the scene not belonging to the model are considered as extraneous landmarks. The result of matching each model object of the library with the scene are summarized in Table 12.1(c). Note that the specialty plier cannot be recovered owing to heavy occlusion. Again, the models that correctly match with the scene have the smallest match errors. Figure 12.10 shows the result of mapping the spacecraft, Luzon, Borneo, Halmahera, and New Guinea into the scene shown in Figure 12.9.

12.5 CONCLUSIONS

There has been an upsurge of research in neural networks. As an application, the Hopfield neural network has been modified to perform partial shape recognition. It has also been shown that when the connection matrix is not symmetric, the network also converges with a different updating rule. Through experimental results, it has been demonstrated that the new approach can handle occlusion quite well. The performance depends on the quality of the extracted scene landmarks and the number of correct landmarks in a scene that are detectable. The match error is undetermined if two or less landmarks of a model are correctly matched with the scene landmarks. Therefore, when matching landmarks of a model with those in a scene, at least three landmarks in a scene that correspond to the model must be detectable. As compared to reference [4], which cannot handle scale variations, the new approach can recognize objects with different scales. As compared to reference [5], in which the search is sequential, the new approach can be implemented in parallel.

REFERENCES

[1] M. W. Koch and R. L. Kashyap, Using polygons to recognize and locate partially occluded objects, *IEEE Trans. on Pattern Analysis and Machine Intelligence*, PAMI-9(4), 483–494 (July 1987).

[2] D. P. Huttenlocher and S. Ullman, Object recognition using alignment, *Proc. IEEE 1st Conf. on Computer Vision*, 102–111 (1987).

[3] R. C. Bolles and R. A. Cain, Recognizing and locating partially visible objects: The local feature focus method, *Internat. J. Robotics Res.*, 1(3), 57–82 (Fall 1982).

[4] L. Wei and N. M. Nasrabadi, Object recognition based on graph matching implemented by a Hopfield-style neural network, *IEEE Internat. Joint Conf. on Neural Networks*, Vol. II, 287–290 (June 1989).

[5] N. Ansari and E. J. Delp, Partial shape recognition: A landmark-based approach, *IEEE Trans. on Pattern Analysis and Machine Intelligence*, on PAMI-12(5), 470–483 (May 1990).

[6] L. S. Davis, Shape matching using relaxation techniques, *IEEE Trans. on Pattern Analysis and Machine intelligence*, PAMI-11(1), 60–72 (January 1979).

[7] B. Bhanu and O. D. Faugeras, Shape matching of two-dimensional objects, *IEEE Trans. on Pattern Analysis and Machine Intelligence*, PAMI-6(2), 137–155 (March 1984).

[8] K. E. Price, Matching closed contours, *Proc. 7th Internat. Conf. on Pattern Recognition*, 990–992 (July 30–August 2, 1984).

[9] N. Ayache and O. D. Faugeras, HYPER: A new approach for the recognition and positioning of two-dimensional objects, *IEEE Trans. on Pattern Analysis and Machine Intelligence*, PAMI-8(1), 44–54 (January 1986).

[10] B. Bhanu and J. C. Ming, Recognition of occluded objects: A cluster-structure algorithm, *Pattern Recognition*, 20(2), 199–211 (1987).

[11] J. L. Turney, T. N. Mudge, and R. A. Volz, Recognizing partially occluded parts, *IEEE Trans. Pattern Analysis and Machine Intelligence*, PAMI-7(4), 410–421 (July 1985).

[12] T. F. Knoll and R. C. Jain, Recognizing partially visible objects using feature indexed hypothesis, *IEEE Trans. on Robotics and Automation*, RA-2(1), 3–13 (March 1986).

[13] A. Kalvin, E. Schonberg, J. T. Schwartz, and M. Sharir, Two-dimensional model-based, boundary matching using footprints, *Internat. J. Robotics Res.*, 5(4), 38–55 (Winter 1986).

[14] G. J. Ettinger, Large hierarchical object recognition using libraries of parameterized model sub-parts, *Proc. IEEE Comput. Soc. Conf. on Computer Vision and Pattern Recognition*, 32–41 (June 5–9, 1988).

[15] W. E. L. Grimson, On recognition of curved objects, *IEEE Trans. on Pattern Analysis and Machine Intelligence*, PAMI-11(6), 632–643 (June 1989).

[16] Y. Lamdan, J. T. Schwartz, and H. J. Wolfson, Object recognition by affine invariant matching, *Proc. IEEE Conf. Computer Vision and Pattern Recognition*, 335–344 (June 5–9, 1988).

[17] Y. Lamdan, J. T. Schwartz, and H. J. Wolfson, "On recognition of 3-D objects from 2-D images," *Proc. IEEE Internat. Conf. Robotics and Automation*, 1407–1413 (April 1988).

[18] N. Ansari, "Shape Recognition: A Landmark-based Approach," Ph.D. thesis, School of Electrical Engineering, Purdue University, West Lafayette, In. (August 1988). Also issued as School of Electrical Engineering, Purdue University, Tech. Rep. TR-EE-88-31 (July 1988).

[19] W. E. L. Grimson and T. Lozano-Perez, Model-based recognition and localization from sparse range or tactile data," *Internat. J. Robotics Res.*, 3(3), 3–35 (Fall 1984).

[20] P. J. Besl and R. C. Jain, Three-dimensional object recognition, *ACM Computing Surveys*, 17(1), 75–154 (1985).

[21] J. J. Hopfield, Neurons with graded response have collective computational properties like those of two-state neurons, *Proc. Natl. Acad. Sci. USA*, 81, 3088–3092 (May 1984).

[22] J. J. Hopfield and D. W. Tank, Neural computation of decisions in optimization problems, *Biol. Cybern.*, 52, 141–152 (1985).

[23] J. J. Hopfield, Neural networks and physical systems with emergent collective computational abilities, *Proc. Natl. Acad. Sci. USA*, 79, 2554–2558 (1982).

[24] N. Ansari and E. J. Delp, On detecting dominant point, *Pattern Recognition*, 24(5), 441–451 (1991).

[25] N. Ansari and E. J. Delp, On the distribution of a deforming triangle, *Pattern Recognition*, 23(12), 1333–1341 (1990).

[26] F. Attneave, Some informational aspects of visual perception, *Psychol. Rev.*, 61(3), 183–193 (1954).

[27] V. Torre and T. A. Poggio. On dege detection, *IEEE Trans. on Pattern Analysis and Machine Intelligence*, PAMI-8(2), 147–163 (March 1986).

[28] D. Gans, *Transformations and Geometries*, Appleton-Century-Crofts, New York, (1969).

CHAPTER 13 ─────────────

Directed and Undirected Segmentation of Three-Dimensional Ultrasonograms

RONALD H. SILVERMAN

13.1 INTRODUCTION

A variety of biomedical imaging procedures (CT, MRI, confocal microscopy) scan tissues in serial planes, which may be postprocessed to reconstruct three-dimensional structures. Our laboratory has recently introduced the use of 3-D ultrasonic imaging in clinical ophthalmology.

A significant issue relating to the processing of three-dimensional scan series is the isolation of anatomic structures from each other (segmentation). Such operations are conventionally performed by gray-scale histogram and gradient thresholding. These procedures may not always be sufficient, especially in the case of data affected by low signal/noise ratios or other forms of degradation. This paper describes use of neural networks for segmentation of three-dimensional ultrasonic images, including use of competitive learning as an undirected learning procedure and backpropagation for directed learning.

While natural objects are generally three-dimensional in structure, both the retina and electronic display devices present two-dimensional surfaces. In the case of the retina, higher cortical functions process the incoming stimulus patterns from both eyes to provide the psychological effect of three-dimensions.

In recent years, radiological techniques such as computed tomography (CT), magnetic resonance imaging (MRI), and ultrasound (US) have allowed acquisition of digital data that is inherently three-dimensional in structure. Such data is most

Fast Learning and Invariant Object Recognition, By Branko Souček and the IRIS Group.
ISBN 0-471-57430-9 © 1992 John Wiley & Sons, Inc.

Supported in part by NIH grant EY03183, the Dyson Foundation, the St. Giles Foundation, the Rudin Foundation and Research to Prevent Blindness, Inc.

commonly presented to the diagnostician in the form of two-dimensional sections from several, possibly orthogonal, planes.

While software packages designed to create "three-dimensional" perspective images of 3-D scenes are currently available, they have not as yet found widespread acceptance in the radiological community. The crucial operation of such packages must be segmentation, that is, representation on a two-dimensional display of three-dimensional structures so that relevant features may be distinguished from one another. The most common operations now in use include thresholding, contrast, transparency, and gradient transforms. The object of their use is the isolation of anatomical components such as a tumor or a vascular tree from background tissues.

Radiologic images often are affected by low contrast and marginal signal to noise ratios. Ultrasonic imaging suffers from additional forms of image degradation related to signal attenuation, lateral spread of beam cross section with axial distance, scattering, and poor delineation of boundaries that are oblique to the beam axis.

Because of the complexities involved in segmentation of 3-D radiologic images in general, and 3-D ultrasound images in particular, novel approaches are of interest. This paper describes use of neural networks for segmentation and reconstruction of images of the eye obtained from scanning in serial sections.

Two procedures will be described: segmentation via regularity detection by use of competitive learning [1–4] and directed segmentation of a feature of interest by use of back propagation [5].

13.2   METHODS

Ultrasonic scans of the eye were obtained with a 10-MHz weakly focused transducer whose position was controlled with XY mounted stepper motors. The transducer was coupled to the eye with a saline transmission medium, and serial slices were made under computer control. Scans were 25.6 mm in width and 31 mm in axial depth, with an interval of 0.5 mm between slices. Each slice consisted of 128 scan lines (0.2 mm apart) of 2048 8-bit samples each. The stored samples consisted of unrectified radio frequency echo data.

After acquisition, scans were processed by rectification and averaging to produce 128×128 images with real valued pixel (or more precisely, voxel) elements ranging from 0 to 1.

A serial scan series of a human eye with a total retinal detachment and diffuse vitreous debris was segmented using both directed and undirected learning procedures. The scan series consisted of 32 serial slices.

The undirected learning procedure was a form of competitive learning. The network, shown schematically in Figure 13.1, consisted of 10 competing units, which received excitation from successive $9 \times 9 \times 5$ regions from the scan series, where the first two dimensions refer to a square region within a slice and the last dimension refers to the range of slices. In physical dimensions, the input region is

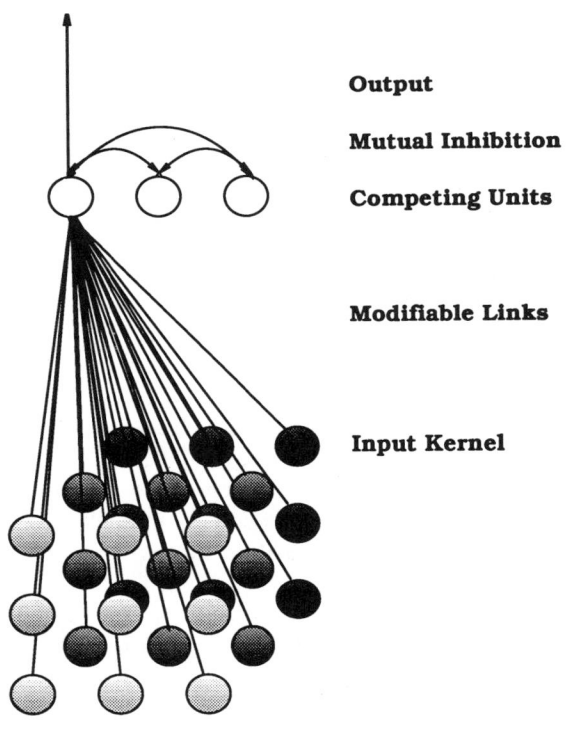

Output

Mutual Inhibition

Competing Units

Modifiable Links

Input Kernel

Figure 13.1 *Schematic of the competitive learning network. For clarity, the actual 9 × 9 × 5 input kernel is shown as 3 × 3 × 3, and links are shown to only one competing unit. Similarly, only three of the 10 actual competing units are shown. For each stimulus pattern, only one output unit fires.*

approximately $1.6 \times 2 \times 2$ mm in size. Prior to training, link weights were randomized to range between 0.1 and 0.5.

During training, the input kernel was "rastered" through the 3-D data structure, with a learning step occurring at each successive position. The following equation describes the excitation of competing units by the voxel intensities of the input kernel:

$$x_j = \sum_{i=0}^{n} (y_i - w_{ij})^2 \qquad (13.1)$$

In Eq. (13.1), y_i refers to the level of the ith element of the input vector, w_{ij} is the (modifiable) weight of the link from unit i to unit j, and x_j is the excitation level of the jth competing unit. The input element y_0 is a bias unit, always having a value of unity.

Equation (13.1) thus defines the excitation of each competing unit as the sum of squares of the differences between input values and corresponding link weights. The task of the network is to minimize this difference so that link weights form templates of input patterns typically present in the data set.

On each trial, the unit with the minimum excitation (i.e., the best match between link weights and input pattern) is the "winner." After each trial, units adapt as follows:

$$\Delta w_{ia} = k_a(y_{ia} - w_{ia}) \tag{13.2}$$

$$\Delta w_{ib} = k_b(y_{ib} - w_{ib}), \quad b \neq a \tag{13.3}$$

where the index a refers to the winning unit, and k_a and k_b are learning rate constants such that $k_a \gg k_b$.

Upon initiation of training, $k_b = 0.01 \, k_a$. The value of k_b assigned to each unit was allowed to vary so that in units with a very low firing rate, k_b was increased, and in units with a high firing rate, k_b was decreased. This procedure allowed poorly adapted units to gradually move toward valid stimulus patterns. Additionally, units that had successfully adapted to a specific class of patterns were not desensitized by readjustment of link weights in response to other (competing) patterns. The training cycle consisted of a single pass through the training set. Due to boundary constraints, the effective size of the training set was $28 \times 120 \times 120$, yielding approximately 4×10^5 trials.

Directed learning was implemented using the back-propagation algorithm, as described by Rumelhart, Hinton, and Williams [5] and using the delta-bar-delta procedure for accelerated convergence, as described by Jacobs [6], in combination with a momentum term. Thus, the modification of link weights is described by the following equation,

$$\Delta w_{ij}(t) = \beta \Delta w_{ij}(t - 1) - c_{ij}(1 - \beta)\partial E/\partial w_{ij} \tag{13.4}$$

where c_{ij} is the modifiable learning rate term, β the momentum constant, and $\partial E/\partial w_{ij}$ is the dependence of the global error (the squared difference between actual and desired output) on the link from unit i to unit j. Prior to training, link weights were randomized in the range -0.5 to 0.5. A value of 0.75 was used for β, and c_{ij} was initially set to 0.0025. During training, c_{ij} was allowed to increase by increments of 0.0001 when $\partial E/\partial w_{ij}$ had the same sign as its running average. If these had opposite signs, c_{ij} was decreased by 20%.

Directed learning requires that teaching patterns be paired with stimulus patterns during training. In this case, the teaching patterns consisted of a series of 32 128×128 images in which the positions of the detached retina had been manually demarcated. Nonspecific image locations were set to 0.05 and detached retina to 0.95.

The back-propagation network, shown schematically in Figure 13.2, consisted of a $9 \times 9 \times 5$ input kernel, nine hidden units, and a single output unit. Each layer had an additional bias unit with constant output of unity. The network was trained to minimize the squared difference between the actual network output and the value of the teaching vector corresponding to the central voxel of the $9 \times 9 \times 5$ input region.

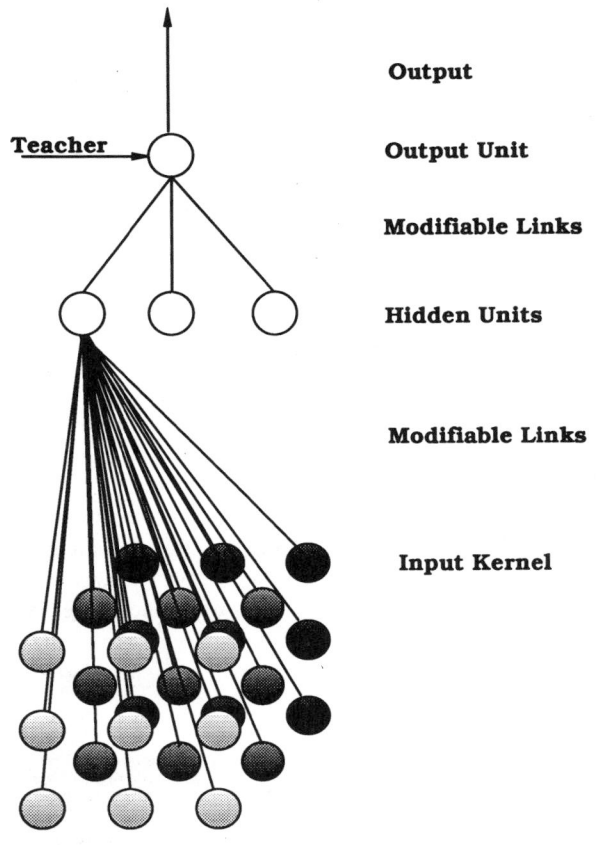

Figure 13.2 *Schematic of the back-propagation network. For clarity, the actual 9 × 9 × 5 input kernel is shown as 3 × 3 × 3 and links are shown to only one hidden unit. Similarly, only three of the nine actual hidden units are shown.*

Because of the large size of the training set and the fact that active teaching elements comprised less than 1% of this set, the following strategy was used during training: prior to link weight modification, the dependencies of the global error on local link weights were accumulated for all active teaching vector positions plus twice this number of randomly selected positions. Five-hundred training cycles were performed, by which time convergence had occurred.

After completion of training, link weights were fixed. For the competitive learning network, output images were formed by determination of the winning unit at each position in the scan series. Discrete output levels were assigned to each unit, so that output images could be represented in ten shades of gray, or ten different colors. For back propagation, the output must, by definition, be a real number between 0 and 1. The output at each image position was then rescaled to range between 0 and 255 for display in gray scale.

13.3   RESULTS

Figure 13.3 is an example of a single slice from a 3-D ultrasound image series of the eye. The eye is oriented such that the anterior segment is on the left and the posterior (orbit) is on the right. Normally, the vitreous compartment is acoustically clear (i.e., black), but in this case a detached retina and vitreous debris are present.

Figure 13.4 is a perspective representation of the eye reconstructed from 3-D gray-scale data. This image was constructed using thresholding, transparency and contrast operations so as to display the three dimensional extent and structure of the detached retina and the globe. While the 3-D rendering is useful, especially when rotated in an interactive fashion, the static image remains less than easily understandable.

Figure 13.5 illustrates the use of the competitive learning network for processing of this 3-D series. A 3-D rendering of the eye, where voxels are coded in the different gray levels assigned to each of the ten competing output units, is shown in Figure 13.5(*A*). Figure 13.5(*B*) is a single slice taken from this rendering. It was found that a single output unit had become specific to the detached retina. A 3-D reconstruction and a single slice of the output of this unit are shown in Figures 13.5(*C*) and 13.5(*D*), respectively. While this unit was sensitive to the detached retina, it also was sensitive to other ocular structures, including the lens, the anterior margin of the globe, and the posterior boundary of the orbit.

Figure 13.6 illustrates the use of back propagation for segmentation of this

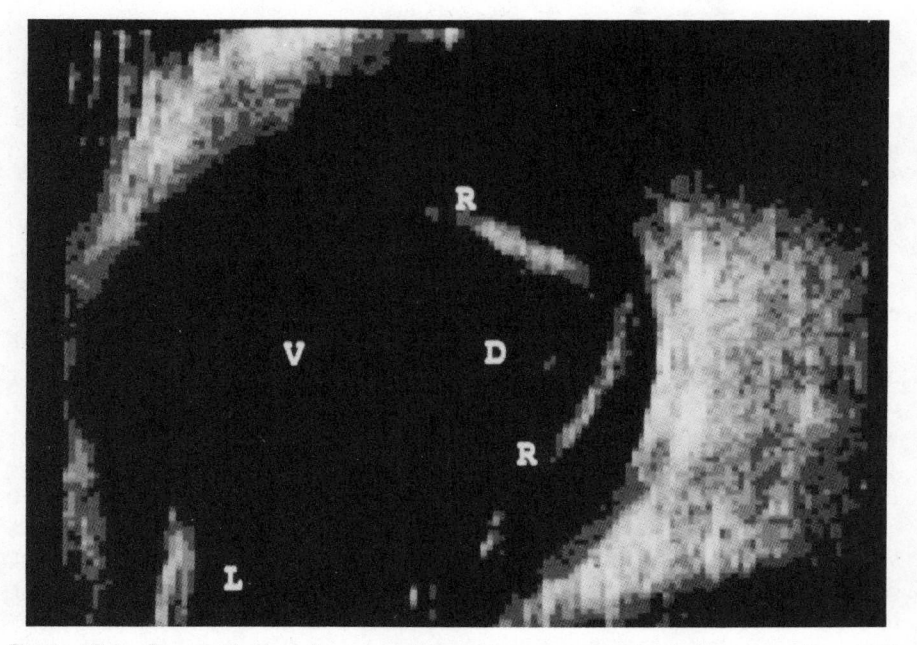

Figure 13.3   *One of 32 slices from an ultrasound scan series of a human eye with a total retinal detachment. V = vitreous chamber; L = lens; R = detached retina; D = vitreous debris.*

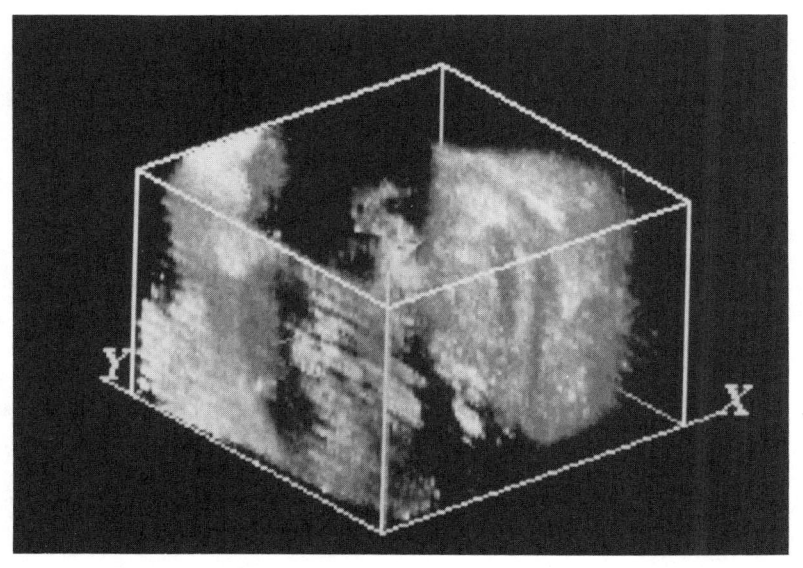

Figure 13.4 *Volume rendering of scan series. X-axis refers to axial depth. Y-axis is horizontal, and Z-axis is vertical.*

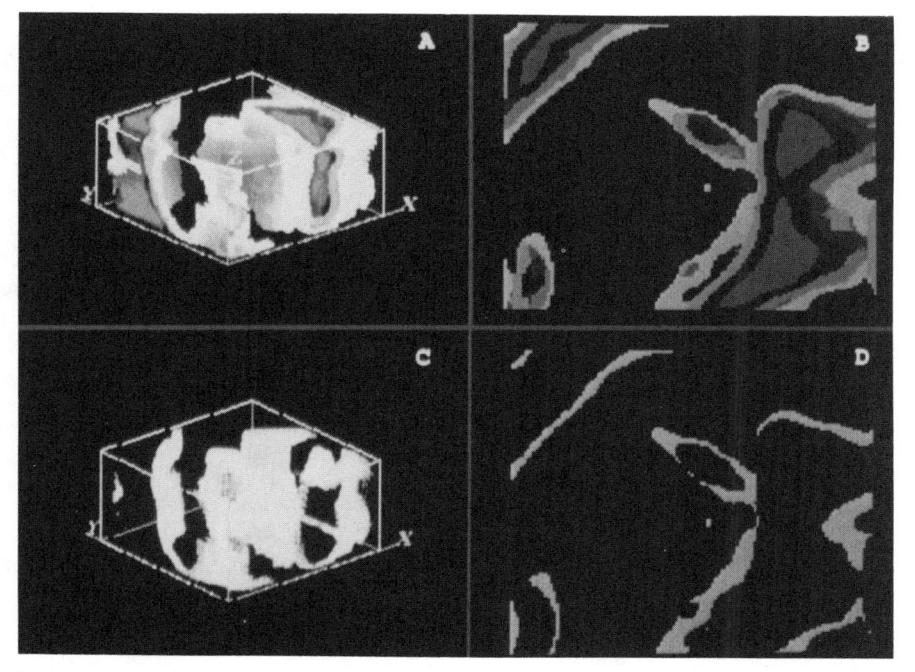

Figure 13.5 *Illustration of competitive learning: (A) Three-dimensional reconstruction where each shade of gray indicates output of "winning" unit at each X-Y-Z position. (B) A single horizontal cross section through (A). (C) Three-dimensional reconstruction of output of the unit found to be most sensitive to the detached retina. (D) A single horizontal cross section through (C).*

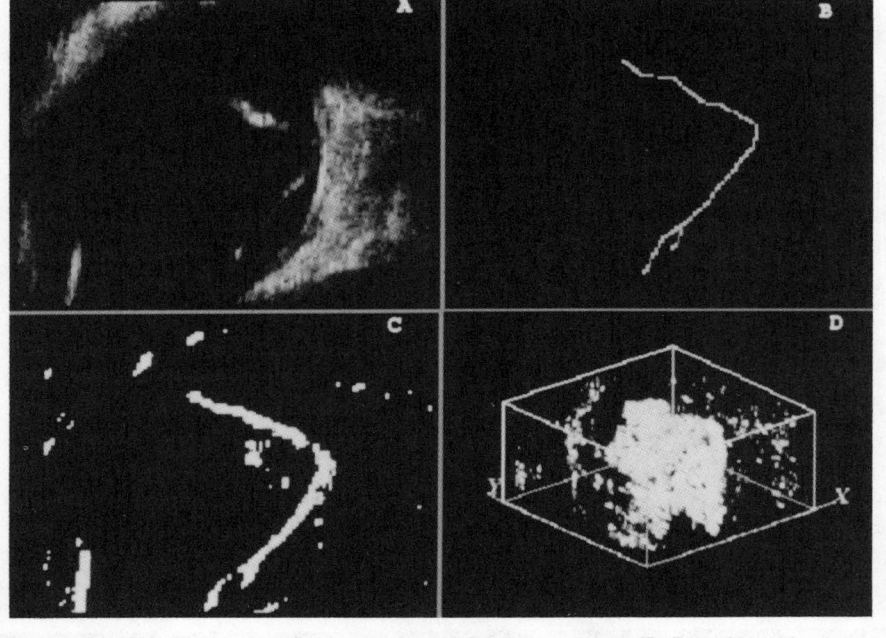

Figure 13.6 *Illustration of back-propagation (A) Single input slice. (B) Paired teaching image in detached retina is set active. (C) Output of trained network for slice shown in A and B. (D) Three-dimensional reconstruction based on back-propagation output.*

series. Figure 13.6(*A*) shows a single input slice from this series while Figure 13.6(*B*) shows the paired teaching image in which the detached retina has been manually delineated. Figure 13.6(*C*) shows the network output after training for this slice. A 3-D reconstruction based on network output is shown in Figure 13.6(*D*). The output of the back-propagation network is far more specific than that of the competitive learning network. The output unit was sensitive to the detached retina, but also to the lens boundaries.

13.4 DISCUSSION

While use of gray-scale thresholding and gradient operations is useful as a means for segmentation for the purpose of 3-D display of anatomical structures, these techniques may often lack the specificity necessary to isolate structures in images where contrast is low and/or gradients are weak.

Undirected self-organizing neural networks, based on competitive learning, have the virtues of simplicity and the capability to rapidly adapt to regularities in pattern sets. Their limitations, however, are twofold: First, because learning is undirected, one cannot be certain that a single unit or combination of units will act to segment the feature of interest from background; and second, because the network consists of only a single modifiable layer of connections, the complexity of the functions that can be implemented by the network is limited.

Directed learning with back propagation has virtues and limitations that are the converse of competitive learning. The presence of hidden layers permits networks to implement logically complex functions, but the learning rate in back propagation is notoriously slow, especially considering the size of the input pattern sets likely to be encountered when dealing with images, let alone three-dimensional image structures.

Directed learning has the advantage of aiming to specifically segment the feature (or features) of interest from background, but the disadvantage of requiring the definition of a teaching pattern set by manual feature delineation before training can take place.

Neural networks provide a modality whereby image segmentation operations based on pixel gray-scale levels and their spatial distributions may be performed. Furthermore, these techniques may be extended to three-dimensional image sets, where such operations may be of particular value. As 3-D radiologic imaging techniques become more and more dominant, the importance of algorithms capable of segmenting these huge sets of data into anatomically relevant images becomes imperative. The ability of neural networks to adapt to pattern structure makes them of special interest for such operations.

REFERENCES

[1] C. von der Malsberg, Self-organizing of orientation sensitive cells in the striate cortex, *Kybernetik*, 14, 85–100 (1973).

[2] D. E. Rumelhart and D. Zipser, Feature discovery by competitive learning, *Cognitive Sci.*, 9, 75–112 (1985).

[3] S. Grossberg, Adaptive pattern classification and universal recoding: Part I. Parallel development and coding of neural feature detectors, *Biological Cybernetics*, 23, 121–134 (1976).

[4] T. Kohonen, "Clustering, Taxonomy, and Topological Maps of Patterns," in M. Lang, Ed., *Proceedings of the Sixth International Conference on Pattern Recognition*, IEEE Computer Society Press, Silver Spring, Md., 114–125 (1982).

[5] D. E. Rumelhart, G. E. Hinton, and R. J. Williams, Learning representations by back-propagating errors, *Nature*, 323, 533–536 (1986).

[6] R. A. Jacobs, Increased rates of convergence through learning rate adaptation, *Neural Networks*, 1, 295–307 (1988).

Implementation of Neural Networks on Parallel Architectures and Invariant Object Recognition

MANAVENDRA MISRA
VIKTOR K. PRASANNA

14.1   INTRODUCTION

The past decade has seen a resurgence in the field of neural networks. This renewed interest has manifested itself in hectic research, as well as in the development of commercial applications that employ neural principles. Research in the field has resulted in the application of artificial neural networks in diverse application areas such as computer vision, medical diagnosis, signal processing, business, weather forecasting, and robotics [1].

   A number of different approaches can be used to implement neural models in the context of specific applications. The simplest and most straightforward of these approaches is to simulate the particular model in software that runs on a serial machine. This method provides a readily available tool for learning about neural networks and for demonstrating the concepts behind neural processing. Many commercial products based on this approach are currently available in the market. Although this approach possesses the positive attributes of simplicity, flexibility, and ease of use, most real applications use networks with sizes that far exceed the limited capabilities of these programs. One way to enhance the speed of these simulations is to use coprocessor boards that have been especially designed for these applications. These boards make it possible for a conventional machine to handle somewhat larger networks. However, since ANN theory is based on massive parallelism, it is evident that parallel machines have to be used to exploit this inherent parallelism. Adopting this line of thinking, researchers have developed a

Fast Learning and Invariant Object Recognition, By Branko Souček and the IRIS Group.
ISBN 0-471-57430-9   © 1992 John Wiley & Sons, Inc.

number of special purpose parallel machines to implement larger networks. Both analog and digital technologies (or a combination of both) have been used in such machines. These machines can be optimized for the particular application that they have been designed for and can yield extremely good results. The drawback in such schemes, however, is that these designs are very inflexible and work for only the specific model for which they have been designed. An attractive compromise between speed and flexibility is provided by programmable, general purpose, digital parallel architectures. Implementations on these machines have the advantage that myriads of ANN models of varying sizes, and using different learning mechanisms, can be simulated on the same architecture with reasonable efficiency.

Over the past few years, we have directed our research efforts toward developing algorithms to simulate neural networks on such architectures [2, 3, 4]. Our interest has been in issues such as the time and space complexities of the algorithms, the interprocessor communication requirements, and the routing of data in the machine. This chapter presents a summary of some of our work in the field before describing new results.

The chapter consists of two parts. Part I presents algorithms for implementing general neural network models on the Reduced Mesh of Trees (RMOT) architecture. An RMOT of size n is an SIMD architecture with n PEs and n^2 memory modules arranged in an $n \times n$ array. The ith PE has access to the memory modules in the ith row and the ith column of the memory array. A fully connected, single layer neural model with n neurons can be mapped onto an RMOT of size n in a very natural fashion. An update of activation values in this case requires $(n + 2)$ time steps. The chapter shows how to simulate models with sparse connectivity among neurons on an RMOT of size $\sqrt{n + e}$ in $O(\sqrt{n + e})$ time, where e is the number of nonzero weights in the connection matrix of the network. Preprocessing is carried out on the connection matrix of the given sparse network resulting in data movement that has an optimal asymptotic time complexity and a small constant factor. Finally, it is shown how multilayer networks can be simulated efficiently on the architecture. The RMOT is thus shown to be an attractive architecture for implementing various neural models.

One particular area where ANNs have been finding great application is computer vision. Central to the development of an artificial vision system is its ability to recognize objects in a translation and rotation invariant manner. The Dynamic Link Architecture [5] is a neural system that provides this invariance capability. In the framework of this model, objects are represented by labeled graphs and recognition amounts to a process of labeled graph matching. The second part of the chapter describes this model and shows how it can be implemented on a linear array of processors. The linear array of processors provides an extremely simple parallel framework for the implementation of the model, and we present an algorithm to implement labeled graph matching (the major computational component of the model) on this architecture. If N_A is the number of nodes in the incoming labeled graph, N_B is the total number of nodes of all stored graphs, and p is the number of processors in the array, the algorithm has a time complexity of $O(N_A \log N_A + N_A N_B / p)$.

PART I: PARALLEL IMPLEMENTATION OF GENERAL NEURAL NETWORK MODELS

This part of the chapter presents a discussion of the issues involved in the implementation of general neural network models on parallel, general purpose architectures. It is organized as follows. A definition of the problem and the models being considered is presented first. The state of the art in the area is then presented, followed by a description of the Reduced Mesh of Trees Architecture. This is followed by the algorithms for simulating the general models on this target architecture.

14.2 ARTIFICIAL NEURAL NETWORKS

The problem being addressed in this part of the chapter is that of the implementation of artificial neural network models on general purpose, programmable, parallel digital architectures. In the rest of this section, we define the kinds of model we are trying to implement. We are interested in the algorithmic and architectural issues that emerge when these general models are implemented. Of particular interest are the time and space complexities of the algorithms being used, the mapping techniques, interprocessor communication requirements, and data routing issues. These are also the criteria that are used to compare algorithms and architectures against each other.

14.2.1 Biological Inspiration

The animal brain is a large conglomeration of very richly interconnected simple processing elements called neurons. Typically, the nervous system has about 10^{11} neurons, each having an average of 10^3–10^4 inputs and outputs, giving rise to 10^{15} interconnections. It is theorized that the immense computing power of the brain is a result of the parallel and distributed computing carried out by these neurons.

There is a great variety in the structure of neurons found in the nervous system and, if looked at microscopically, neurons can be very complex. The biological model of the neuron, however, captures all the salient features of a real neuron in a simple model (Fig. 14.1). Dendrites form the input channels of a neuron, while the axon forms the output channel. Axons of other neurons impinge upon the dendrites of a neuron through junctions called synapses. Synapses can be either excitatory or inhibitory and have weights associated with them. Signals are passed electrically through axons and then are transmitted chemically across synapses. A weighted sum of all the signals being received by a neuron's dendritic structure is formed at the cell body, and this determines the membrane potential of that cell. The output of a neuron is a train of pulses sent out on the axon. The magnitude of these pulses remains constant and information is conveyed in the firing rate of the neuron. A continuous monotonically nondecreasing function relates the membrane potential to the firing rate of the neuron.

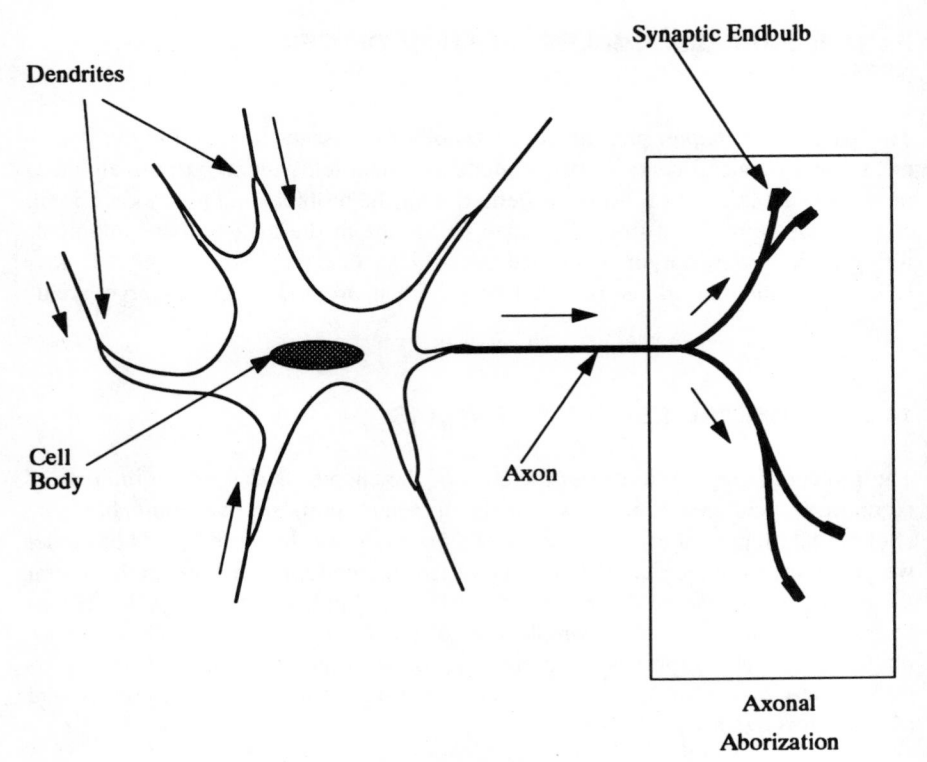

Figure 14.1 The biological model of a neuron.

14.2.2 Model of the Neuron

The computational model of the neuron used in ANNs is an abstraction of the characteristic properties of the biological neuron. The earliest neural model was developed in the 1940s by McCulloch and Pitts (Fig. 14.2).

The McCulloch–Pitts neuron [6] is a simple two state device. It forms a weighted sum of its inputs and yields a binary output, depending on whether the weighted sum is greater than or less than a threshold θ.

$$
a_i = \begin{cases} 1 & \text{if } \sum_{j=1}^{n} w_{ij} a_j > \theta_i \\[2mm] 0 & \text{if } \sum_{j=1}^{n} w_{ij} a_j < \theta_i \end{cases} \tag{14.1}
$$

where a_i is the activation of the ith neuron, w_{ij} is the weight of the connection from neuron j to neuron i, and θ_i is the threshold of the ith neuron. To mimic the biological model more closely, this transfer function could be replaced by a continuous, monotonically nondecreasing function, which corresponds better with bi-

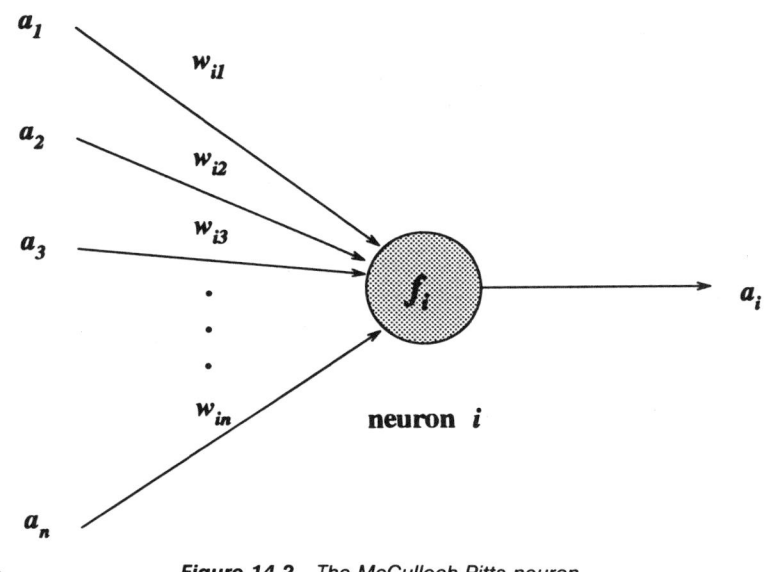

Figure 14.2   *The McCulloch-Pitts neuron.*

ological data. One such function that is often used is the Sigmoid function:

$$S(x) = \frac{1}{1 + e^{-cx}} \qquad (14.2)$$

where c is a constant. Neurons with continuous transfer functions are called *graded response neurons* [7].

14.2.3   The General Model

Several ANN models have been proposed in literature [8]. These models can be differentiated on the basis of

- Whether the network is a single or a multilayer network
- Whether it is a feedforward network or it has feedback
- Whether the network incorporates learning* or not

The computations involved in most ANN models, however, conform to a common form. The neural networks addressed here adhere to the following general model. A neural network consists of interconnected simple neurons. The input signals received by a neuron are multiplied by appropriate weights and summed to yield the overall input to the neuron. The output of the neuron is produced by applying a function f, called the activation function, to the weighted sum.

*Learning is defined to be the updating of synaptic weights.

The update step can be formally described as

$$a_i^{k+1} = f_i \left(\sum_{j=1}^{n} w_{ij} a_j^k \right) \tag{14.3}$$

where the index k indicates time steps.

The neurons in the network could form a single layer with feedback connections or could form the input, output, and hidden layers of a multilayer network. In a single layer network, a neuron computes its new activation value after receiving inputs from other neurons, and communicates the updated activation value to neurons its output connects to. In a multilayer network, the activation values are communicated to the next layer. A forward pass of data from the input layer to the output layer (which does not involve changes of weights) is referred to as a *recall operation* or the *search phase*. Learning can either be executed in the forward pass by carrying out additional computations in the neurons or may require a separate pass of data in the opposite direction (as in the back-propagation model).

14.2.4 Learning

Learning is defined as the modification of synaptic weights that encodes patterns into the ANN. Learning can either be supervised or unsupervised. In unsupervised learning (e.g., Hebbian Learning [9]), the weight of a link is updated based on local information available to the neurons connected by the link. Supervised learning [10], on the other hand, requires the presence of an external "teacher." The teacher modifies the weights based on the error between a desired response and the actual response to an input.

One of the most popular learning schemes for multilayer neural networks is the back-propagation algorithm [11]. Back propagation is a supervised learning mechanism that minimizes the mean squared error between the desired and actual output values. There are two phases to the back-propagation algorithm. In the forward pass, a training pattern is input to the network and activations of the neurons are updated layer by layer till the output emerges at the output layer. This output is compared with the desired output for that pattern, and the error signals are propagated back through the network and the weights are updated. The computational complexity of the backward phase is the same as that of the forward phase.

At the start of a training run, a training pattern is input to the input layer of the multilayer ANN. Let the actual output of the jth neuron of the output layer be a_j. Let the desired (or target) output at that neuron be t_j. Then $(t_j - a_j)$ defines the error ϵ_j at that neuron. In general, the change in weight w_{ij} is given by

$$\Delta w_{ij} = \eta \delta_i a_j \tag{14.4}$$

where w_{ij} is the weight of the connection from neuron j to neuron i, η is the learning rate, and δ_i is the error signal. The error signal is defined as follows. If neuron j

is an output unit, then

$$\delta_j = \epsilon_j f_j'(x_j) \tag{14.5}$$

where x_j is the weighted sum of inputs to neuron j and f_j' is the derivative of the activation function. The error signals for the hidden units are computed recursively:

$$\delta_j = f_j'(x_j) \sum_k \delta_k w_{kj} \tag{14.6}$$

where the index k covers neurons in the next layer.

It should be noted that the major computation in the back-propagation algorithm requires the computing of a weighted sum (Eq. (14.6)) which makes the structure of the computation very similar to that of the search phase.

14.3 STATE OF THE ART

The late eighties saw a series of articles describing research on the implementation of ANNs on parallel digital architectures. In [12, 13], S. Y. Kung and J. N. Hwang describe a scheme for designing special purpose systolic ring architectures to simulate neural nets. By recognizing that neural algorithms can be rewritten as iterative matrix operations, the authors have been able to apply well known techniques for mapping iterative matrix algorithms directly onto systolic architectures. This method, however, is efficient only for fully connected networks. Simulating sparsely connected networks requires the storing of zero weights for all the missing interconnections and unnecessary computations involving these weights. A considerable amount of space and time is thus wasted. Also, the existence of wraparound connections is an undesirable feature of these architectures.

H. T. Kung et al. [14] have simulated feedforward neural networks that employ the back-propagation learning algorithm on the CMU Warp. The Warp is a programmable systolic machine with ten powerful PEs and thus provides a coarse grain of parallelism. This coarse grain of parallelism makes it difficult to completely exploit the parallelism in all but the smallest of neural networks. Of the two algorithms described in the paper, the network partitioning scheme is inefficient for large networks, while the data partitioning scheme is effective during the learning phase but not in the search phase.

The Connection Machine is seen by many researchers as the perfect ''neural engine'' because of its fine grain architecture. A simulation of multilayer ANNs running the back-propagation learning algorithm on the Connection Machine CM-2 is presented in [15] by Zhang et al. The authors describe how to implement a *multiply–accumulate–rotate* iteration for a fully connected network, a process quite similar to the one described in [12], using the 2-D mesh connections of the CM-2.

Przytula et al. [16, 17] describe algorithmic mapping schemes to map ANN models onto fine grained SIMD arrays. The implementations apply to connectionist networks of arbitrary topology in which search and learning operations can be expressed in terms of matrix and vector computations. The mapping methods developed are simple and general enough to be used on a number of commercial and existing machines. As a specific instantiation, the mapping methodology is shown for the Hughes SCAP machine.

A number of other researchers have also contributed to this rapidly developing research field that brings together parallel processing and neural networks. In [18], Diamantara et al. describe the implementation of neural network algorithms on the P^3 associative processor. Hammerstrom [19] has designed a digital VLSI chip for neural processing. Tomlinson et al. [20] have used a different approach by using digital pulse trains to simulate biological pulse trains. Ramacher and Beichter [21] describe a modular systolic chip for emulating ANNs. Ranka et al. [22, 23] have developed an ANN simulator for the Connection Machine and are working on a distributed implementation of back-propagation on a LAN. Shams and Przytula [24] present a method for mapping multilayer ANNs onto 2-D SIMD arrays. Tomboulian [25] uses a method developed to route arbitrary directed graphs on SIMD architectures to simulate ANNs. Wah and Chu [26] describe a mapping methodology for mapping ANNs onto multicomputers. Watanabe et al. [27] and Wilson [28] present ways to implement ANNs on specific array processors.

Recently, several researchers have considered alternative interconnection schemes for parallel computations [29, 30, 31]. This chapter presents techniques for simulating ANNs on one such organization, the Reduced Mesh of Trees organization. A Reduced Mesh of Trees (RMOT) of size n is an SIMD architecture with n PE's and n^2 memory modules arranged in an $n \times n$ array. The ith PE has access to the memory modules in the ith row and the ith column of the memory array. The RMOT has been shown to be very efficient for applications requiring dense data transfer operations [31]. It can provide optimal performance for many image and graph algorithms. This part of the chapter presents a summary of our research on implementing ANNs on the RMOT. A fully connected, single layer neural model with n neurons can be mapped onto an RMOT of size n in a very natural fashion. An update of activation values in this case requires $(n + 2)$ time steps. The chapter presents an algorithm to simulate models with sparse connectivity among neurons on an RMOT of size $\sqrt{n + e}$ in $O(\sqrt{n + e})$ time, where e is the number of nonzero weights in the connection matrix of the network. Preprocessing is carried out on the connection matrix of the given sparse network resulting in data movement that has an optimal asymptotic time complexity and a small constant factor. Finally, it is shown how multilayer networks can be simulated efficiently on the architecture.

14.4 SIMULATING NEURAL NETWORKS ON THE REDUCED MESH OF TREES ARCHITECTURE

A summary of our research on the implementation of ANN models on the RMOT [2, 3, 4] is presented in this section. It describes the RMOT and shows how neural network models with varying connectivities can be implemented on this target architecture.

14.4.1 The Reduced Mesh of Trees Architecture

An $n \times n$ Mesh of Trees (MOT) consists of an $n \times n$ array of processing elements (PEs) in which each row and each column of PEs form the leaves of a binary tree. The root and the internal nodes of each tree are also PEs. Thus, a Mesh of Trees of side n has a total of $3n^2 - 2n$ PEs. The reduced VLSI architecture considered in this paper consists of n PEs each having row and column access to an $n \times n$ array of memory modules, such that PE_i can access the modules in the ith row and ith column of the array. The memory module in the ith row and the jth column of the array is denoted by M_{ij}. Note that M_{ij} acts as a shared space between PE_i and PE_j. The proposed organization can be looked upon as a Mesh of Trees organization, in which the n^2 leaf PEs are replaced by n^2 memory locations, and each row (column) tree is replaced by a single PE with a row (column) bus. This organization has been called a Reduced Mesh of Trees [31]. The organization of such an architecture is shown in Figure 14.3 for $n = 4$. The PEs have arithmetic/logic capabilities and memory registers. Also, each memory module consists of a fixed number of $O(\log n)$ bit routing registers. Notice that $O(\log n)$ bits are necessary and sufficient to specify a memory address among n^2 memory modules. The advantages of the RMOT over the MOT are that it has a reduced number of PEs and can be laid out in lesser VLSI area and yet can provide optimal performance for a number of graph and image computations requiring dense data movements.

Memory Access and Operation Modes In normal operation, each PE can read or write one unit of data from a single memory location in its row or column. A single bit is used to indicate whether the access is *row-access* or *column-access*. Memory contention is avoided by allowing all PEs to do either a row-access or a column-access, but not both, in one cycle. Each PE specifies a $\log n$ bit address to select the memory module to be accessed. In addition, if each memory module contains k registers or memory locations, then each PE specifies a $\log k$ bit address to select a register within the module.

It should be noted that other research groups have been working with similar orthogonal arrays of PEs [29, 30].

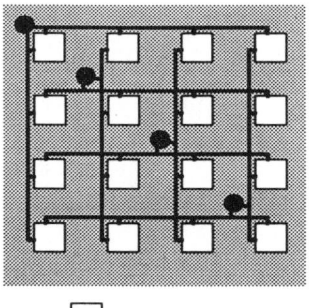

☐ Memory Module

● Processing Element

—— Row/Column Bus

Figure 14.3 *Organization of an RMOT with four PEs.*

14.4.2 Simulation of Fully Connected Networks

This section describes how a fully connected, single layer neural network is simulated on the RMOT.

Mapping   An RMOT of size n is used to simulate a fully connected network with n neurons. Each of the neurons in the network has n connection weights associated with it. PE i of the RMOT stores the current activation value of the ith neuron. The connection weights are stored in the $n \times n$ array of memory modules in row major order (connection weight w_{ij} is stored in memory module M_{ij}). Thus, the mapping of the activation values and connection weights onto the RMOT is done in the most natural fashion.

Update of Activation Values   As shown in Eq. (14.3), an update of the activation value of the ith neuron can be written as

$$a_i^{k+1} = f_i\left(\sum_{j=1}^{n} w_{ij} a_j^k, \theta_i \right) \tag{14.7}$$

where k is the iteration index and f_i is the activation function (step function, sigmoid function, etc.).

Equation 14.7 can be rewritten as

$$a_i^{k+1} = f_i(x_i^k, \theta_i) \tag{14.8}$$

$$x_i^k = W \cdot \mathbf{a}^k \tag{14.9}$$

where W is the $n \times n$ matrix of connection weights and $\mathbf{a}^k$ is the $n \times 1$ vector storing the activation values during the kth iteration. The update of activation values can, therefore, be thought of as a matrix–vector multiplication.

The computation represented by Eq. (14.7) can be carried out in three steps:

1. The activation value of the jth neuron, a_j, is communicated to all memory modules that contain the weights of the connections emanating from neuron j (i.e., all w_{ij}'s).
2. The value of $\Sigma_{j=1}^{n} w_{ij} a_j$ is computed for each neuron i.
3. The neuron's activation value is updated by applying the activation function to the weighted sum.

The mapping of activation values and connection weights onto the RMOT described in the previous subsection facilitates the above three steps. They are carried out as follows.

- **Broadcast:** The kth iteration begins with each PE j broadcasting the stored activation value a_j^k to all memory modules in the column j. The broadcast of

```
begin
   for each PE i in parallel do
      begin
         PS := 0;
         for j := 1 to n do
            begin
               read w_ij and a_j from memory module j in row i;
               PS := PS + (w_ij * a_j)
            end
      end
end.
```

Figure 14.4   *The multiply and add phase.*

data to modules in a column can be done in just one time step by using the column busses in the RMOT. At the end of the broadcast step, the memory module storing w_{ij} also has a_j.

- **Multiply and Add:** In this phase, a PE accesses each memory module in its row, multiplies the two values (w_{ij} and a_j) and adds the product to a partial sum register (PS). At the end of this phase, the register has the sum $\sum_{j=1}^{n} w_{ij}a_j^k$. Since there are n memory modules in each row, this phase takes n time steps. The steps of this phase are shown in Figure 14.4.
- **Activation Function Application:** After the multiply and add phase, the register PS has the required weighted sum. The activation function f_i is then applied to this sum to yield the new activation value of that neuron.

The complete update step therefore takes $n + 2$ time steps.

14.4.3   Simulation of Sparsely Connected Networks

If a single layer ANN has a few links missing, it is possible to carry out the search phase processing in the manner described in the previous section. In this approach, a zero is stored as the weight of a missing connection. If, however, the number of missing connections is very large, a considerable amount of space and time is wasted in storing and computing with the zero weights. An efficient method of carrying out search phase computations for sparse neural networks is presented in this section.

Initial Data Mapping   We assume that the neural network to be simulated has n neurons and e nonzero connections. An RMOT having $\sqrt{n + e}$ PEs and a $\sqrt{n + e} \times \sqrt{n + e}$ array of memory modules is used to simulate the network. The memory locations in a module are either used as data registers or as routing registers. The initial activation values are assigned to the first n PEs in row major order (an example is shown in Fig. 14.5). This mapping can be mathematically described as follows: Each memory module M_{ij} ($1 \le i, j \le \sqrt{n + e}$) is assigned an index given by $[(i - 1) * n] + j$. Starting with $i = 1$ and going to $i = n$,

$$\mathbf{W} = \begin{bmatrix} X & 0 & 0 & 0 & X & 0 \\ 0 & 0 & 0 & X & 0 & 0 \\ 0 & 0 & X & 0 & 0 & 0 \\ X & 0 & 0 & 0 & 0 & 0 \\ 0 & X & X & 0 & 0 & X \\ X & 0 & 0 & 0 & 0 & X \end{bmatrix}$$

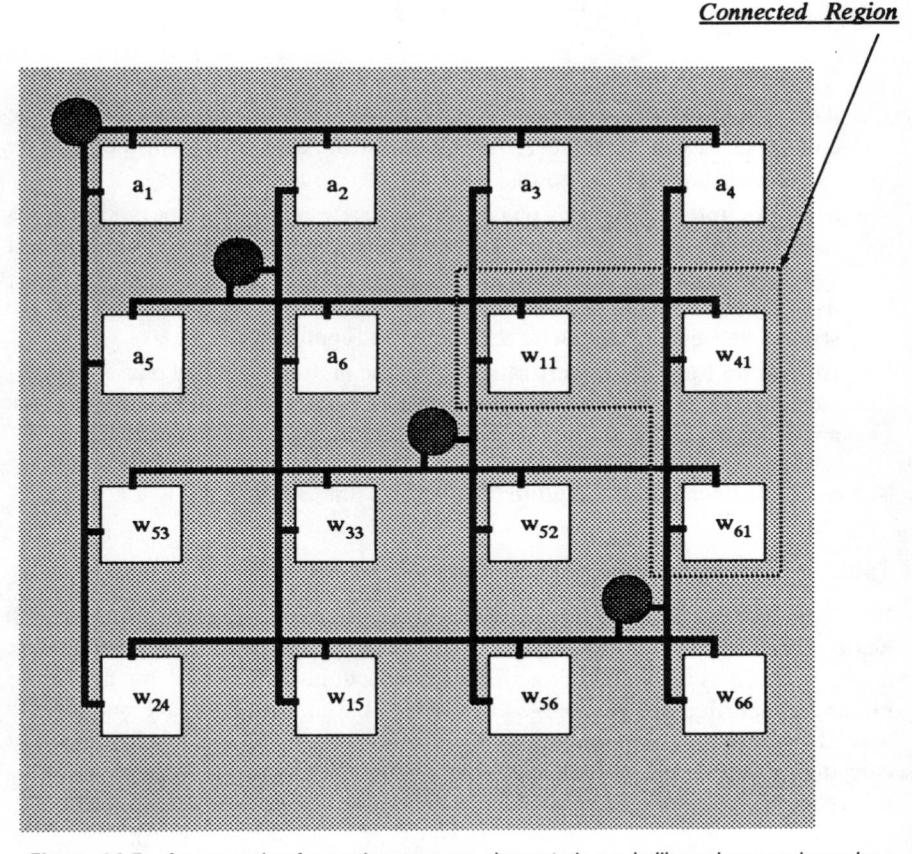

Figure 14.5 *An example of mapping nonzero elements in snakelike column major order.*

activation value a_i is mapped onto the memory module with the smallest index that doesn't have an activation value mapped onto it yet.

Given the sparse connection–weight matrix for the network, the nonzero entries are mapped onto the memory array in snakelike column major order (Fig. 14.5). Snakelike column major ordering is formally defined as follows: Each memory module M_{ij} is assigned an index. If i is odd, the index is given by $[(i - 1) * n] + j$, else the index is $[(i - 1) * n] + (n - j + 1)$. Starting with $j = 1$ and going to $j = n$, choose the nonzero entry in column j of the weight matrix with the least row index that hasn't been mapped onto the memory array yet. Map it onto the memory module with the least index (as determined earlier) that does not have a weight assigned to it yet. This mapping ensures that nonzero entries belonging to a particular column of the weight matrix form a connected region (Fig. 14.5). In each iteration of the algorithm, the $(w_{ij} * a_j)$ products corresponding to a row of the weight matrix have to be collected and summed. This would be facilitated by having these products in a connected region. This in turn, requires the realization of a permutation that arranges the elements in snakelike row major order. A snake-like row major ordering is similar to a snakelike column major ordering, except that the nonzero elements to be mapped are chosen row by row (instead of column by column). Each data element to be routed has three routing tags associated with it. Routing tags are calculated for each entry and stored in the routing registers. The computation of these routing tags can be done in $O((n + e) [\log (n + e)]^2)$ time on a serial computer [32] and in $O(\sqrt{n + e})$ time on a $\sqrt{n + e} \times \sqrt{n + e}$ mesh connected computer [33].

Recall that an iteration of the algorithm consists of the computation

$$a_i^{k+1} = f_i\left(\sum_{j=1}^{n} w_{ij}a_j^k, \theta_i \right), \quad \text{for } 1 \le i \le n$$

During an iteration, the following steps transpire:

1. a_j $(1 \le j \le n)$ is sent to all the memory modules that contain nonzero elements from the jth column of the weight matrix.
2. The product of w_{ij} (the element in the memory module) and a_j is to be routed to a module such that in the new distribution of elements, the products corresponding to a row form a connected region.
3. The data in each new connected region are summed to yield the weighted sum.
4. This sum is sent to the appropriate memory module. An application of the activation function on this weighted sum yields the updated activation value.

Data Routing   During each iteration, three kinds of data routing problems arise:

1. The broadcast of a_j to all elements of the jth column of the connection weight matrix.
2. Transformation from a snakelike column major order distribution to a snake-like row major order distribution.
3. Transportation of the sums $(\Sigma_{j=1}^{n} w_{ij}a_j^k)$ to the memory modules that store the appropriate activation values.

We develop an efficient method that uses preprocessing done on the structure of the weight matrix to solve the above routing problems in $O(\sqrt{n} + e)$ time per iteration. A description of the general routing technique follows.

The problem of data transport among memory modules is essentially that of realizing a permutation of the elements contained in the modules. More formally, if M_{ij} has to send data D_{ij} to M_{i*j*}, then the permutation to be realized is $\pi: (i, j) \rightarrow (i*, j*)$. An approach toward realizing such a permutation is to apply the following two steps: In the first step, the elements are moved within their columns until they are in their respective destination rows. In the second step, the elements are moved within their rows until they are in their correct positions. This method, however, could result in many elements accumulating in one module at the end of the first step (e.g., if all the elements of a column have the same destination row, they will all end up in the same module). To avoid this kind of congestion, the elements are first permuted within their rows in such a manner that when the permutations along the columns are carried out, no two elements end up in the same module [34].

The "three-phase" routing method can therefore be described as follows:

Phase I: Permute the elements within their rows so as to avoid congestion in Phase II.

Phase II: Permute the elements within columns so as to get them to their destination rows.

Phase III: Permute the elements within their destination rows so as to get them to their final positions.

The theoretical foundation of the algorithm is presented in detail in [3]. Each piece of data has three routing registers associated with it (one for each phase): RR_I, RR_{II}, and RR_{III}. The values of these routing registers are computed off line and this computation can be done in the times specified earlier.

Using the procedures shown in Figure 14.6, the broadcast, redistribution and update problems are solved by procedures called BROADCAST, RE-DISTRIBUTE, and UPDATE, respectively, [3]. These procedures are then used in the overall algorithm as shown in the next section.

The Algorithm   The complete algorithm to update activation values of the neurons of a sparsely connected neural network is presented in this section. In the preprocessing stage shown in Figure 14.7, the memory array is set up to perform the iterations. The iterations are performed as shown in Figure 14.8.

14.4.4   Simulating Multilayer Networks

In this section, we describe how multilayer ANNs employing a back-propagation learning scheme are simulated on an RMOT. Initially, we assume that each layer of the network has an equal number of neurons, and all possible connections between layers exist. The method can be modified for other cases too. The compu-

```
procedure PHASE(RR, phase-number)
  begin
    if phase-number=I or phase-number=III then
      for each PE(i) in parallel do
        for j:= 1 to √n + e do
          begin
            read data and its destination, RR(i,j), from M_ij;
            write data in destination module in the same row
          end
    else
      for each PE(j) in parallel do
        for i:= 1 to √n + e do
          begin
            read data and its destination, RR(i, j), from M_ij;
            write data in destination module in the same column
          end
  end.
procedure ROUTE
  begin
    PHASE(RR_I, I)
    PHASE(RR_II, II)
    PHASE(RR_III, III)
  end.
```

Figure 14.6   *The procedures ROUTE and PHASE.*

1. Compute the mapping of the nonzero elements of *W* onto the memory array in snakelike column major order and store it.
2. Identify the "leader" modules in the connected regions formed in step 1. Set the limit registers in these modules to define the boundaries of the connected regions.
3. Compute the mapping of the nonzero elements of *W* onto the memory array in snakelike row major order and store it.
4. Identify the leader modules in the connected regions formed in step 3. Set the limit registers in these modules to define the boundaries of the connected regions. Set the routing registers of the modules that correspond to the update step so as to get these data to the modules storing the components of *a*.
5. Store initial components of a^0 in the first *n* modules in row major order. Compute the routing tags to route these elements to the leader modules identified in step 2 and store them in the routing registers corresponding to the broadcast step.
6. Map the nonzero elements of *W* onto the memory array in snakelike column major order according to the mapping computed in step 1. Compute the routing tags for these modules for routing data so as to achieve a permutation from the mapping in step 1 to the mapping in step 3.

Figure 14.7   *Preprocessing steps.*

repeat

1. Broadcast the elements of a using the procedure BROADCAST. The routing registers, already set, determine which modules the elements go to.
2. Use RE-DISTRIBUTE to get the product terms in the new connected regions.
3. Use UPDATE to form the weighted sums, route them to the modules storing the components of a and update the activation values by applying the activation function to the weighted sum.

until (convergence).

Figure 14.8 *Iteration steps.*

tations involved in the search phase of a multilayer network are similar to those for a single layer ANN. The major difference is that layer numbers are used as iteration indices instead of time steps.

Notation and Mapping The ANN is assumed to have N layers, numbered from 1 to N with m neurons per layer. The neurons in each layer are numbered from 1 to m. The ith neuron in the lth layer has an activation value labeled by a_i^l $(1 \le l \le N, 1 \le i \le m)$. The weight from the jth neuron in the kth layer to the ith neuron in the $(k + 1)$st layer is labeled as w_{ij}^k $(1 \le i, j \le m, 1 \le k \le N - 1)$.

The mapping of the activation values and the connection weights is done in a manner similar to that for fully connected single layered networks. We notice that updates are done on a layer by layer basis and parallelism is only required between the neurons of a particular layer. Thus, it is sufficient to use an RMOT with m PEs. The ith PE stores the activation values $a_i^1, a_i^2, \ldots, a_i^N$ in its registers. The derivatives f_i' are computed along with the activation values and are stored in the PEs too. The PEs also have registers allocated for storing the error functions (δ's) for each neuron during the backward pass. The memory module M_{ij} stores w_{ij}^1, $w_{ij}^2, \ldots, w_{ij}^{N-1}$.

Search Phase The computations for the update of the activation values for the search phase are given by

$$a_i^l = f_i \left(\sum_{j=1}^m w_{ij}^{l-1} a_j^{l-1} \right) \tag{14.10}$$

This can be rewritten as

$$a_i^l = f_i(x_i^l) \tag{14.11}$$

where (x_i^l) represents the weighted sum of the inputs to neuron i of layer l. Thus, the computations of derivatives, $f_i'(x_i)$, to be used in the learning phase, can also be done at this time.

Equation (14.10) is quite similar to Eq. (14.7) and so the search phase computations can be carried out in a manner quite similar to that described for fully connected single layered networks. Details are omitted because of the similarity.

Learning Phase The learning phase is composed of the following steps:

1. Computation of error signals for the output layer. In terms of our notation, the computation is given by

$$\delta_i^N = (t_i - a_i^N) f_i'(x_i^N), \quad 1 \le i \le m \tag{14.12}$$

This computation can be done locally within each PE.

2. Update of weights going from layer $N - 1$ to layer N. This computation is given by

$$w_{ij}^{N-1} \leftarrow w_{ij}^{N-1} + \eta \delta_i^N a_j^{N-1} \tag{14.13}$$

This will require the broadcast of δ_i^N down a row and then each PE computes the new weight for each of the modules in its column.

3. For all other layers (on a layer by layer basis), computation of error signals and the update of weights. This is done according to

$$\delta_i^l = f_i'(x_i^l) \sum_k \delta_k^{l+1} w_{ki}^l \tag{14.14}$$

$$\Delta w_{ij}^{l-1} = \eta \delta_i^l a_j^{l-1} \tag{14.15}$$

The calculation of δ_i^l is similar to a matrix vector multiplication operation and so can be done in a manner similar to that of Section 14.4.1. However, the broadcast of δ_i^{l+1} is done along a row and the sums are formed for the elements of a column.

14.5 DISCUSSION

The RMOT is shown to be an attractive architecture for simulating artificial neural networks. Fully connected single layer ANNs are mapped and simulated on an RMOT with n PEs, in a straightforward manner in $(n + 2)$ time steps. Single layer ANNs with sparse connectivity can be simulated on an RMOT with $\sqrt{n} + e$ PEs in $O(\sqrt{n} + e)$ time, if preprocessing is carried out on the connection weight matrix of the ANN. It is shown that multilayer ANNs that employ the back-propagation algorithm for learning patterns can be efficiently simulated on an RMOT too. In comparison to the linear systolic array simulation of fully connected ANNs [13], the RMOT implementation uses the same number of PEs and updates take the same amount of time. Notice that $\Omega(n)$ time is needed to carry out these sim-

TABLE 14.1 Simulation of Fully Connected Single Layer Networks

	No. of PEs	Total Storage	Time per Update
Linear Array [13]	n	$O(n^2)$	$O(n)$
MCC	n^2	$O(n^2)$	$O(n)$
RMOT	n	$O(n^2)$	$O(n)$

TABLE 14.2 Simulation of Sparsely Connected Single Layer Networks

	No. of PEs	Total Storage	Time per Update
Linear Array [13]	n	$O(n^2)$	$O(n)$
MCC	$n + e$	$O(n + e)$	$O(\sqrt{n + e})$
RMOT	$\sqrt{n + e}$	$O(n + e)$	$O(\sqrt{n + e})$

TABLE 14.3 Simulation of a Multilayer Network with *N* Layers and *m* Neurons/Layer

	No. of PEs	Total Storage	Time per Update
Linear Array [13]	$m \times N$	$O(m^2 N)$	$O(mN)$
MCC	m^2	$O(m^2)$	$O(mN)$
RMOT	m	$O(m^2)$	$O(mN)$

ulations. In addition, the RMOT is shown to have an efficient algorithm for handling sparse networks. The linear array simulation [13] of sparse ANNs will use $O(n^2)$ storage (as all the zero weights have to be stored), and an update takes $\theta(n)$ time in the worst case (because of the limited bandwidth, all the n activation values have to traverse one link, thus fixing a lower bound of n time steps). An $n \times n$ Mesh Connected Computer (MCC) could also be used to simulate fully connected ANNs in the same amount of time (using sort as a basic routine), but the MCC would have n^2 PEs as compared to only n PEs in the RMOT. These results are tabulated in Tables 14.1, 14.2, and 14.3. With attempts being made to actually build such massive memory machines, it will soon be possible to use ANNs for real life applications by implementing them on the RMOT.

PART II: IMPLEMENTATION OF THE DYNAMIC LINK ARCHITECTURE ON PARALLEL MACHINES

Central to the development of a good model of the human visual system is the ability to recognize objects in a translation and rotation invariant manner. The Dynamic Link Architecture [5] is an attempt to model the architecture of the human brain. It breaks away from more traditional neural network models in that it employs rapid modification of synapses during the recognition phase itself. This provides the model with a capability to recognize objects in spite of translations and rotations of the objects in the visual field.

This part of the chapter describes the motivation and the theoretical framework behind the model and then discusses the various issues involved in implementing the model on parallel machines. For the sake of completeness, a brief description of the model is presented here. Details of the model can be found in [5, 35, 36]. A major component of the model is determining the best match of an incoming labeled graph from amongst a set of stored graphs. This chapter presents an algorithm to implement this labeled graph matching on a linear array of processors.

14.6 TRANSLATION INVARIANT OBJECT RECOGNITION

Human memory is organized in an associative manner. Unlike inputs to digital computer memory, inputs to human memory are not addresses but sensory patterns or parts of patterns. Given this input, the memory has the ability to recognize an input as being similar to some stored pattern. A striking example of this associative recall is the ability to recollect the words of a song after hearing a snatch of the tune. The visual system, too, is capable of recognizing an object in the presence of distractors or even when part of the object happens to be occluded. Efforts to incorporate these properties in artificial systems have been quite successful and a number of associative memory models have been suggested. Hopfield [37] has mathematically analyzed neural associative memories and using techniques from statistical mechanics, has proved stability and convergence properties of such structures. Artificial associative memories have the desirable properties of generalizing over Hamming distance and pattern completion. The human visual system, however, has abilities that far exceed those of these simple associative memories. Shown a scene, a human subject is able to recognize most of the objects in the scene independent of where they may be in the visual field. Recognition of objects by the human visual system is invariant to a set of transformations of the input image. The object can be translated anywhere within the visual field, rotated or distorted to a certain degree, or scaled up or down without degrading the accuracy of recognition. Most artificial associative memories do not provide these properties of invariance, and it is desirable to incorporate these properties in artificial systems.

The next section describes a model that achieves translation and rotation invariance in an object recognition system.

14.7 DYNAMIC LINK ARCHITECTURE

To clearly distinguish how the dynamic link model differs from conventional associative memory, a description of the dynamics of associative memory is presented before the description of the dynamic link model.

Associative Memory. The following formalization of associative memory is due to J. J. Hopfield [37]. The associative memory is constructed with a set of neurons *B*. The elements of *B* are indexed by natural numbers $\{1, \ldots, N\}$. A function σ assigns activation values to the individual neurons $\sigma: B \rightarrow \{-1, +1\}$. A neuron with $\sigma_i = -1$ is inactive, while one with $\sigma_i = +1$ is active. Corresponding to a state of the network, we construct an energy function

$$H = -\tfrac{1}{2} \sum_{i,j} T_{ij} \sigma_i \sigma_j \tag{14.16}$$

where T_{ij} is the weight of the connection from neuron *j* to neuron *i*. The values of T_{ij} are chosen so as to yield minima of the energy for each of the memory states that represent stored patterns ξ^α, where $\alpha \in \{1, \ldots, M\}$. The rule for changing the weights, so as to store a particular pattern ξ^α is given by

$$\Delta T_{ij} = \frac{1}{N} \xi_i^\alpha \xi_j^\alpha \tag{14.17}$$

where ξ_i^α represents the activity of neuron *i* in pattern ξ^α.
Thus

$$T_{ij} = \frac{1}{N} \sum_\alpha \xi_i^\alpha \xi_j^\alpha \tag{14.18}$$

To use this abstract model of associative memory for storing and recalling real patterns, features are assigned to the individual neurons. The features are chosen from a set of feature types *F*, and a function $\mathcal{F}$ assigns a feature to each neuron $\mathcal{F}: B \rightarrow F$. Objects are therefore represented by the activities of feature specific neurons at each *position* of the input image. This associative memory has the desirable properties of generalization over Hamming distance, pattern completion, and fault tolerance. Translation invariance, however, is not an inherent property of this model. We now describe a model that is capable of translation invariant object recognition.

Dynamic Links. To achieve translation invariance, von der Malsburg and Bienenstock [35, 36] have proposed a model in which they discard information pertaining to the absolute position of a feature in the input and store an object as a relational structure. Thus, the object is represented by a connected graph in which the nodes are labeled by features.

Unlike the model of associative memory described above, the activation values σ_i are no longer the primary variables. The temporal correlations of these values $\langle \sigma_i \sigma_j \rangle_t$ are more important. New primary variables J_{ij} are introduced. These variables interact with the second order correlations and encode spatial relations between features. These connection strengths change on a rapid time scale unlike the "permanent" connections T_{ij}, which are fixed when the patterns get stored. An additional constraint, $J_{ij} \le T_{ij}$ $\forall i, j$, is imposed so that only synapses that exist get activated. A pair of decoupled energy functions describe the dynamics of the system

$$H_J(\sigma) = -\sum_{i,j} J_{ij} \sigma_i \sigma_j \tag{14.19}$$

$$H(J) = -\sum_{i,j} J_{ij} \langle \sigma_i \sigma_j \rangle + \gamma \sum_i \left(\sum_j J_{ij} - p \right)^2 \tag{14.20}$$

where the dynamics of σ_i's are on a fast time scale while the dynamics of the J_{ij}'s are on a slower time scale. For the dynamics of Eq. (14.19), the variables J_{ij} are considered fixed, and it is assumed that the new values of $\langle \sigma_i \sigma_j \rangle$ have been computed before each change in J takes place. The first term in Eq. (14.20) biases the system toward higher values of J_{ij} for pairs of neurons with a higher $\langle \sigma_i \sigma_j \rangle$. The second term biases the system toward a state where each neuron has p active links. Since graphs in the model have a 2-D grid connectivity, each neuron has four nearest neighbors and p is set equal to 4. The parameter γ is the weight of this term.

A given image is stored by the system in the following way. It is first scanned to determine the local feature types. For each occurrence of a local feature f, a neuron $i \in B$ is chosen *randomly* such that $\mathcal{F}(i) = f$. The connection pattern is set up by assigning $T_{ij} = 1$ when the features $\mathcal{F}(i)$ and $\mathcal{F}(j)$ occur as neighbors in the image. A number of images, $1 \le \alpha \le M$, can be superimposed by using the same set of neurons B for storing them. The values of the permanent connections for each pattern are determined as above and the final values are given by

$$T_{ij} = \max_\alpha T_{ij}^\alpha \tag{14.21}$$

The selection of neurons from B is governed by a "mixing requirement" [35], which demands that neurons that are neighbors in pattern α are far apart (in the graph theoretic sense) in any other stored pattern β.

To make this basic model computationally more tractable, it is modified. The computation of the temporal correlation of signals proves a formidable task, and so $\langle \sigma_i \sigma_j \rangle$ is approximated by a term from its high temperature expansion, which involves only J_{ij}'s.

The system is now defined by a two layer structure. Input patterns are presented to layer A, while stored patterns are retrieved from layer B. The dynamics of the system are as follows. The object to be recognized is presented to layer A as a labeled graph. The input graph is represented by a set of J_{ij}'s that remain fixed while the system evolves. The objects in layer B are represented by the permanent connections T_{ij} between neurons. Permanent connections exist from neurons in layer A to neurons in layer B that have the same feature types: for $i \in B, j \in A$, $T_{ij} = 1$ if $\mathcal{F}(i) = \mathcal{F}(j)$, $T_{ij} = 0$ otherwise. Figure 14.9 gives an idea of the connectivity within as well as between the two layers.

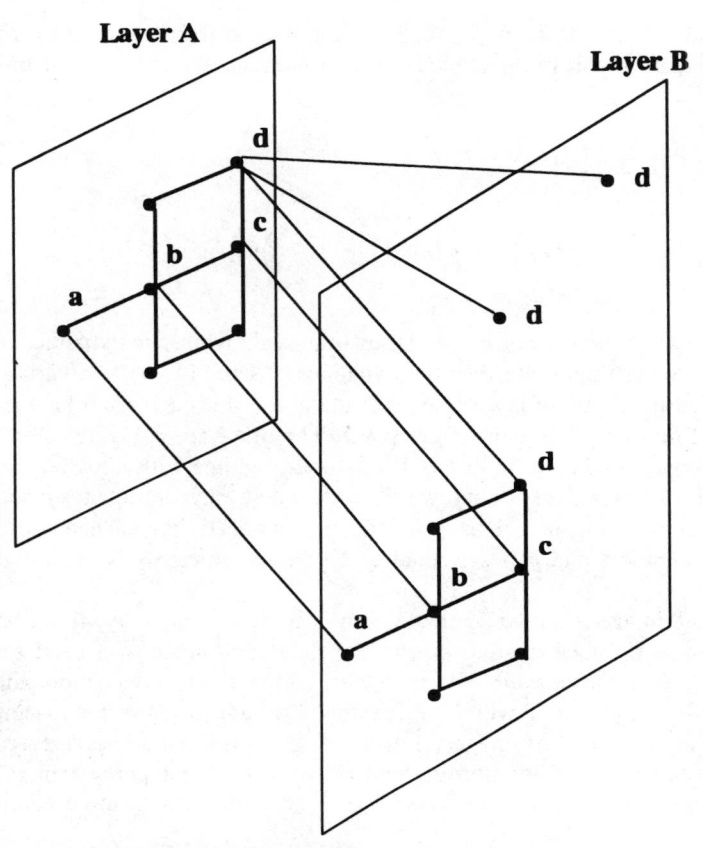

Figure 14.9 *Label preserving connections between layer A and layer B. Letters indicate feature types.*

J_{ij} connections (where $i \in B$ and $j \in A$ or B) are the variables of the system and are governed by the constraint $J_{ij} \leq T_{ij}$. Graph matching of the input graph in A with a stored graph in B is achieved by the minimization of the following energy function

$$H^{AB}(J) = - \sum_{i,j \in B, k, l \in A} J_{ij} J_{jl} J_{ik} J_{kl} + \gamma' \sum_{i \in A} \left(\sum_{k \in B} J_{ki} - p' \right)^2$$

$$+ \gamma' \sum_{k \in B} \left(\sum_{i \in A} J_{ki} - p' \right)^2 \qquad (14.22)$$

The first term approximates the second order correlation of signal activations. It is a cooperation term that favors 4-cycles of the form shown in Figure 14.10.

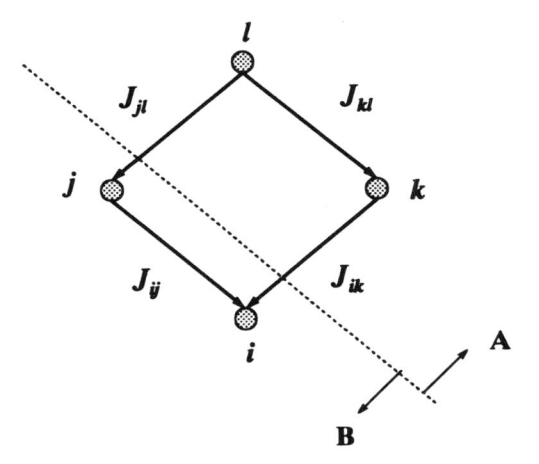

Figure 14.10 *The type of 4-cycle favored by H^{AB}.*

Since links between neurons now have directions assigned to them, there are two terms in the energy function that constrain the connectivity at a node. The second term in Eq. (14.22) is minimized when each neuron in layer A has p' outgoing links to layer B and the third term is minimized when each neuron in layer B has p' incoming links from layer A. For a 1–1 match between graphs, p' will have to be set equal to 1.

Subgraph retrieval from layer B is achieved by the minimization of an energy function with a structure similar to H^{AB}

$$H^{BB}(J) = - \sum_{i,j,k,l \in B} J_{ij} J_{jl} J_{ik} J_{kl} + \gamma \sum_{i \in B} \left(\sum_{k \in B} J_{ki} - p \right)^2$$

$$+ \gamma \sum_{k \in B} \left(\sum_{i \in B} J_{ki} - p \right)^2 \tag{14.23}$$

To solve both the graph matching and the subgraph retrieval problems, a new energy function $H(J)$ is constructed

$$H(J) = H^{BB}(J) + \delta H^{AB}(J) \tag{14.24}$$

Minimizing H solves both problems simultaneously. The parameter δ can be used to weight the function toward one or the other of the factors.

The pattern recognition task begins by the presentation of an input image to A. This activates a labeled graph $\{J_{ij}\}_{i,j \in A}$. A set of feature preserving permanent connections are established that link each neuron in A to all neurons in B that have the same feature type. The aim is to retrieve a labeled subgraph in B (say T^1) that best matches the input graph. The global minimum of H is then the graph $\{J_{ij}\}$ such that

1. $J_{ij} = T_{ij}^1$ for $i, j \in B$.
2. $\{J_{ij}\}_{i \in B, j \in A}$ realizes a label preserving isomorphism, that is, a neuron j in the input graph is connected to a neuron i in B that has the same label, and neighbors in the input graph are connected to neighbors in the retrieved graph.

$H^{BB}(J)$ has M minima of equal energy corresponding to the M stored patterns. The introduction of H^{AB} breaks this symmetry and only one of the stored graphs allows a label preserving isomorphism with the input graph. The energy valley corresponding to this pattern is deepened.

14.8 IMPLEMENTATION ISSUES

This section discusses the various issues involved in implementing the dynamic link model on a parallel machine. An implementation of the model on a multiprocessor system has been designed as a demonstration of the capabilities of the model [38]. Transputers are used as the processing elements in this system. To aid the implementation of the model in the framework of the transputer machine being used, a number of simplifications have been made which force the sacrifice of some of the salient features of the model. The architecture used is a tree of transputers with one master and many workers. Each worker carries out comparisons between the input labeled graph and stored patterns using conventional techniques. Thus the neural approach to the problem is lost in an effort to simplify the implementation.

Most of the computation in recognizing objects using the Dynamic Link Architecture goes in carrying out the labeled graph matching. The important question to be asked in this regard is: How are the dynamics of the system, resulting in the minimization of $H(J)$ (Eq. (14.24)), implemented efficiently on a parallel machine? An attempt to directly implement the minimization of the energy function does not yield an efficient implementation as it requires global communication. An alternative mechanism that achieves parallelism on a fine scale while avoiding global communication is desired. The next section describes an algorithm to implement the model on a linear array of processors that addresses this issue. Although it is a first step toward a full scale parallel implementation of the model, the algorithm has many attractive features.

The implementation is done on a linear array of processors. The linear array is a very simple parallel architecture that is amenable to VLSI implementation. Depending on the number of processors available in the machine being used, the implementation can vary from fine grain to relatively coarse grain. The algorithm stores graphs in the form of individual nodes with information about the node's feature type and about its neighbors. Comparisons can now be carried out on a node by node basis as opposed to a graph by graph basis as is done in the transputer implementation [38]. This provides for more parallelism in the graph matching, and this fine grain parallelism can be exploited to varying degrees depending upon the number of processors in the machine being used. The storing of graphs in terms of individual nodes and not monolithic entities is also closer to the original model where neurons are chosen at random from a fixed set B to represent nodes of graphs. The time complexity for matching an input object graph to stored graphs is $O(N_A N_B/p)$, where N_A is the number of nodes in the input graph, N_B is the total number of nodes in layer B, and p is the number of processing elements (PEs). This time complexity is to be expected since, in the worst case, N_A nodes have to be compared with $O(N_B)$ nodes and this work is distributed over p PEs.

14.9 LABELED GRAPH MATCHING ON A LINEAR ARRAY OF PROCESSORS

This section presents the algorithm for implementing labeled graph matching on the target architecture.

14.9.1 Data Representation

A graph G is formally defined as $G = \{V, E\}$ where V is the set of vertices (or nodes) and $E \subset V \times V$ is the set of edges between the nodes. A number of data structures can equivalently be used to represent graphs [39]. The choice of one particular data structure is dependent on its suitability for the application at hand. For the case being considered in this chapter, the adjacency list representation is used to represent labeled graphs. In this format, each node of a graph is represented by a linked list. The header of the list consists of the node's id-number and information about its feature type. Subsequent elements of the list contain information about the node's neighbors and their feature types (Fig. 14.11).

One of the steps in the algorithm involves the comparison of two nodes. This translates to a comparison of the two linked lists that represent the nodes. The data format chosen to represent graphs imposes a sequentiality in the comparison of two nodes. This sequentiality is not inherent in the problem itself but is due to the choice of data structure. The target architecture being considered here does not have the fine granularity needed to exploit parallelism at this level and, thus, this choice does not introduce extra inefficiency. However, there is nothing sacrosanct about the data structure chosen and, given a different architecture, it can be replaced by another more suitable structure.

The choice of the adjacency list representation is made because of its simplicity. It does not turn out to be an overly expensive choice in the given context because of two valid assumptions that are based on the graph structures being considered. The first assumption is that graphs in this framework will have only a few nodes. The number of nodes is small because one needs to determine the features at only a few salient points in an object to represent the object with a sufficient degree of

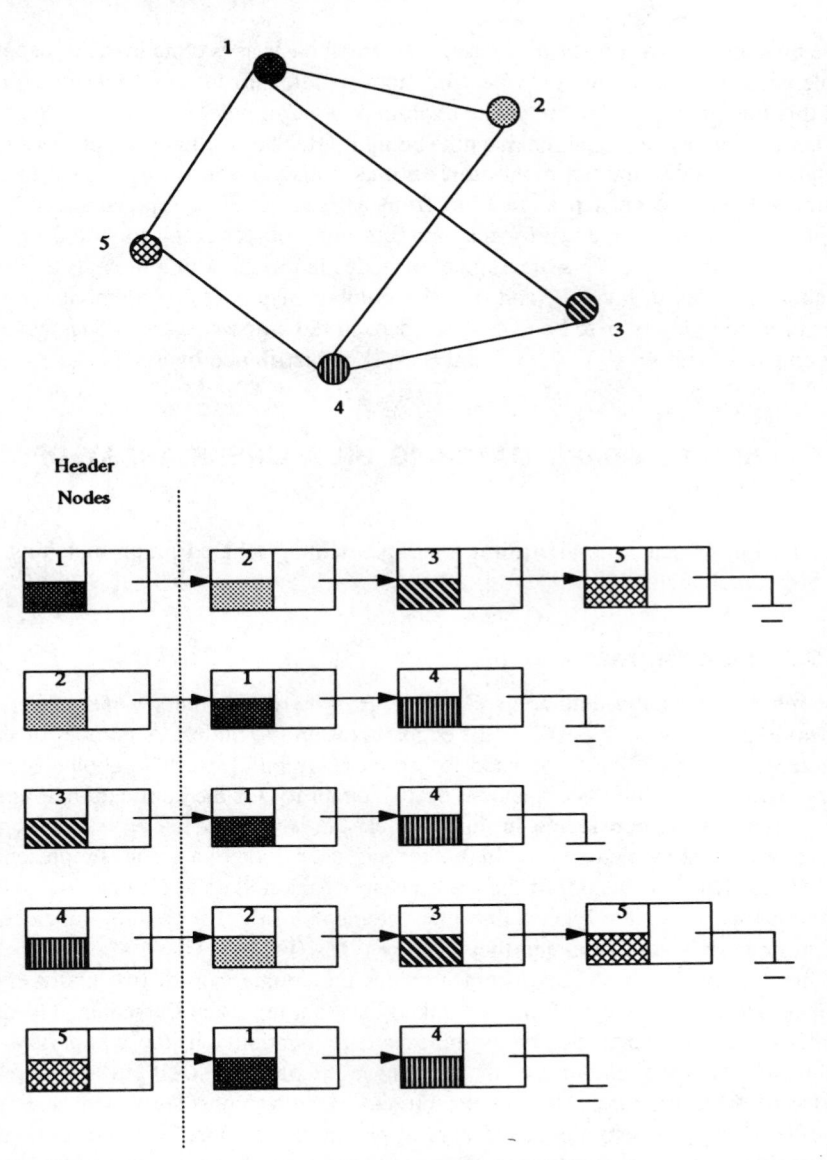

Figure 14.11 *Linked list representation of labeled graphs. Feature types of nodes are represented by shades.*

accuracy. The second assumption is that the graph representation of an object will be sparse. Again, neighborhood relations between a few nodes are sufficient to represent the object. (In [38], a 7 × 10 grid with four nearest-neighbor connections proved sufficient to represent a face). The two assumptions together imply that only a few linked lists, each with a few nodes, are sufficient to represent an object.

14.9.2 Mapping Layer *B* Graphs onto the array

This section describes the scheme employed to map labeled graphs that constitute the data base of memorized objects, onto the linear array of PEs. In addition to the information stored by linked lists as described above, linked lists that represent nodes from layer *B* graphs also store an object id which is necessary for the final identification of the recalled object. Instead of storing the layer *B* graphs as monolithic entities, they are dismantled and their nodes are stored on the basis of their feature types. Thus, establishing the data base of object graphs involves sorting the linked lists on the basis of feature types of the header nodes and storing them in appropriate PEs. Graph nodes are assigned to PEs in a manner such that nodes of the same feature type form a "connected region" on the linear array. This implies that nodes with a certain feature type are mapped onto the same PE as far as possible, and when it becomes necessary to use more PEs, neighboring PEs are chosen. Thus, a typical distribution of the linked lists representing the nodes might appear as shown in Figure 14.12.

If N_B is the total number of nodes in all the graphs in layer *B*, then $O(N_B/p)$ linked lists are stored per PE.

Object graphs can be added to an existing data base of graphs by merely sorting the nodes of the graph to be stored and assigning them to the appropriate PEs.

14.9.3 Matching Algorithm

Preprocessing for the algorithm involves the sorting of all the layer *B* nodes on the basis of their feature types and the mapping of the linked lists onto the individual PEs according to the mapping scheme described above. Using a sequential sorting algorithm, this can be done in $O(N_B \log N_B)$ time.

Once the layer *B* nodes have been mapped onto the array, each incoming object can be processed in parallel to determine the best match among the stored objects.

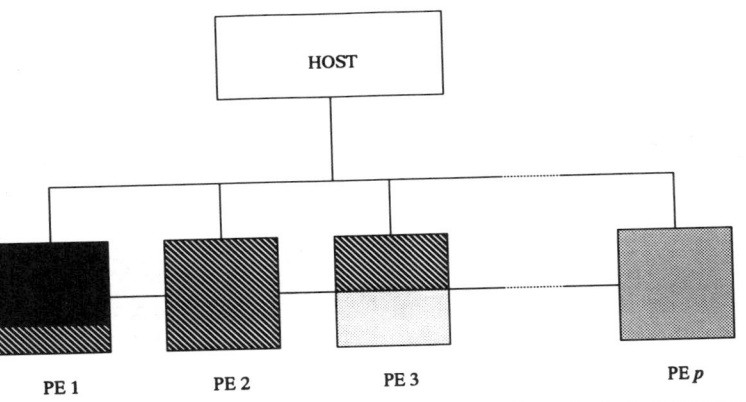

Figure 14.12 *Mapping layer B nodes onto the linear array. Each shaded region represents a set of nodes with the same feature type.*

This is done by the following algorithm: An input object graph is represented by a collection of linked lists as described above. These lists are sorted by the host and directed to appropriate PEs, as the first step of the algorithm. If the input graph contains $O(N_A)$ nodes, this is done in $O(N_A \log N_A)$ time. Within an individual PE, an incoming linked list is processed in a sequential manner. It is compared with each of the stored lists that have the same feature type, and each of these comparisons generates a "confidence of match." The comparison of two linked lists can also be done in a sequential manner, with each element of the incoming list being compared with every element of the stored list. The confidence of the match is determined by the number of nodes in the input list that have the same feature types as some nodes in the stored list. Since we have assumed sparse connectivity among nodes, the number of elements of a list is less than some small constant k. This implies that the comparison of two lists can be done in $O(1)$ time. Once an input list has been compared with the appropriate stored lists, the object id of the stored node with the highest confidence level is sent to the host. This overall operation has an asymptotic time complexity of $O(N_A N_B / p)$. The host thus receives the best match ids for each of the input graphs nodes. Given the information about best matches for the input nodes, the host can decide as to which stored object best matches the input object. This decision is produced by a winner-take-all kind of operation, which can be performed in $O(N_A)$ time.

As can be seen from above, the overall asymptotic time complexity for determining the best match for a labeled graph is $O(N_A \log N_A + N_A N_B / p)$. In most typical cases $N_A \ll N_B$ and, therefore, the time complexity is dominated by the N_B / p term.

14.9.4 Discussion

Although the algorithm described in this part of the chapter is a first step toward a complete parallel implementation of the Dynamic Link Architecture, it possesses many attributes that make it attractive. The first among these attributes is the simplicity of the algorithm. Because the algorithm has been designed for the linear array, it can be implemented very easily. A number of parallel machines based on the linear array architecture are currently available (e.g., the CMU Warp), and the algorithm can be implemented on these machines in a very straightforward manner. The linear array is very amenable to VLSI implementation. In addition to this, the algorithm requires very simple computational capabilities of the individual PEs (the PEs need to store the linked lists and carry out comparisons between lists). This means that the internal structure of each PE is very simple, making the architecture even more amenable to VLSI implementation. The algorithm can be run on linear arrays with a wide range of granularities resulting in a corresponding trade-off in performance. As is shown by the expression of the asymptotic complexity of the algorithm, the performance of the algorithm increases if the number of PEs in the array increases. The performance can be further enhanced if comparisons between individual nodes can be done in parallel. The algorithm achieves the requirements of the Dynamic Link Architecture model (discarding information about the absolute location of features but retaining the relational structure of the features) by storing relational information in the form of adjacency lists for each node. At the same time, the algorithm avoids an expensive global communication that would be necessary if an attempt to minimize the energy function $H(J)$ (Eq. (14.24)) were made on a parallel machine. In the algorithm, a comparison of two nodes involves comparing the feature types of all their neighbors. This takes the determination of best matches for individual nodes beyond a mere check for 4-cycles to one for a check for all neighbors having the same feature type. This will result in a smoother energy landscape than would result if only 4-cycles were favored.

Overall, the algorithm presents a first step toward a parallel implementation of the Dynamic Link Architecture. A number of issues still need to be tackled before it can result in a complete implementation, but the ideas presented here can form a foundation for such an implementation.

14.10 CONCLUSION

This chapter has presented an overview of our research in the area of parallel digital implementation of artificial neural networks. The first part of the chapter showed the Reduced Mesh of Trees Architecture to be an attractive architecture for implementing neural models with various connectivity schemes between neurons. The second part presented an algorithm to implement labeled graph matching (which forms the major computational component of the Dynamic Link Architecture) on a linear array of processors.

Our current work is directed toward developing a complete parallel implementation of the dynamic link model, which retains the neural flavor of the model, while providing performance that can be used for real-life invariant pattern recognition tasks. A number of issues still remain open and are being tackled. Prominent among them are the choice of features used to label graph nodes, how these features can be computed on the same parallel machine that carries out the labeled graph matching, and how the labeled graph representation of an object can be computed automatically. Work is currently underway at the Brain Simulation Lab at the University of Southern California to develop an C++ environment that provides a researcher working in this area with the ability to develop rapid prototypes to test new ideas. It is envisioned that these prototypes will be ported onto a network of transputers and tested. Other work related to the theme of this chapter can be found in [40].

REFERENCES

[1] A. J. Maren, C. T. Harston, and R. M. Pap, *Handbook of Neural Computing Applications*, Academic Press, New York, 1990.

[2] Manavendra Misra and V. K. Prasanna Kumar, "Implementation of Neural Networks on Massive Memory Organizations," Tech. Rep. CENG 89-30, Dept. of EE-Systems, University of Southern California (November 1989).

[3] Manavendra Misra and V. K. Prasanna Kumar, Massive memory organizations for implementing neural networks, *Internat. Conf. Pattern Recognition* (June 1990).

[4] Manavendra Misra and V. K. Prasanna Kumar, Neural network simulation on a reduced mesh of trees organization, *SPIE/SPSE Symp. Electronic Imaging* (February 1990).

[5] C. von der Malsburg, Pattern recognition by labeled graph matching, *Neural Networks*, 141–148 (1988).

[6] W. S. McCulloch and W. H. Pitts, A logical calculus of the ideas immanent in nervous activity, *Bull. Math. Biophys.*, 5, 115–133 (1943).

[7] J. J. Hopfield, Neurons with graded response have collective computational properties like those of two-state neurons, *Proc. Nat. Acad. Sci. USA*, 81, 3088–3092 (1984).

[8] R. P. Lippman, An introduction to computing with neural nets, *IEEE ASSP Magazine*, 4–22 (April 1987).

[9] D. O. Hebb, *The Organization of Behavior*, Wiley, New York, 1949.

[10] D. E. Rumelhart, G. E. Hinton, and R. J. Williams, "Learning Internal Representations by Error Propagation," in D. E. Rumelhart and J. L. McClelland, Eds., in *Parallel Distributed Processing: Exploration in the Microstructure of Cognition*, vol. 1, MIT Press, Cambridge, Mass. 1986, pp. 318–362.

[11] D. E. Rumelhart and J. L. McClelland, Eds., *Parallel Distributed Processing: Exploration in the Microstructure of Cognition*, Vol. 1. MIT Press, Cambridge, Mass., 1986.

[12] S. Y. Kung, Parallel architectures for artificial neural nets, *Internat. Conf. Systolic Arrays*, 163–174 (1988).

[13] S. Y. Kung and J. N. Hwang, A unified systolic architecture for artificial neural nets, *J. Parallel and Distributed Computing*, 6, 358–387 (1989).

[14] H. T. Kung, D. A. Pomerleau, G. L. Gusciora, and D. S. Touretzky, How we got 17 million connections per second, *Internat. Conf. Neural Networks*, Volume II, 143–150 (1988).

[15] X. Zhang, M. McKenna, J. P. Mesirov, and D. Waltz, An efficient implementation of the backpropagation algorithm on the connection machine CM-2, Conference proceedings of *Neural Information Processing Systems*, (1989).

[16] K. W. Przytula and V. K. Prasanna Kumar, Algorithmic mapping of neural networks models on parallel SIMD machines, *Internat. Conf. Application Specific Array Processing* (1990).

[17] K. W. Przytula, W.-M. Lin, and V. K. Prasanna Kumar, Partitioned implementation of neural networks on mesh connected array processors, *Workshop on VLSI Signal Processing* (1990).

[18] K. I. Diamantara, D. L. Heine, and I. D. Scherson, Implementation of neural network algorithms on the P^3 parallel associative processor, *Internat. Conf. Parallel Processing*, Vol. I, 247–250 (1990).

[19] Dan Hammerstrom, A VLSI architecture for high-performance, low-cost, on-chip learning, *Internat. Joint Conf. Neural Networks*, Vol. II, 537–544 (1990).

[20] M. S. Tomlinson Jr., D. J. Walker, and M. A. Sivilotti, A digital neural network architecture for VLSI, *Internat. Joint Conf. Neural Networks*, Vol. II, 545–550 (1990).

[21] U. Ramacher and J. Beichter, "Systolic Architectures for Fast Emulation of Artificial Neural Networks," in J. McCanny, J. McWhirter, and E. Swartzlander Jr., eds., *Systolic Array Processors*, Prentice Hall, Englewood Cliffs, N.J., 1989, pp. 277–286.

[22] Sanjay Ranka, "A Distributed Implementation of Backpropagation" Manuscript, Department of Computer Science, Syracuse University (1990).

[23] Sanjay Ranka, N. Asokan, R. Shankar, C. K. Mohan, and K. Mehrotra, A neural network simulator on the connection machine, *Fifth IEEE Internat. Symp. Intelligent Control* (1990).

[24] Soheil Shams and K. W. Przytula, Mapping of neural networks onto programmable parallel machines, *Internat. Symp. Circuits and Systems* (May 1990).

[25] S. Tomboulian, "Introduction to a System for Implementing Neural Net Connections on SIMD Architectures," Tech. Rep. ICASE No. 88-3, Institute for Computer Applications in Science and Engineering, NASA Langley Research Center (January 1988).

[26] B. W. Wah and L.-C. Chu, Efficient mapping of neural networks on multicomputers, *Internat. Conf. Parallel Processing*, vol. I, 234–238 (1990).

[27] T. Watanabe, Y. Sugiyama, T. Kondo, and Y. Kitamura, Neural network simulation on a massively parallel cellular array processor: AAP-2, *Internat. Joint Conf. Neural Networks* (June 1989).

[28] Stephen S. Wilson, Neural computing on a one dimensional SIMD array, *Internat. Joint Conf. Artificial Intelligence*, 206–211 (1989).

[29] P. S. Tseng, K. Hwang, and V. K. Prasanna Kumar, A VLSI based multiprocessor architecture for implementing parallel algorithms, *Internat. Conf. Parallel Processing* (1985).

[30] I. D. Scherson and S. Sen. Parallel sorting on two-dimensional VLSI models of computation, *IEEE Trans. Computers*, C-38, 238–249 (February 1989).

[31] Hussein M. Alnuweiri, "Communication Efficient Parallel Architectures and Algorithms for Image Computations," Ph.D. thesis, Dept. of EE-Systems, University of Southern California (August 1989).

[32] G. Lev, N. Pippenger, and L. Valiant, A fast parallel algorithm for routing in permutation networks, *IEEE Trans. Computers*, C-30(2), 93–100 (February 1981).

[33] David Nassimi and Sartaj Sahni, Parallel algorithms to set up the Benes permutation network, *IEEE Trans. Computers*, C-31(2), 148–154 (February 1982).

[34] C. S. Raghavendra and V. K. Prasanna Kumar, Permutations on ILLIAC-IV type networks, *IEEE Trans. Computers*, C-37(7), 622–629 (July 1986).

[35] Christoph von der Malsburg and E. Bienenstock, A neural network for the retrieval of superimposed connection patterns, *Europhysics Lett.*, 3, 1243–1249 (1987).

[36] E. Bienenstock and Christoph von der Malsburg, A neural network for invariant pattern recognition, *Europhysics Lett.*, 4, 121–126 (1987).

[37] J. J. Hopfield, Neural networks and physical systems with emergent collective computational abilities, *Proc. Nat. Acad. Sci. USA*, 79, 2554–2558 (1982).

[38] Joachim Buhmann, Jorg Lange, Christoph von der Malsburg, Jan C. Vorbruggen, and Rolf P. Wurtz, "Object Recognition in the Dynamic Link Architecture—Parallel Implementation on a Transputer Network," in Bart Kosko, Ed., *Neural Networks: A Dynamical Systems Approach to Machine Intelligence*, 1990.

[39] A. V. Aho, J. E. Hopcroft, and J. D. Ullman, *The Design and Analysis of Computer Algorithms*, Addison-Wesley, Reading, Mass., 1974.

[40] Manavendra Misra, "Implementation of Neural Networks on Parallel Architectures—Work in Progress," Ph.D. thesis, Dept. of EE-Systems, University of Southern California (1992).

INDEX

269